Special Educational Needs Review

Special Educational Needs Review

Volume 1

Edited by

Neville Jones

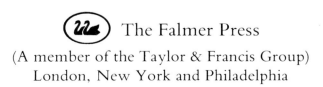

The Falmer Press

(A member of the Taylor & Francis Group)
London, New York and Philadelphia

UK   The Falmer Press, Falmer House, Barcombe, Lewes,
East Sussex, BN8 5DL

USA   The Falmer Press, Taylor & Francis Inc., 242 Cherry Street,
Philadelphia, PA 19106–1906

First published 1989

British Library Cataloguing in Publication Data

Special educational needs review.—(Education
 & alienation series).
 Vol. 1
 1. Great Britain. Special education
 I. Jones, Neville, *1930–* II. Series
 371.9′0941

ISBN 1-85000-488-9
ISBN 1-85000-489-7 Pbk

**Library of Congress Cataloguing in Publication Data is available
on request**

Jacket design by Caroline Archer

Typeset in 10/12 Garamond by
Mathematical Composition Setters Ltd, Salisbury

*Printed in Great Britain by
Redwood Burn Limited, Trowbridge, Wiltshire*

Contents

Preface

Oxfordshire Disaffected Pupil Programme

The positive approach of the Oxfordshire Disaffected Pupil Programme (DPP) draws attention to what can and is being achieved in our schools to improve the experience of pupils who are, or who may feel, alienated in school. The focus of the Programme is towards the kinds of good teaching and effective management for all pupils, which in themselves prevent disaffection, and which can actively engage in the processes of restitution and re-engagement for those pupils who are already alienated. This is to recognize that in spite of ideas for individual pupils, and education as a whole, such ideas cannot always be reached and regularly maintained. No matter how effective and skilled teachers are in their teaching and the management of their schools, there will always be some pupils who are more than a little disaffected with their school experience, and some who as a consequence become actively alienated.

The Programme, however, is essentially about the prevention of disaffection. This can be achieved through curriculum innovation, the ethos and values of schools, effective leadership, through teachers refining their teaching skills together with effective classroom management — all within a context of positive teacher-pupil relationships, by the involvement of parents and others from the local community — and indeed, through organizational planning within schools which can in itself so easily marginalize pupils and their learning.

Disaffection is a normal human sentiment but it has connotations that are both positive and damaging. Disaffection can be a spur to re-evaluating personal goals and a motivating force to achieve these: it can damage self-esteem, confidence and worthwhileness, when it becomes expressed in severe, complex and persisting forms. It is when pupils feel they cannot resolve their dissatisfactions, or feel they are not receiving help to do so, that they are then at risk of becoming educationally alienated. The Disaffected Pupil Programme, as part of its enquiry, liaison, and dissemination aspect, is engaged in bringing attention, through publications, to the innovatory work now being carried out throughout the education service in Britain. This volume is part of that work.

The Review is the first volume in a new series of publications, bringing together a collective knowledge and expertise from known authorities in their respective fields, both in this country and overseas. The aim in this book is to provide a forum for the dissemination of current thinking and ideas about the education of pupils with special educational needs. While the main emphasis is on the prevention of disaffection through the curriculum in ordinary schools we intend to include and share experiences of those working in specialist institutions, units, special schools and centres, as well as government and voluntary research agencies, and voluntary organizations.

This Preface provides an opportunity to express an appreciation to many colleagues in the field of education in general, and special education in particular, for their advice and counselling as to the style and emphasis that would be enhancing for a book series of this kind. It is not possible to name individuals. But it would be inappropriate not to record thanks and appreciation to my Editor, Christine Cox at Falmer Press, for her early enthusiasm and encouragement at the planning stage, and a never failing support and guidance, a calming expertise, to bring this book and the series into existence.

Neville Jones
Director, Disaffected Pupil Programme
Oxfordshire
June 1988.

Introduction

Margaret Peter

Many of the chapters in this opening volume hint at a shared concern: how to make a divided system less divisive. Whether they travel the past hundred years reviewed by Ron Gulliford, when the divide was largely between the 'haves' and the 'have-nots', or whether they discuss the past ten to twenty, when the divisions have had more to do with *where* and *how* than *who* receives education, they reflect the quest for a unified and equal system which has spurred on many reformers.

When pupils with severe learning difficulties entered the education system in 1971, pressures for the integration of the majority of pupils into ordinary schools intensified, and they found expression ten years later, albeit guardedly, in Section 2 of the 1981 Education Act. The last four years have, perhaps, been the most 'comprehensive' this century. The percentage of children with special educational needs segregated in special schools has fallen faster than the school population as a whole. Comprehensive secondary education has continued to expand, and grammar schools to decline, even though the proportion of children in the separate independent school system has risen slightly over the same period. Will the period from 1984 to 1988 be seen in retrospect as the high point in integration before divisiveness began to set in again, in the wake of a new 1988 Education Act? Questions of where, how and for whom will be asked about more children more often, not least about the disaffected pupils who are the focus of this new series. Seamus Hegarty, in the opening chapter, refers to 'the growing uncertainty over the political will to maintain integrated education or even to consider the implications of proposed reforms for special educational provision'.

The problem about legislation and other efforts to reduce divisiveness is that they can sharpen awareness of inequalities elsewhere in the system, heighten existing differences, and create new divisions where none existed. Ten years ago the Warnock Report rejected statutory categories of handicap in favour of a wider definition of 'special educational needs' and encouraged integration. Both principles were embedded, at differing depths, in the 1981 Education Act. However, in its efforts to translate the Warnock Report proposals into a system of assessment which would safeguard extra provision for the minority of children with the most acute needs, the 1981 Act widened awareness of the gulf between the wider group of pupils with special needs, the notional 18 per cent, and the protected 1 to 2 per cent with legally binding statements of special educational needs under the Act. More than seven of the Act's fourteen pages were devoted to the assessment of the minority, only one or two Sections to the wider group.

The reaction was predictable. Even before the 1981 Act provisions became active in 1983, and certainly within a year of its implementation, misgivings began to be expressed. Previously, children considered to be in need of special educational provision had largely been out of sight, and out of mind, in separate schools or units. Now more of them were becoming conspicuous in ordinary schools, bringing statements and extra provision with them — five hours of specialist teaching here, half a classroom assistant there. They were often seemingly indistinguishable in their degree of need from other children in the class whose extra help, if any, had not been legally protected by a statement under the 1981 Act. 'What about the needs of the 18 per cent?' was the response of teacher organizations like the National Association for Remedial Education and the National Council for Special Education. The question was taken up by the House of Commons Education, Science and Arts Committee in its report on the implementation of the 1981 Act published in 1987. From other quarters, including the evidence of the National Union of Teachers to the same Parliamentary Committee, came misgivings about provision for children of high ability whose needs were unrecognized in the 1981 Act.

Divisiveness, inherent in the wording of the 1981 Act, was intensified by the way the majority of local authorities felt compelled to translate its sections into lengthy and cumbersome procedures, and sometimes to invent some of their own. Educational psychologists and, to a lesser extent, advisers and teachers felt too many resources were being devoted to a minority of children, to the neglect of a larger group. The impression is confirmed by Jennifer Evans and her colleagues reporting in Chapter 3 on their research into the implementation of the 1981 Act. They found that much time, energy and resources were being spent on statutory assessment and provision for children with statements and that a larger share of educational spending than before was going to special education. Fears were expressed in some LEAs that this was at the expense of 'remedial' or 'special needs' departments in mainstream schools. Two of the ironies of the Warnock-into-81 Act metamorphosis are that legislation which was intended to reflect Warnock's support for integration should become divisive, and that the delays in assessment under the pre-1983 system, of which the Warnock Committee complained, could turn out to be even longer under the 1981 Act.

To what extent did the way the Warnock proposals were translated into law and practice contribute to the arrival, ten years later, of an Education Reform Act which puts many of the Warnock Report's aims into jeopardy? Have so much time and effort been invested in the 1.7 per cent of children with statements and in trying to contain, if not satisfy, the needs of the 18 per cent, including those with emotional and behavioural difficulties, that children of higher ability have been seen as increasingly neglected? The Report's implementation may have been a contributory factor. Divisiveness at one end of the education system may have helped to promote divisiveness at the other. The Reform Act's provisions for grant-maintained schools and open enrolments encourage schools to select children according to ability, aided at around secondary stage by national testing at eleven, reviving the ordeal of the 'eleven plus'.

Has the growth of integration encouraged by both the Warnock Report and the 1981 Act been another factor in the government's upheaval of education? Children who might previously have been segregated are now, with or without statements, more likely to stay in the mainstream. Although a recent paper by Will Swann in the *Oxford Review of Education* suggests that the evidence for a national trend towards integration is very slight, and the impact of the 1981 Act's integration section in doubt, it is too soon to dismiss the law's influence as negligible. Given the disincentives to integration (the advent of the GCSE, the welter of other curriculum and training initiatives, the scantiness of in-service training, for example), a seemingly small movement may be significant. Without such deterrents the shift towards integration might have been greater.

Whatever the statistical evidence about integration, the *perceived* increase in children with learning difficulties in ordinary classrooms may be more significant. Irene Bowman's chapter on a UNESCO study suggests that teachers' attitudes to integration seem to vary according to their training, experience of pupils with special educational needs, and the support available. As well as the 29,037 children with statements of special educational needs now being educated in ordinary schools in England according to the latest available figures, and the numerous pupils with mild learning difficulties, pupils with disruptive behaviour are diverting teachers' attention from others of above average ability. While Delwyn Tattum is at pains to emphasise in Chapter 9 that research into the incidence of disruptive behaviour is 'beset with problems', and claims of increasing disruption likewise, he accepts the view of teaching unions on indiscipline and disruption that they 'do represent the perceptions of very many members of the profession and so must be taken seriously ...'. Though some LEAs have developed a range of support for teachers coping with difficult behaviour, others have failed to give enough help to enable teachers to stimulate pupils in the higher ability ranges.

Has the continued rise in spending on special education also strengthened the government's determination to create divisions at the other end of the ability range? Hansard, as usual, is revealing. In a rare utterance on special educational needs since she became Prime Minister, Margaret Thatcher told the House of Commons in March last year that spending per pupil had risen by 19 per cent in real terms within four years. There were, she said, more teachers, fewer pupils, and more money being spent on each pupil. The percentage rise, like those for books and equipment reported in Hansard last July, is noticeably higher than that for pupils in primary and secondary schools. The latest figures for 1986, show the annual average cost of a special school place in England as £4,444 compared with £1,339 for secondary schools and £897 for primary schools. The findings of Jennifer Evans and her colleagues in Chapter 3 confirm this trend at local authority level. 72 per cent of the authorities surveyed reported that the proportion of the total education budget going to special education had increased. Perhaps an underlying feeling of 'enough is enough' on resources for special education was one of the attitudes lurking behind the government's apparent fit of absent-mindedness about references to special educational needs in the Education Reform Bill.

While trends in special educational provision may have contributed in only a small way to the coming of the Education Reform Bill, the new legislation is likely to have a disproportionate impact on children with special educational needs. In proposing the reforms the government appears to be standing a familiar quotation on its head. By dividing we stand, by uniting we fall — it is a disturbing transposition. As Seamus Hegarty suggests, unless the issues inherent in a common curricular framework are tackled in a concerted way 'the effects of introducing a national curriculum could be to undo the advances of recent years and return pupils with special needs ... to marginal status in the school system'. He also warns of the adverse effects which could arise for such pupils when schools opt out of local authority control and achieve greater financial autonomy. Integration, balanced school intakes, the level of advisory and support services and planning and provision in general for special educational needs, could all suffer.

The Education Act does bring at least one change which should unite rather than set apart. This is the inclusion of pupils with special educational needs within the national curriculum rather than, as originally planned, their automatic exclusion. The extent to which this brings cohesion rather than differentiation may depend largely on the regulations governing the sections in the Act which allow for modifying or disapplying the requirements of the National Curriculum for individual children and groups of pupils. It is also possible that, through other changes created by the Act, teaching staff who find they are losing pupils to grant-maintained and to other schools under the open-enrolment policy may be more responsive to developing a whole-school approach and integrating children with learning difficulties.

In some ways the Act has already widened unity. Professional and parent bodies, charities and individuals have joined forces to oppose, or to propose improvements to, clauses in the Bill hostile to children with special educational needs. More than thirty were represented at a series of meetings held at the National Children's Bureau at Bill stage. The implementation of the Act could also create or fortify other alliances such as parent support and self advocacy groups mentioned by Philippa Russell in Chapter 4.

Laws can have opposite effects to those intended and, as Ron Gulliford points out, 'their implementation has always fallen short of their intentions'. It is just possible that the effects of the Education Reform Act will be less divisive than we can now foresee?

Part One
Special Needs and Integration

1
Past, Current and Future Research on Integration: an NFER Perspective

Seamus Hegarty

Introduction

In 1987 a major set of studies on integration was completed at the National Foundation for Educational Research (NFER). These had gone on for more than a decade and spanned a wide compass. They included large national studies and purely local investigations; they examined institutions and services as well as pupils with diverse special needs; and they employed a wide range of qualitative and quantitative research techniques. Despite this diversity, the studies were mutually complementary and have helped to build up a comprehensive understanding of the process of integration.

It must be acknowledged that the studies were not planned as part of an interrelated programme — and the coherence and common directions are more in evidence with the benefit of hindsight than they ever were along the way. The various studies were conducted in the ad hoc way characteristic of educational research in Britain. They were carried out by changing terms of researchers, to commissions from several different sponsors. The remarkable thing perhaps is that they fit together at all.

The purpose of this paper is to outline the basic features of this programme and to suggest what might follow it. It traces three main topics which were addressed in turn: the feasibility of integrated provision; classroom and other curricular implications; and the kinds of support ordinary schools require to educate pupils with special needs. These topics were not totally discrete in practice since they overlapped in the different studies, but they do offer a useful way of categorizing the studies in terms of their main focus. The paper concludes by taking stock and noting some pointers for the future.

Feasibility of integration

The first study of integration at NFER ran from 1972 to 1974. It dealt with educational provision for pupils with visual impairment in the light of the growing controversy over educating these pupils in ordinary schools. It was in part a methodological venture in that it espoused the techniques of illuminative evaluation and sought to test their relevance to special education.

Within the general goal of contributing to the integration debate, it had five aims:

1. to document developments in the education of the visually impaired;
2. to investigate examples of integration programmes at work;
3. to elucidate features of classroom life when blind or partially sighted pupils were taught alongside those with normal vision;
4. to explore the relationships between home and school; and
5. to examine a number of policy concerns and discuss practical and theoretical issues associated with implementing integration.

These were addressed by gathering a wide variety of interview and some observational data and subjecting them to detailed analysis. The project report (Jamieson *et al.*, 1977) combines description with interpretive and critical comment. It documents the experience of integration, particularly from the pupil's perspective, juxtaposes different points of view, examines the assumptions underlying practice and explores the ways in which numerous factors converge to shape an individual's schooling.

The next study was a major project which focused on the feasibility question for pupils with the full range of special needs, those with emotional and behavioural difficulties excepted. This was a national study, funded by the Department of Education and Science, and ran from 1977–80. It was reported in detail in Hegarty and Pocklington (1981 and 1982) and in summary form in Hegarty (1982). The study used a mixture of qualitative and quantitative techniques to amass data on prevailing experience of educating pupils with special needs in ordinary schools. It documented a wide range of practice — individual integration programmes, special classes and units, and links between special schools and ordinary schools. Analysis of these data helped to build up a detailed account of the process. This is presented in the reports, with copious illustrations, under six broad headings: initiating programmes; staffing; practicalities — costs and resources; curriculum development and implementation; social dimension — interactions, development, perceptions and attitudes; and the attitudes and roles of parents.

The firm conclusion of the study was that integration was possible. Special educational needs could be met in ordinary schools, and to a far greater extent than was currently the practice. Integration was not an easy option however and there were numerous difficulties to be resolved. In particular, the ordinary school had to make significant changes in both structure and working practices. The study attempted to spell these out and, by implication, set out an agenda for school reform that would enable pupils to be educated in ordinary schools who would otherwise continue to be educated in special schools.

A third study was concerned specifically with language unit provision for pupils with speech and language difficulties. Such units began to be established in ordinary schools from the late seventies onward. A focused study looked in detail at one such unit over a two year period (1980–82). The project report (Pocklington and Hegarty, 1982) recounted the main events in the early running of the unit and set the emerging provision in context. The aim was to provide sufficient contextualized detail so that practitioners and policy makers elsewhere could make better informed decisions about their own provision.

Implications for the curriculum

Each of the studies mentioned so far referred to the curriculum in various ways. It would be difficult to explore the feasibility of educating pupils with special needs in ordinary schools without taking account of the curricular implications. The next two studies focused explicitly on the curriculum and sought to collect information that would help schools and teachers in the task of improving or extending their provision for pupils with special needs.

The first of these was concerned with provision for slow learners in secondary schools. It was funded by the NFER and ran from 1979–81. The focus was on pupils who were already in the school and whose education was without question the responsibility of the ordinary school. The impetus for the study came from previous NFER work on mixed ability teaching in secondary schools in which the problems of slow learning pupils were very commonly voiced by heads and class teachers. The proliferation over the 1970s of slow learner and other 'remedial' provision in schools provided another context for the study.

The study consisted of two distinct phases: questionnaire surveys and case studies. A questionnaire was sent to a 20 per cent sample of all maintained secondary schools in England and Wales requesting information on school policy and organization and on slow learner provision. A follow-up questionnaire was sent to teachers of slow learners in these schools to obtain details on how slow learners were taught and what tests and teaching materials were in use. This was followed by intensive case studies in seventeen schools, chosen to exemplify the different ways in which slow learner provision might be organized. The case studies included interviews with the headteacher and the teacher in charge of slow learner provision and a full day's observation of a pupil. A reading test was also administered to every pupil in the intake year group.

The project gathered two quite different kinds of data. The first, drawn from the questionnaire responses (85 per cent response rate), presented the national picture on secondary school policy for slow learners and the organizational structures used to meet their needs. The second focused on the classroom implications of these structures for both teacher and pupil. The findings are reported in Clunies-Ross and Wimhurst (1983). Successive chapters are concerned with: the organization of provision; how pupils are identified as slow learners; administrative structures and the role of the teacher-in-charge; backgrounds of the teachers who taught slow learners and their views on the training required; the curriculum, years 1–3 and years 4 and 5; and pointers for future provision.

The second study here was concerned specifically with the classroom implications of integration. It was funded jointly by the NFER and by the Schools Council within its Programme on Individual Pupils. It ran for a period of two years from January 1982. This study sought to identify classroom strategies relevant to managing the learning of pupils with a wide variety of special needs and illuminate the processes whereby the curriculum could be modified to take account of their needs. These aims were addressed primarily in an empirical way. The effort was to see what individual teachers and schools were doing in practice, not what they would like to do or what curriculum theorists would have them do. Initially, the team visited a large number of ordinary schools to map out the range of practice and select a number of schools for detailed case study. The latter entailed interviewing teachers, ancillaries and peripatetic staff and observing pupils in a range of settings. In the event, twenty-six schools were chosen. All of these had pupils who were spending at least part of each day being taught alongside age peers in a mainstream setting. Both primary and secondary schools were included, and the pupils in question had a wide variety of special needs.

The findings are reported in detail in Hodgson *et al.* (1984) and in summary form in Hegarty (1985). They are grouped under four main headings: academic organization; modification of curriculum content; staffing; and teaching. Thus, they range from in-service training arrangements and the deployment of ancillary staff, through timetabling and pupil grouping, to classroom organization and monitoring the effectiveness of teaching. The net result is to give a wide-ranging but realistic picture of the steps being taken at classroom and school level to ensure that pupils with special needs receive a good education while still participating in the normal activities of the school.

Support for the ordinary school

The study referred to in the Introduction had to do with different aspects of supporting the ordinary school in the task of meeting special educational needs. It was one of three funded by the Department of Education and Science in the wake of the Education Act 1981. The other two were concerned respectively with in-service training (University of Manchester and Huddersfield Polytechnic) and the implementation of the Act (University of London Institute of Education); they are the subject of separate reports in this volume.

The NFER study focused on the theme of support. Ordinary schools have had to pay more attention to special needs in recent years: many existing pupils were failing to benefit from their schooling, while pupils arriving through integration programmes necessitated a radical rethink of the curriculum on offer. All of this has meant that schools were having to take on new tasks for which many were not adequately equipped. The 1981 Act was a further source of pressure.

Exceptions apart, it called for all pupils with special needs to be educated in ordinary schools, and required that they should participate in the normal activities of the school to the greatest extent possible.

Ordinary schools required a good deal of support if pupils with special needs were to benefit to the full from the new arrangements. Some were developing relevant initiatives, but it was clear that many schools were floundering in uncertainty over how best to provide for these pupils. So it was decided to focus on three aspects of provision where schools can receive major assistance in educating pupils with special needs: local authority services; links between special schools and ordinary schools; and in-service training. A summary of the findings is given in Moses *et al.* (1987).

Initial information was gathered by means of questionnaires sent to all local education authorities in 1984. These covered each of the three aspects as well as other features of special needs provision such as extra-district placements and designated special needs posts in ordinary schools. Responses were obtained from seventy-seven authorities. On the basis of the information received it was decided to pursue the three areas of interest separately.

Further survey data were obtained on the different local authority services for pupils with special needs: learning support service; hearing impaired service; visually impaired service and advisers. These were amplified with information obtained by interviewing members of the services. The general picture was one of modest expansion, partly to meet the requirements of the 1981 Act, particularly in respect of statementing, and partly reflecting real growth in services to schools and pupils. One of the most significant changes was in the character of the local authority remedial service. Traditionally a relatively self-contained service focusing on individual pupils' reading difficulties, it was evolving into a broader learning support service whose clients were teachers as well as pupils and which sought to address learning problems across the curriculum. Full details on this and on developments in the other services are given in Moses *et al.* (1988).

Link arrangements were studied in two ways: a questionnaire to a 25 per cent sample of special schools in England and Wales (90 per cent response); and case studies of nine settings, each comprising a special school and its associated ordinary school(s). This gave a national picture of the prevalence of link arrangements, and also provided details on how schemes worked in practice. Link arrangements turned out to be far more common than had previously been realized, with three-quarters of the special schools responding currently involved in a link of some kind. There were numerous types of scheme, involving pupils, teachers and resources in various combinations. The most common type of scheme was where pupils went from a special school to an ordinary school for part of the school day, with or without staff support from the special school. Full details on the study are given in Jowett *et al.* (1988).

The third aspect of support investigated had to do with in-service training, specifically the one-term courses on Special Educational Needs in the Ordinary School introduced by DES Circular 3/83. Information was gathered by interview and questionnaire from 23 of the 25 courses running in 1984/5. Interviews were also held with the local authority training coordinators and with course members.

The courses consisted of four main elements: core taught component, covering current thinking on special educational needs and how ordinary schools could respond to them; visits to schools and other institutions; introduction to the work of local authority support services; and a school project. The project was a key element and in most courses was allocated one or two days a week. The aim was to develop an aspect of special needs provision in the course member's own school. The focus of the project was decided before the course started, in agreement with the headteacher, local authority coordinator and course tutor. Time was spent on the course assembling the information required to draw up a detailed plan for implementing in the school after the course was over. Topics chosen covered a wide span — developing particular areas of the curriculum, establishing an assessment and diagnostic system, promoting the integration of particular pupils and so on. While not all projects were successful, many were taken forward and seemed likely to result in lasting change in their schools.

Local authorities played a greater part in these courses than is customary with externally provided training. Each appointed a coordinator, usually a special needs adviser, to liaise with the training institution and be generally responsible for the authority's students on the course. The authorities' involvement with the courses encompassed planning, teaching and feedback. The local authority input to teaching was variable, averaging between 10 and 20 per cent of lecture time and concerned mostly with the work of the support service. Local authority staff also selected candidates for the courses from their teaching force. Full details are given in Hegarty and Hodgson (1988).

Future research needs

Where to next? Does research still have a place on the agenda for reform? Now that we know that integration is possible, that ordinary schools *can* educate pupils with special needs, and have identified some of the key forms of support they require in order to do so, what further information would enhance the participation of pupils with special needs in ordinary schools?

Any answers to these questions must take account of the full body of research that has taken place in recent years. The NFER studies have by no means been the only ones; there have been various other studies, particularly concerned with pupils' experience of integration, attitudes to pupils with special needs and whole-school case studies. It is necessary also to take account of new ways of regarding special educational needs and of developments in special education and practice that bear on special needs provision: the priorities and questions are not necessarily the same now as they were ten years ago.

Against this background, two sets of issues stand out: one specific and building on the research to date; and one general, arising out of the changing sociopolitical context of schooling. These point to quite distinct research agendas.

The questions they imply point in separate directions and need to be addressed in quite different ways.

Building on existing research

The first set of questions falls within the mainstream of educational research. They capitalize on previous research and seek to refine and extend it. The concern is to assist practice by producing more precisely targeted information. This can be done in three ways.

1. Examine the component parts of the process in more detail.

This entails a whole set of questions at both micro and macro levels. Integration, or more accurately equipping ordinary schools to provide an appropriate education for pupils with special needs, is a multi-faceted process, and while we now know a certain amount about it there are numerous questions to be asked about each component of the process. These questions can for convenience be grouped at three levels: classroom, teacher and school — though other groupings are possible. In addition to the questions themselves, there has to be a concern, either implicit or explicit, running through each for the pupils' perspective and for the role of parents in their children's education.

Classroom

How can teachers modify the curriculum and manage pupil learning so that pupils at very different stages of development achieve to their full potential?

What is the nature of the social and academic interaction between pupils with special needs and their classmates?

What effect does intervention, e.g. to promote interaction, have?

How is the self-concept of pupils with special needs affected by being part of the mainstream?

Teacher

What is the role of the teacher in the face of growing involvement of other workers — peripatetic specialist teachers, ancillary staff, speech therapists, physiotherapists, educational psychologists, advisers and parents?

How are the different role components to be fitted together?

What shifts in attitude are required, and how are they best achieved?

How are tasks and responsibilities to be assigned when two or more adults are working in a classroom?

How do teachers further their own professional development to best effect?

How can they share expertise with colleagues?

School

How are curricular and other resources to be allocated in respect of pupils who have very different learning needs?

What are the management implications when two schools have a substantial programme of exchange or other shared activity?

2. Ask more specific questions.

We have to move beyond general statements to more precise accounts that relate to pupils' ages and special needs and the types of school they attend. Teaching a visually impaired pupil in an ordinary class is different from teaching one who has considerable learning difficulties. The situation for either is very different depending on whether they are aged 5 or 11 or 15, and on whether the school they attend is rigidly streamed with a strong academic orientation or classes are mixed ability with staff deployed flexibly according to pupil need. The nature and extent of the social interaction possible for individual pupils are governed by factors such as hearing impairment and other communication difficulties, whether they can physically join in activities with classmates and whether they reach puberty later than their peers.

We know from existing studies that much is possible and that much more can be achieved. What we need now is a deeper understanding of individual differences in respect of every facet of integration and a better awareness of the different steps that need to be taken with different groups to ensure that they participate to the full in the life of the school.

3. Pay more attention to the process as a whole.

Many of the inquiries to date have focused on particular aspects of educating pupils with special needs in ordinary schools. Such studies are useful, and essential to any detailed understanding, but they are not enough. They must be backed up with broader studies that examine how the different elements fuse together into a single functioning whole.

Schools are complex systems, composed of several interlocking components — staffing, curriculum, academic organization, assessment procedures. Changes in one part of a system necessitate changes in the other parts as well, in ways that cannot always be predicted clearly. New developments in schools have to be accommodated within existing structures and networks. This applies to special needs provision no less than to any other aspect of school life.

Hence, it is essential to look at provision for special needs and the changes it entails within a whole-school perspective.

How does the curriculum on offer to pupils with special needs relate to the school's mainstream curriculum?

How can we ensure that any differences are justified and appropriate?

If there are integration programmes for specific groups, how do these relate to the school's total provision for pupils with learning difficulties and what is the impact on it?

Can schools monitor and record pupils' progress within a common framework?

How does provision for special needs relate to other developments in schools such as examination reform, multi-cultural education and teacher appraisal?

What steps can be taken to ensure that all teachers appreciate the professional challenges of special needs work, and that this work is accorded its due status within the school?

How can schools move away from earmarking resources for particular categories of pupils and ensure that differential provision according to need is made for each pupil as part of the school's normal provision?

Dealing with the new realities

The second set of questions starts from a very different perspective and necessitates a radically different way of looking at special needs provision. Unlike the questions above, these do not grow out of prior questions in a well-ordered way. The effort is not to add incrementally to an existing body of knowledge but rather to scrutinize the same matters within quite another context. This enterprise may take account of existing knowledge and lines of inquiry, but equally it may ignore them or even dismiss them as irrelevant.

Schools are currently subject to pressures from many sources — falling rolls, changing patterns of post-16 provision, large-scale youth unemployment, new information technologies. Special needs provision is not — nor should it be — exempt from these pressures and the changes they bring in tow. We have to take account of how these factors impinge on integrated education, which is not necessarily the same as their impact on mainstream schooling. There is, therefore, an important subset of questions here, such as:

How do the new opportunities and constraints affect the process by which young people with special needs become adults?

What does integration mean in the context of specific vocational training?

How are young people with special needs affected by structural changes in job opportunities?

These questions are neither totally new or unexpected since the underlying issues have been emerging for a considerable period of time. There is a further subset of questions however with major significance for integrated education, that surfaced for the first time in 1987. These arise from the Government's legislative programme for education.

The proposed imposition of a national curriculum with designated subjects is at the core of this programme. The Consultative Document issued in August 1987 virtually ignored pupils with special needs and left numerous question marks regarding all special needs provision, not just integrated education. Some of the questions are simply a matter of clarifying the Government's intentions. When this has been done however, there will still be numerous operational points to resolve. The goal of a common curriculum *framework* may have widespread support, but it is not something that can be conjured up by legislative fiat. There are many pedagogical, structural, resource and training problems. These need to be addressed for all pupils including those with special needs in a concerted way. This will not be easy, especially as professional and theoretical concerns are being compounded with political ones, but it has to be done. If it is not, the effect of introducing a national curriculum could be to undo the advances of recent years and return pupils with special needs to marginal status in the school system.

A further proposal by the Government is to allow schools to opt out of local authority control and assume independent status. This could raise problems for the pupils with special needs at several levels and make it more difficult for them to receive education in ordinary schools. The precise details of the opting out arrangements are not yet available, nor is it known to what extent schools will avail themselves of them. If the Government's intention of a sizeable proportion of schools opting out is to be realized however, the context in which special education is provided will be changed dramatically. Many questions will have to be answered. At the school level, admission policies will be a primary concern. How will pupils with special needs, of different kinds, fare? Will schools dedicated to academic excellence — in the sense of high examination results as opposed to developing each individual's potential to the full — be willing to accept less academically able pupils? Will schools remaining in local authority control receive a higher proportion of pupils with special needs than before? If pupils with special needs are admitted to opting out schools, will there be appropriate educational provision for them and will they be able to participate in the life of the school?

At local authority level, planning and the provision of adequate choice will be major concerns. If a significant number of schools opt out, local authorities may have to cater for the same number of pupils with special needs in fewer ordinary schools. Apart from the pressure this would put on individual schools, it might lead some authorities to maintain and even expand their special school sector. Questions would also have to be addressed concerning advisory and support services. How should staffing levels be determined in the light of a reduction in the total number of pupils, but not in the number requiring extra support, for which the authority is responsible? Will the structure and mode of working of the support services need to be modified following on changes in the distribution of pupils with special needs?

A further proposal is to give schools greater financial autonomy. They will be allocated a total budget and, within certain limits, will be free to spend it as they see fit. This devolving of financial responsibility will be welcomed by many and it should help to ensure better targeting of resources.

Special needs provision will require the most careful consideration under these new arrangements. There will be issues to resolve at two levels: the calculation of total budgets; and the allocation of funds within the school. Experience from pilot projects has shown how difficult it is to establish a formula for setting budgets for schools of different sizes and drawing on different catchment areas. Some appropriate way must be found of including pupils with special needs in the formula since they draw on school resources to a disproportionate extent. This in turn requires mechanisms for establishing categories of need, gathering empirical information and translating individual pupils' need of resources into financial allocations. Within the school, the problems of earmarked funding in a unified system will have to be addressed. Earmarking funds for a limited period may be legitimate but it can be out of keeping with a whole-school philosophy if maintained over a long period.

Conclusion

Special educational provision in ordinary schools has developed a good deal over the past ten years. Pupils with special needs have greater opportunities now to receive an appropriate education and to participate in the life of ordinary schools. The contribution of research has been to show that this was possible and how in practical terms to achieve it. From an initial concern with particular aspects of integrating pupils with special needs, the research focus has moved on to the ways in which ordinary schools have to change in order to accommodate pupils with special needs. The deeper understanding of the interactive nature of learning difficulties and how schools can prevent them, that flowed from this, has benefited both pupils with special needs and many others not usually regarded as the concern of special education.

Under normal circumstances, the primary need now would be to refine the research questions so as to produce a deeper and more specific understanding of the process of integration. The more special educational provision is seen within ever wider contexts however, the less adequate this is as a research strategy.

The proposed educational reforms pose a particular challenge to special needs provision. If schools become more specialized and competitive, the traditional rationale for integrated education in terms of expanding comprehensive schooling will be less relevant. What price special needs when schools are driven by market forces? The feasibility question, which was apparently disposed of, could well be back on the agenda: what is possible for a neighbourhood school striving to offer comprehensive education may not be possible for a school that has opted out of local authority control and has to compete in a selective market-place. At a broader level, this reflects growing uncertainty over the political will to maintain integrated education or even to consider the implications of proposed reforms for special educational provision.

References

CLUNIES-ROSS, L. and WIMHURST, S. (1983) *The Right Balance*, Windsor, NFER-Nelson.
DEPARTMENT OF EDUCATION AND SCIENCE (1983) The In-service Teacher Training Grants Scheme, Circular 3/83, London, DES.
HEGARTY, S. (1982) 'Meeting special educational needs in the ordinary school', *Educational Research*, **24**, pp. 174–81.

HEGARTY, S. (1985) 'Integration and teaching: some lessons from practice', *Educational Research,* **27**, pp. 9–18.

HEGARTY, S. and HODGSON, A. (1988) 'The one-term Courses', in: Hegarty, S. and Moses, D. (eds.) *Developing Expertise: INSET for Special Needs,* Windsor, NFER-Nelson.

HEGARTY, S., POCKLINGTON, K. and LUCAS, D. (1981) *Educating Pupils with Special Needs in the Ordinary School,* Windsor, NFER-Nelson.

HEGARTY, S., POCKLINGTON, K. and LUCAS, D. (1982) *Integration in Action; case studies in the integration of pupils with special needs,* Windsor, NFER-Nelson.

HODGSON, A., CLUNIES-ROSS, L. and HEGARTY, S. (1984) *Learning Together: Teaching Children with Special Educational Needs in the Ordinary School,* Windsor, NFER-Nelson.

JAMIESON, M., PARLETT, M. and POCKLINGTON, K. (1977) *Towards Integration: A Study of Blind and Partially Sighted Children in Ordinary Schools,* Windsor, NFER-Nelson.

JOWETT, S., HEGARTY, S. and MOSES, D. (1988) *Joining Forces: A Study of Links between Special and Ordinary Schools,* Windsor, NFER-Nelson.

MOSES, D., HEGARTY, S. and JOWETT, S. (1987) 'Meeting special educational needs: support for the ordinary school', *Educational Research,* **24**, pp. 174–81.

MOSES, D., HEGARTY, S. and JOWETT, S. (1988) *Local Authority Support Services,* Windsor, NFER-Nelson.

POCKLINGTON, K. and HEGARTY, S. (1982) *The Development of a Language Unit: an evaluation of Rose-Hill Language Unit, Oxford,* Slough, NFER.

2
The Development of Special Education: Lessons from the Past

Ron Gulliford

Introduction

The 1981 Education Act is the latest in a series of enactments over the last hundred years which have been concerned with the education of pupils whose disabilities or difficulties in learning have been deemed to require some form of special provision. Each of the Acts reflected contemporary attitudes and beliefs as well as professionals' understanding of the problems presented. One simple indication of that can be seen in the change in terminology. At the end of the nineteenth century those concerned with these matters were comfortable with the word 'defective' to refer to learning disability or impairment. Such a description became less acceptable during the 1930s and was replaced following the 1944 Education Act by the term 'handicapped'. By 1981 this also had become unacceptable and was replaced by the term 'special educational needs'. One wonders now whether this term will in its turn prove unacceptable and what — if anything — will replace it. Already, the term 'disability' is being used to designate the specific disorder or disablement whereas the term 'handicap' now refers to the social context within which the disabled child has to live and learn.

The implementation of legislation has always fallen short of its intentions — sometimes markedly so. One recurring reason for that has been economic factors and financial constraints. Another has been the competing demands of other developments on the efforts of administrators and teachers as well as their claim on resources. May there be a risk of this happening in respect of developments from the 1981 Act? In the past there were periods, such as the 1920s and the 1930s, when there were rather few new demands on schools. In the last decade or so, however, schools have been in a continual process of trying to respond to changes in organization and curricula and to a variety of other demands.

Changes in practice and in the legislative framework have always been influenced by the professionals involved — their conceptual framework, their methods of working and the nature of the expertise they bring to the assessment and education of children. At the end of the nineteenth century and well into the twentieth, medical expertise was the main specialist source, and through the school health service the first support service. Very many doctors took an interest, according to their speciality, in pupils then termed defective and it is hardly surprising that the term was used until 1945 since there were no other professionals equipped by training and special expertise to question it until educational psychologists began to be appointed. The Ministry Inspector for special schools was always a doctor until 1933 when the first educationalist with a psychological qualification was appointed.

The teachers who undertook the daily work of teaching pupils in the first special classes and schools were ill-prepared. In the early years some would have been uncertificated having had no teacher training other than experience. In the inter-war years the majority had a two-year training for teaching, but usually with little reference to pupils other than of average ability. There were few books on methods of teaching pupils in special schools and few sources of guidance on teaching backward pupils in ordinary schools. There were few opportunities to attend what we now refer to as short in-service courses. Even in the post-1944 period when one-year or part-time training became available, only a small proportion of teachers were able to receive it. The Warnock Report recorded that only 22 per cent of teachers in special schools, other than those for the blind or deaf, had obtained a special qualification. The main support for teachers in special schools during the first half of the century was the mutual support of associations such as the Special Schools Association, founded in 1903, which attracted teachers of the mentally and physically defective and those for teachers of the blind and the deaf who have long had their own organizations.

The development of psychology as a discipline in its own right advanced considerably in the first half of this century. Emerging from philosophy and biology, and adopting experimental method, psychology had little at first to offer special schools until Binet's tests of intelligence produced in 1905 led to the development of mental and educational testing. This was quickly taken up by Burt, following his appointment to the London County Council in 1913. At the present time when psychological testing is seen as very much less relevant to the identification of children's special needs, it is possible to underestimate what an important step forward testing was at the time. It replaced a number of medical methods and procedures seeking to diagnose mental defect. A report of the Charity Organisation Society (1893) quotes Dr. Warner's description of his procedure:

> the children should be drawn up in ranks ... so that the observer can see each child individually. To fix the eyes of the child ... it is convenient to hold up some object for it to look at. The trained observer can read off the physiognomy of the individual features and their parts, the facial action and expression, the eye movements, the balance of the head and body etc., as quickly as a printed line.

During the inter-war years psychological studies of children's development began to inform practice, a notable example being Susan Isaacs' studies of intellectual and social development in children. Articles drawing upon her work were published in *Teachers World* and subsequently as a book *The Children We Teach* which went through 9 reprints from 1932 to 1948 (Isaacs, 1932). It was notable for its attention to children's learning and adjustment difficulties. The small number of psychologists at work in the few child guidance clinics in the interwar years also contributed to the understanding of backwardness and emotional difficulties but the professional role of the educational psychologist in something like its modern form was mainly a post-1944 development. This is certainly the case in respect of pupils' assessment for special forms of help and for advice on educational methods.

In contrast with the teacher's rather isolated role early in the century, with only the doctor, inspector or administrator giving occasional support, the special education teacher is now likely to have more or less frequent, sometimes daily, working contact with speech therapists, physio-therapists, a variety of social workers, educational advisers and parents.

Finally we should refer to the wide range of ideas, research and innovations in practice which the teacher may be prompted to examine. Sociological concepts and studies have already had an influence on the examination of practices in general and special education in particular. School management has assumed greater importance as schools have faced new demands including the aim of providing better for pupils of a wide range of attainment and ability, an important aspect of which is the management of classrooms to facilitate effective teaching and learning.

Legislation and provision

Since the 1890s provision in special schools and classes has been developing for children with sensory defects and for children who were then termed physically and mentally defective and also for epileptic children. When one reads of the large classes, the poor social and health conditions in urban areas and the teachers' lack of training, one must feel admiration for those who tried to tackle the teaching problem. Legislation provided for the blind and the deaf in 1893. There was permissive legislation in respect of the physically and mentally defective and the epileptic in 1899 which became obligatory in 1914. The School Medical Service was established in 1908 and this was followed by school clinics and by open air schools for delicate children.

The 1914–18 War and the economic difficulties of the 1920s and 1930s constrained development of this basic provision which was mainly in the larger towns. For example, there were 13,000 children in schools for the mentally defective in 1913 and the number had only risen to 17,000 in 1939. Doctors were cautious about certifying a child as feeble minded and were no doubt mindful of possible parental opposition. Teachers were also often reluctant to refer children partly for the same reason and also because, I believe, many were averse to the process of separating a child. In a pamphlet in my possession (written I guess about 1930) a teacher writes about how to help the retarded senior school boy:

> Should such emotionally sensitive boys be forced into special schools? As far as possible they should not. For the sense of shame and the feeling that they have been unjustly humiliated may well be the beginning of an anti-social sentiment that makes them hate all authority and yearn for self-expression and self congratulation through positive criminal acts ... such places may be harmless to semi-human imbeciles but boys who are merely slow at the three Rs should be retained in an atmosphere of culture and normality (Birch, undated).

Pritchard (1963) suggests that the limited increase in provision during the 1920s was partly due to the appointment of the Wood Committee which was set up in 1924 to examine the incidence of feeble-minded children and the need for changes in the system of provision for them (Board of Education, 1929). Local authorities were unwilling to take any action until the committee reported and indeed, a Board of Education circular in 1927 advised them not to set up new schools or enlarge existing ones. The request for figures of incidence was prompted by the considerable variation in numbers on LEA returns to the Board of Education. The report of the committee in 1929 contained the findings of a survey by Dr E. O. Lewis which was conducted in 6 areas, each with a population of 100,000 people. He estimated that nationally there would be 105,000 mentally defective children in terms of the 1914 Education Act. One third of that number had been formally ascertained by LEAs but only 16,000 were attending special schools. The committee estimated that there were about another 10 per cent of pupils in ordinary schools who were educationally retarded and failing to make progress. The committee recommended that a comprehensive provision should be made for all children who though educable in a true sense were unable to profit from the instruction in the ordinary schools (Board of Education, 1929).

The Great Depression in 1929 and the subsequent economic difficulties of the 1930s must be the presumed cause of failure to act on the report's recommendations until they formed the basis of the category of educationally subnormal in the 1945 Regulations following the 1944 Act. The report's concerns for the larger number of educationally retarded children in ordinary schools are reflected in some of the publications of the Board of Education during the later 1930s, notably a booklet on the education of backward children (Board of Education 1938). Mr Lumsden was appointed as Inspector for special schools and his influence was felt in the expression of educational ideas about provision.

There were two other committees of inquiry during the 1930s. One was concerned with distinguishing the educational needs of the partially sighted from those of the blind (Board of Education, 1934). Although methods for the partially sighted were quite well developed, there were still many such pupils in schools for the blind and the committee recommended that they should be educated in special classes in ordinary schools and belong to the 'sighted world'. The second committee (Board of Education, 1938) was concerned with defective hearing, in particular, the need of partially hearing pupils who should be exposed to a normal language environment so far as possible. The committee distinguished:

1. Pupils who could be educated in the ordinary school with special arrangements;
2. Pupils who could be educated in an ordinary school but with hearing aids and visits from a teacher of lip reading;
3. Pupils who should be educated in a special school but in a class for partially deaf children;
4. Deaf pupils whose hearing and speech was so poor that they would need to be educated by methods for those without naturally acquired speech i.e., manual methods.

Post-war legislation and development

The Education Act 1944 and the Handicapped Pupils and School Health Service Regulations 1945 provided a framework for a new phase of development. Previous legislation had been specifically made in respect of the deaf, the blind, the physically or mentally defective, and the epileptic, or like the Education Act 1921 had treated defective pupils as a separate form of provision. The 1944 Act made it a requirement that LEAs should make provision for handicapped pupils as part of their general duty to ensure that pupils were educated in accordance with their age, ability and aptitude and 'to have regard to the need for seeing that provision is made for pupils who suffer from any disability of mind or body by providing either in special schools or otherwise special educational treatment'. It is interesting to note that Section 33 of the Act stated that LEAs should provide, so far as is practicable, for those pupils whose disability is serious, in special schools. This proved a most controversial point in the Parliamentary debate and many MPs objected, not for the reason that one might assume in the 1980s, but because the words 'so far as practicable' would enable authorities to avoid their obligations. The concern of politicians was well founded since the quality and amount of provision varied enormously in different areas of the country. The Regulations which followed the 1944 Education Act defined eleven categories of handicapped pupils, soon to be reduced to ten. They were the blind, the partially sighted, the deaf, the partially deaf (partially hearing from 1962), delicate, diabetic, epileptic, educationally subnormal, maladjusted, physically handicapped, and speech defective.

The list included two groups which had not previously been provided for in legislation: the maladjusted and the speech defective. Awareness of the former had been shown earlier in the century by concern for pupils who were described as 'nervous' but understanding began to develop in the late 1920s when three child guidance clinics on the American model, employing a psychiatrist, psychologist, and social worker were set up in London. The first to be set up by an LEA was at Birmingham in 1932. There were also a few independent schools for disturbed children set up during the 1930s and the first local authority school was established at Leicester in 1932. A class for disturbed pupils had been in existence in Oxford since 1930 and this is now Northern House Special School. An important influence in the recognition of this group was war-time evacuation when hostels were established for evacuated children who proved difficult to place in billets. Moreover, some of the child guidance clinics and their staff had moved into evacuation areas and were used for local as well as evacuated children which disseminated awareness of the problems as well as what could be done. Maladjusted children had not been the subject of any inquiry prior to the war and it was appropriate therefore that the Underwood Committee was set up to grapple with the issues (Ministry of Education, 1955). Since the term maladjustment was not in common use before the war, it is not surprising that the committee, appointed in 1950, took five years to conclude their inquiry reviewing as it did the theory and practice in this country and abroad. This had a bearing on how maladjusted pupils would be regarded. The Committee also surveyed three LEAs to try and establish some degree of incidence for maladjustment in schools. The percentage of children deemed to need attendance at a child guidance clinic ranged from 5 to nearly 12 per cent. By 1970 there were more than 400 child guidance clinics attended by 70,000 children. By 1962 there were 5,000 pupils placed in 43 residential schools, in 13 day schools, 69 classes and 45 hostels. Ten years later in 1972 the total number of pupils was 14,208 placed in 136 residential schools, 61 day schools, 141 classes and 41 hostels.

A growing awareness of speech defects in pupils had been shown during the 1930s by the increasing number of appointments of speech therapists in local authorities. In 1933 a resolution was adopted at the Annual General Meeting of the Association of Education Committees urging the government to make provision for meeting the special needs of these pupils as compulsory. The Ministry of Education envisaged that the majority of pupils with speech defects should attend their own schools and have speech therapy from LEA employed therapists. Two schools were established by the Invalid Children's Aid Association for children with severe receptive and/or expressive aphasia: Moor House in 1947 and a primary school, the John Horniman in 1958. A few other schools have been established since then and from the late 1970s there has been a rapid development of units or special classes for pupils with speech and language disorders. These pupils require regular speech therapy and teaching methods matching their very individual needs.

Two additional categories resulted from the need to distinguish the special teaching for the partially sighted from that of the educationally blind, and the needs of the partially hearing from those of the deaf. At the present time, categories are rightly viewed with disfavour and are seen as restricting, but in the years prior to the 1945 Regulations distinguishing and providing for the needs of the partially sighted and the partially deaf was a real issue. Earlier in the century some special schools and classes had been established for severely myopic pupils and by 1930 there were 37 schools providing for 2,000 pupils. There were many partially sighted children being taught in blind schools, often in residential schools, because there was not a convenient day school for them to attend. The committee of inquiry on the education of partially sighted pupils reported in 1936 and recommended that these pupils should be educated in ordinary schools, have appropriate educational and social contact with pupils in mainstream schools, and that there should be appropriate methods and resources. It also recommended that schools for blind pupils should be reorganized so that some would become schools for pupils who were partially sighted. Little was done about these recommendations until ten years after the new Regulations, when conferences were held for interested schools and organizations for the blind, which resulted in four schools becoming schools for the partially sighted. As building restrictions were lifted during the 1950s, it became possible to establish new schools for the partially sighted. Parents were pleased that their children were not being placed in a school for the blind; teachers were able to concentrate on the development of methods for the partially sighted.

A significant factor in this was a change in medical opinion which had previously imposed restrictions on pupils with myopia in their use of vision for fine tasks such as reading and writing. Also on physical education because of the risk of detached retina. A chapter in the Health of the School Child 1946–47 (Ministry of Education, 1949) provided a thorough discussion of contemporary medical opinion and an outline of appropriate teaching methods. Far from suggesting to medical officers that categorization involved a simple and a straightforward recommendation, the writer concluded that 'deciding how best to educate a partially sighted child is even more complex than it was. There is no easy way out by saying "Send him to a special school". A choice of methods of education is available according to the child's educational needs and choice requires enlightened study of the child and knowledge of alternative modes of action'. This comment would not have been out of place in the 1980s!

The process of developing distinctive special methods has continued, assisted by appropriately planned schools with special lighting and furniture, and also by technological developments. It was also furthered by the formation of an Association for the Education and Welfare of the Partially Sighted which enabled teachers and welfare workers to meet discuss their common aims and problems, to review and assess and to share their experiences. When that desirable process of differentiation had served its purpose, it was possible for another committee of inquiry on the education of the visually handicapped (DES, 1972) to recommend the inclusive term visually handicapped. About the same time, the course for teachers of the blind at the University of Birmingham used the same term and made explicit its training for the full range of visual impairment. The two organizations for teachers of the blind and the partially sighted also merged.

Similar issues arising from the wide range of hearing impairments were also apparent in the field of the education of the deaf. As noted earlier, a committee of inquiry (Board of Education, 1938a) had recommended a classification of the deaf according to the degree of hearing impairment and the appropriate placement for their education. Hence the new category of partially deaf which was changed to partially hearing in 1962. A Department of Education and Science Circular

(10/62) emphasized the variable factors, especially those of speech and language development, which should be taken into account in decisions about placement. It also pointed out that better diagnosis, the opportunities given by improved hearing aids, and an earlier start to auditory training had already been reflected in the proportion of pupils deemed partially hearing. A significant development in the provision for partially hearing pupils had started with four units in ordinary schools in London in 1947. Growth was slow until 1960 but by 1966 there were 162 units in England and Wales. Education Survey No. 1 (DES, 1967) gave a useful account and appraisal of their opportunities and difficulties. The same period saw the development of the service of peripatetic teachers of the deaf which as Education Survey 6 (DES, 1969) reported had shown a widening field of duties which 'extends from the clinics to the child's homes, to their schools and on into employment'. It is of interest to note that just as teachers of the partially sighted felt the need to establish their own organization, so teachers of the partially hearing formed their own society in order to focus on the issues arising in their work, in units in ordinary schools and in peripatetic work. Subsequently the two groups merged into one association for teachers of the deaf. These developments in the field of hearing impairment provided an exploration of the practice of integrated education long before the issue became so prominent in the 1970s. Hegarty *et al.* (1982) quotes the percentage figures for seven European countries (1977–8) of the hearing impaired children being educated in ordinary and special schools. The UK had the highest proportion, 52 per cent, in ordinary schools, a trend which has continued upward.

The separate categories for the partially sighted and the partially hearing might be thought to have been justified in order to assist the development of distinctive approaches and provisions. It would be difficult to argue for the separate categories of diabetic and delicate. The former were considered separately partly as a result of war-time evacuation experience of providing hostels for some diabetic pupils to ensure that their treatment was maintained. In 1958 separate categorization ceased and they were included as delicate. In the case of the delicate, extensive provision for pupils with poor health and nutrition had been made in open air schools since around 1909. There was considerable public concern around the turn of the century about the health of school children when two in three recruits for the Boer War had to be turned down as unfit for service. From 1909 provision of open air schools was made by many urban authorities. It is often referred to as the Open Air School Movement and appropriately so since it aroused a good deal of philanthropic support. Pritchard (1963) refers to the fact that every annual report of the Board's Medical branch from 1908 to 1916 contained a chapter extolling the virtues of the open air schools. By the time of the new Regulations in 1945 the health of school children had already improved and other medical advances in the subsequent decades reduced the need for these schools, and, where they continued to exist, they were used for a diverse group of pupils with special needs.

Improvements in pupils' health and medical treatment had different effects in the case of the population of schools for the physically handicapped. Earlier in the century the chief causes of physical handicap were tuberculosis of bones and joints, chronic rheumatic heart disease, paralysis from poliomyelitis, and congenital defects. By the 1950s there had been a substantial reduction of the first two of these and polio immunization was on the horizon. Considerable attention was being given to the medical, therapeutic and educational treatment of cerebral palsy and a number of schools were established specifically for them. In the 1960s, pupils with another congenital condition, spina bifida and hydrocephalus, began to appear in increasing numbers in the schools as a result of early surgical intervention. Compared with pre-war years therefore, pupils in schools for the physically handicapped were more frequently those with multiple difficulties who required a range of therapies, specialist care and, because of associated learning difficulties, needed rather more specialized educational treatment. A survey showed there was a considerable number of physically handicapped pupils being educated in ordinary schools (DES, 1972b). The survey undertaken in 1968–69 drew upon information from school medical officers in LEAs. At a time when there were 8,500 children in schools for the physically handicapped, it was found that there were 10,200 in ordinary schools, two-thirds of them being in primary schools. Those in the special schools tended to be the most severely and often multiply handicapped but many of those in ordinary schools also required various mobility aids, therapies and ancillary help.

It is of interest to note that only 118 pupils were at that time placed in a special unit — a form of provision which became more available in the 1970s and was the subject of a study by Cope and Anderson (1977) which reported positive findings and identified some of the requirements for integrated schemes. The remaining category, educationally subnormal, was defined as 'pupils who by reason of limited ability or other conditions resulting in educational retardation require some specialised form of education, wholly or partly in substitution for the education normally given in ordinary schools'. The definition was an attempt to put into effect the recommendations of the Wood Report sixteen years before to provide a basis for providing special help to a larger group of educationally retarded pupils. It was suggested that 1 per cent of pupils were likely to need education in a day special school, and perhaps 0.2 per cent in a residential school: about 8 or 9 per cent of pupils would need special help in ordinary schools. The pamphlet No. 5 Special Educational Treatment (Ministry of Education, 1946) commented: 'How this can best be done must be found by experiment ... for as yet there is no unanimity of view on how schools can make the best arrangements for their retarded pupils'. Forty years later there is still no unanimity and we are still experimenting. It is interesting to note that Pamphlet No. 5 devoted eight pages to explanations of the new category and to suggesting in broad terms what was intended. This contrasts with no more than a page on each of the other categories. The Department of Education and Science (1964) restated its views on what constituted educational subnormality: 'Educational backwardness is not regarded as a single sharply defined characteristic as was mental deficiency but rather as a matter of degree and origin and caused by a combination of circumstances ... nor is special education looked upon as a form of education peculiar to special schools'.

Unfortunately the intentions of the new categorization were only partially realized. Special school provision for educationally subnormal pupils began to increase immediately. The abolition of the process of certification probably assisted this and the general sense of making a new start probably helped, especially as new accommodation began to be provided. At first, this did not take the form of new buildings since post-war restrictions prevented it but some old day schools were rehoused in large houses and advantage was taken of the availability of vacant country houses which were converted to residential schools. The improved facilities and educational opportunities contributed to the greater readiness of headteachers to refer pupils, a factor which also operated in areas where there had been no provision pre-war. The number of pupils in special schools for the educationally subnormal increased from 11,000 in 1946 to 35,000 in 1960 and 52,000 in 1970.

Reference was made in Pamphlet No. 5 to the 8 or 9 per cent of educationally subnormal pupils in ordinary schools:

> The problem of finding a way of educating them is one which the modern schools must face and the staff will be justified in trying out enterprising methods and organisation. It is of outstanding importance that such pupils should not be entirely segregated from their fellows and from the corporate life of the school and that whatever course of work they follow it should have real purpose and meaning for them ... There is room here for much thought and experiment.

There were, however, many adverse factors which impeded the intended development of provision in ordinary schools for educationally retarded pupils — which can be regarded as an attempt to do better for the least successful pupils in schools, comparable to the one in five with special educational needs indicated in the Warnock Report (DES, 1978). There was a post-war shortage of teachers even though a thirteen-month Emergency Training Course operated until the end of the 1950s and alleviated the shortage. Two other factors — a large post-war rise in the birth rate and the raising of the school leaving age from 14 to 15 in 1948 — kept the education service stretched. As late as 1961 it was stated in Circular 11/61 that 'it is not to be expected that so long as the present shortage of teachers continues many schools will be able to make fully satisfactory arrangements for their own backward children'. Proposals to employ peripatetic advisory teachers working in special remedial classes or centres, and for area special classes were suggested. Although the teacher shortage eased during the 1960s, there were many other concerns which competed for attention, for example, the reorganization of secondary schools on comprehensive school lines, the assimilation of ethnic minority groups, teaching English as a second language, and preparations for raising the school leaving age (ROSLA) which occurred in 1973. It is hardly surprising that Education Survey 15, *Slow Learners in Secondary Schools*, based on an HMI survey in 1967–68 (DES, 1971), presented a depressing picture of the provision. HMI concluded that 'In a period of rapid educational change, it is perhaps not surprising that in some schools confronted with many difficulties of staff, accommodation, organisation, the needs of the slowest pupils seem to have received less than their fair share of attention'. They went on to refer to the uncertainties about pupils' potential, the nature and extent of their disabilities, about organization, teaching methods and suitable curricula. They concluded that 'In these circumstances it should come as no surprise to find that there is much to be done before the needs of the slow learners in secondary schools can be said to be satisfactorily met'. Nor is it surprising that throughout this period, there were annually about 10,000 pupils recorded as waiting for places in special schools for the educationally subnormal and that the number of pupils so placed increased not only through the primary years but well into the secondary age groups.

The failure to provide satisfactorily for educationally retarded pupils in ordinary schools was not only due to the various factors referred to above. A fundamental problem was uncertainty about aims, objectives and methods for 'slow learners'. At the time of the 1945 Regulations there was rather little experience and few publications about the education of backward pupils on which to draw. A Board of Education publication in 1937 could only suggest that 'The methods employed will demand a greater amount of physical activity. They will involve more frequent movement, a good deal more practical work in all subjects and a much fuller use of pictures, models and objects'. A common organizational response was the 'backward class' about which that 1937 publication said; 'Experience showed that children put into such classes seldom continued over a period of years to make such progress as would justify their segregation from the rest of the school' and 'there was little difference in the treatment of children whose backwardness was due to innate dullness and of those whose retardation could be attributed to some extraneous and removable cause'. Nevertheless the backward class or stream continued to be used into the 1970s.

It was the work of Schonell through his publications and his readiness to contribute to courses for teachers which began to disseminate knowledge of how pupils' potential and difficulties could be understood and provided for. He developed methods and materials to assist teachers beginning with a book on spelling (Schonell, 1932) and arithmetic (Schonell, 1937), and went on to produce the first major British book on teaching basic subjects to backward children (Schonell, 1942). In 1948 he established at Birmingham the first course in an English university education department for training educational psychologists and a course in child development which included much attention to children's educational difficulties. He also established a remedial education centre where students could be trained in methods of assessment and remedial teaching. Many of the students went on to establish the first remedial teaching services in LEAs which increased steadily in number during the 1950s and 1960s (Sampson, 1975).

Although Schonell was interested in backward pupils in general, he was at pains to explain to teachers that all backward pupils were not dull — a point which really did need to be made; that some were of average or even superior intelligence but for a variety of social, emotional and environmental factors as well as specific learning difficulties were failing to make progress. He distinguished between general backwardness and retardation, the latter being indicated when there was a marked discrepancy between a pupil's score on a non-verbal group test not requiring reading or an individually given test and his score on an attainment test. This was an important idea to communicate since as The Handbook of Suggestions (Board of Education, 1937) had said 'there was little difference in the treatment of children whose backwardness was due to innate dullness and of those whose retardation could be attributed to some extraneous and removable cause'. Although a simplistic interpretation of this distinction and its implications for practice soon came under criticism both in terms of statistical and psychometric interpretation, it had an influence in drawing attention to the need for special measures to tackle the problem of failure in acquiring basic educational skills. Remedial teaching services developed during the next twenty years, in spite of negative or inconclusive evidence of the effects of remedial teaching. The word remedial became widely adopted to refer to pupils, teachers and classes in both primary and secondary schools.

The first signs of a different view of what 'remedial' pupils needed in their education came in the Bullock report (DES, 1975) which both at primary and secondary level was obviously concerned about the danger that special arrangements for giving additional help to pupils with low attainment in basic skills could be at the expense of the pupils' experience of the normal curriculum and of their own teachers and their class groups. A Scottish Education Department report (1978) gave an even firmer expression to this idea by stressing that every teacher is responsible for recognizing and providing for the pupils with learning difficulties. Which — ironically — brings us back forty years to the warning in a Board of Education publication on the *Education of Backward Children* in 1937: 'the creation of a new class of specialist peripatetic teachers as a permanency would be as likely to hinder as well as to help the spread of knowledge and skill in handling backward pupils, because of the danger that would beset the teachers in the schools to depend on such outside help rather than upon their own resources'. Fortunately there is now a strong drive in many schools, particularly in secondary schools where the problem is the most difficult to solve, to develop systems of support to teachers and pupils with special needs so that separate special help may not be needed — or can be minimized.

The acceptance of the mentally handicapped into education effected by the 1970 Education Act is perhaps the most notable advance — if only because it was so long delayed. When the new category of educationally subnormal was described and explained in Pamphlet No. 5 it was made clear that children with IQs below about 55 cannot be educated at school. 'In the past, numbers of children who have been recognised ... to be ineducable or detrimental to others have, on sentimental grounds, been allowed to attend school. In future this practice should cease.' It goes on at considerable length and detail to refer to objectionable habits and other circumstances which would distract the other pupils, occupy the teacher's attention and bring the school into disrepute. There were at that time few classes for mentally handicapped pupils and those that there were often took place in church halls run by keen but untrained staff. Matters improved during the 1960s when a number of health authorities built new junior training centres and a training council was set up to monitor the training of staff. Meanwhile, from around 1950, in a field previously dependent on medical knowledge and interest, psychologists appointed to mental deficiency hospitals or to research work into the learning and habilitation of the subnormal child or adolescent began to publish findings which demonstrated that the mentally handicapped could learn under appropriate conditions of reward and with breakdown of the tasks to be learnt. As this work progressed and the work in training centres developed, the evidence accumulated that these pupils would respond to an appropriately planned education. The Education Act 1970 brought them into the education service. New pre-service courses of teacher training brought young, enthusiastic and often very well qualified young people into this field of special education. A further significant development was the Hester Adrian Research Centre, established to undertake research into the education of the mentally handicapped. The new schools developed distinctive curricula and methods. One measure of the progress made is that many — perhaps most — schools have integration programmes whereby pupils have experience of activities or learning with ordinary pupils. Some are educated in ordinary schools and in most areas there are further education opportunities in colleges. The contrast between the 1945 view and the reality of the present is a measure of the progress.

Rethinking special education

In the early 1970s many of the intentions of the 1945 Handicapped Pupils Regulation had been achieved or partially so. There was a much more adequate provision for most children with marked disabilities and, compared with 1944, it was more evenly spread over the country. The categorization of handicapped children was increasingly questioned and there was also a strong current of opinion that pupils should not be separated from normal experiences of learning and living. It also was being made clearer that a much larger number of children than had commonly been realized had difficulties which affected their learning and development. The National Child Development Study's report (Pringle *et al.*, 1966) had surprised the public by showing that some 13 per cent of seven year olds were deemed to need some form of special help though 0.4 per cent at that age were in special schools and only 5 per cent were being helped in their ordinary schools. The Isle of Wight survey (Rutter *et al.*, 1970) had made a thorough study of more than 2,000 children aged between 9 and 11 years of age and had identified 16 per cent as having either intellectual or educational retardation, physical handicaps or emotional or behaviour difficulties. A study carried out in London using similar methods and criteria (Rutter *et al.*, 1975) had found much higher figures. The report of the 1970 study concluded with a discussion of its implications for services, emphasizing the importance of multi-disciplinary cooperation and also suggesting that 'special schooling should be reconsidered from the point of view of the actual needs of handicapped children'. The term 'special needs' had already been used in a book by Lesley Webb (1967) called *Children with Special Needs in the Infant School*. The report of a multi-disciplinary Working Party at the National Children's Bureau (Younghusband, 1970) was much concerned with the personal and social needs of children, the needs of the family and also referred to special educational needs. At the same time, the conviction that those with handicaps should have as normal an experience of living, working and being educated as possible was strengthened from many sources. In brief, many ideas were current about the recognition and assessment of handicapped children, about the coordination of services, and the forms of provision of special help. These led in 1974 to the establishment of the Warnock Committee of Inquiry and in 1981 to the Education Act.

Implications

The development of special education which has been outlined extends over 100 years. The intentions for provision as expressed in legislation were only partly realized. In the first period, pre-war, the concept of defect, the separate legislation, the lack of professionals other than doctors and teachers, and the latter's relative lack of specialist knowledge, were limitations on development. War and economic difficulties retarded development. In the second period, post-war, regulations distinguished categories which had not been previously recognized and others where differentiation was felt to be needed at that time. The idea of provision for a larger group with learning difficulties was imperfectly realized in practice during the next forty years partly because remedial education was, in a sense, a wrong turning and also because schools faced so many other preoccupations.

What lessons might there be for the future? If there are any, I do not think that they can be safely drawn from a brief and selective outline of the past. Historical studies are needed which not only trace developments in legislation and practice but do so in the context of the knowledge, beliefs and circumstances of the time. It is easy for non-historians to judge the past from the viewpoint of the present and its much broader base of theory such as the psychological and sociological.

But it is clear that in the past legislative intentions frequently took a long time to work through into practice and were often only partially realized. Ten years after the Warnock Report and five years after the date of implementing the 1981 Education Act, the need for a new approach seems fairly widely understood and accepted. We are, however, at an early stage in the necessary development of the new practice i.e. the development of the teaching and organizational skills of ordinary teachers and of support systems in schools. One lesson from the past is that the development of better forms of provision in ordinary schools has had to compete for attention and resources with many other changes and new initiatives. The future prospect looks very similar and it will surely be important to ensure that the unfinished task of developing new systems of provision for children and young people with special needs is given the attention and resources which are needed.

One necessary resource is the teacher who has had the opportunity for further study and training, provisions for which came rather late in the period outlined. It is difficult to believe that the development of an appropriate form of education for the mentally handicapped could have been developed so successfully if special courses of training had not been organized. A similar claim could be made in respect of teaching the hearing impaired and the visually handicapped. It is also worth noting that in the case of all three disabilities, the establishment of centres for research contributed to the development of special methods. It is essential to ensure that the new arrangements for funding and organizing the in-service education and training of teachers prove effective in providing a coherent view of pupils' difficulties and needs and of desirable modifications of educational procedures.

References

BIRCH, A. C. (undated) *How to Help the Retarded Senior Schoolboy*, London, Watts.

BOARD OF EDUCATION and BOARD OF CONTROL (1929) *Report of the Joint Departmental Committee on Mental Deficiency*, The Wood Report, London, HMSO.

BOARD OF EDUCATION (1934) *Report of the Committees of Inquiry into Problems Relating to Partially Sighted Children*, London, HMSO.

BOARD OF EDUCATION (1937) *Handbook of Suggestions for Teachers*, London, HMSO.

BOARD OF EDUCATION (1938a) *Report of the Committee of Inquiry into Problems Relating to Children with Defective Hearing*, London, HMSO.

BOARD OF EDUCATION (1938b) *The Education of Backward Children*, London, HMSO.

CHARITY ORGANISATION SOCIETY (1893) *The Feeble-Minded Child and Adult*: A report on an investigation of the physical and mental condition of 50,000 children, with a suggestion for the better education and care of the feeble minded children and adults, London, Swan and Sonnenschein.

COPE, C. and ANDERSON, E. (1977) *Special Units in Ordinary Schools*, London, Institute of Education.

DEPARTMENT OF EDUCATION AND SCIENCE (1961) *Special Educational Treatment*, Circular 11/61.

DEPARTMENT OF EDUCATION AND SCIENCE (1962) *Children with Impaired Hearing*, Circular 10/62.

DEPARTMENT OF EDUCATION AND SCIENCE (1964) *Slow Learners at School*, Education Pamphlet No. 6, London, HMSO.

DEPARTMENT OF EDUCATION AND SCIENCE (1967) *Units for Partially Hearing Children*, Education Survey No. 1, London, HMSO.

DEPARTMENT OF EDUCATION AND SCIENCE (1969) *Peripatetic Teachers of the Deaf*, Education Survey No. 6, London, HMSO.

DEPARTMENT OF EDUCATION AND SCIENCE (1971) *Slow Learners in Secondary Schools*, Education Survey 15, London, HMSO.

DEPARTMENT OF EDUCATION AND SCIENCE (1972a) *The Education of the Visually Handicapped*, Vernon Report, London, HMSO.

DEPARTMENT OF EDUCATION AND SCIENCE (1972b) *The Health of the School Child*, Report of the Chief Medical Officer of the Department of Education and Science 1969–1972, London, HMSO.

DEPARTMENT OF EDUCATION AND SCIENCE (1975) *A Language for Life*, Bullock Report, London, HMSO.

DEPARTMENT OF EDUCATION AND SCIENCE (1978) *Special Educational Needs*, Warnock Report, London, HMSO.

HEGARTY, S., POCKLINGTON, K., with LUCAS, S. (1982) *Educating Pupils with Special Needs in the Ordinary School*, London, NFER/Methuen.

ISAACS, S. (1932) *The Children We Teach*, London, University of London Press.

MINISTRY OF EDUCATION (1946) *Special Educational Treatment*, Pamphlet No. 5, London, HMSO.

MINISTRY OF EDUCATION (1949) *The Health of the School Child* 1946–7, London, HMSO.

MINISTRY OF EDUCATION (1955) *Report of the Committee on Maladjusted Children*, Underwood Committee, London, HMSO.

PRINGLE, M. L. K., BUTLER, N. R. and DAVIE, R. (1966) *11,000 Seven Year Olds*, London, Longmans.

PRITCHARD, D. G. (1963) *Education and the Handicapped 1760–1960*, London, Routledge and Kegan Paul.

RUTTER, M., TIZARD, J. and WHITMORE, K. (1970) *Education Health and Behaviour*, London, Methuen.

RUTTER, M., COX, A., TUPLING, C., BERGER, M. and YULE, W. (1975) 'Attainment and adjustment in two geographical areas: the prevalence of psychiatric disorders', *British Journal of Psychiatry*, **126**, pp. 493–509.

SAMPSON, O. (1975) *Remedial Education*, London, Routledge and Kegan Paul.

SCHONELL, F. J. (1932) *Essentials in Teaching and Testing Spelling*, London, Macmillan.

SCHONELL, F. J. (1937) *Diagnosis of Individual Difficulties in Arithmetic*, Edinburgh, Oliver and Boyd.

SCHONELL, F. J. (1942) *Backwardness in the Basic Subjects*, Edinburgh, Oliver and Boyd.

SCOTTISH EDUCATION DEPARTMENT (1978) *The Education of Pupils with Learning Difficulties in Primary and Secondary Schools in Scotland*, Edinburgh, HMSO.

WEBB, L. (1967) *Children with Special Needs in the Infant School*, London, Colin Smythe.

YOUNGHUSBAND, E., BIRCHALL, D., DAVIES, R. and PRINGLE, M. L. K. (1970) *Living with Handicap*, London, National Bureau for Cooperation in Child Care.

3
The Implementation of the 1981 Education Act

Jennifer Evans, Brian Goacher, Klaus Wedell and John Welton

Introduction

The 1981 Education Act, implemented on April 1st 1983, brought into effect many of the recommendations contained in the Warnock Report (Department of Education and Science, 1978). The Report had the following remit:

> To review the educational provision in England, Wales and Scotland for children and young people handicapped by disabilities of body or mind, taking account of the medical aspects of their needs, together with arrangements to prepare them for entry into employment; to consider the most effective use of resources for these purposes; to make recommendations.

The setting up of the committee was a response to widespread criticisms of the system for identifying and making educational provision for children with special needs from all quarters: parents and their organizations; psychologists; teachers; and doctors. Their main concerns were that there was undue emphasis placed on the differentness of children deemed handicapped and that a medical model of diagnosis and treatment prevailed. The system was highly influenced by the medical profession, who registered children as 'handicapped persons' and had a pivotal role in deciding on their education. Parents had limited rights to have their views heard.

This medical model was already changing, as had been acknowledged by the introduction in 1975 of new procedures for identifying children and assessing them for special educational treatment. These involved the use of special education forms introduced by means of Circular 2/75 (Department of Education and Science, 1975). These new procedures gave a much greater role to educational psychologists and advisers in assessing children and deciding on suitable provision. The Circular also laid emphasis on the importance of inter-service cooperation in making provision for such children, and on the importance of involving parents in discussions about their child's needs.

The key recommendations of the Warnock Report, subject as they were to widespread debate, were as follows:

1. The concept of a continuum of special needs should replace the arbitrary division of children into two populations — the handicapped and the non-handicapped. It should be recognized that up to one in five children would have special needs at some time during their school career;
2. The ten categories of handicap into which children had been assigned in order to receive their special education should be replaced by a single term, 'learning difficulties', which would focus attention on the *educational* implications of disabilities;
3. The views of parents should be actively sought. Parents should be treated as partners. A 'named person' should be assigned to support parents of children with special needs;
4. Children with learning difficulties should, as far as possible, be educated in ordinary schools;
5. Children who had been assessed as requiring education in a special school should have a record of needs. Parents should have access to this;
6. Attention should be given to the transition from school to adult life. Pupils' needs should be assessed at least two years before they were due to leave school;
7. Teacher training, both initial and in-service was required to improve teachers' skills in identifying and meeting special educational needs;
8. Advisory and support services in LEAs should be enhanced to provide help for teachers with pupils with special educational needs;
9. Cooperation between education, health and social services should be improved. Health authorities should appoint a named doctor and nurse for each special school. Social services should appoint a liaison officer to link with the careers advisory service;
10. Inter-professional training for those concerned with meeting special educational needs should be promoted;
11. There should be closer coordination in the planning and delivery of services for children and young people with special needs;
12. Voluntary organizations should be given a greater role in the provision of services.

The publication of the Warnock Report caused a great many LEAs to review their practices and to attempt to put some of the principles which underpinned the report into effect. Before the 1981 Act was passed there had, therefore, been some shift in outlook and attitude, which prepared those working in the three services for the new demands to be made upon them.

The 1981 Education Act represents an attempt to put into a legislative framework some of the ideas and principles outlined in the Warnock Report. The ten categories of handicap were abolished, and replaced by a single term 'special educational needs'. This term can only be understood by reference to three key definitions:

1. learning difficulty
2. special educational provision
3. special educational needs

Learning difficulty

A child has a learning difficulty if he or she:

> has significantly greater difficulty in learning than the majority of children of his or her age;
> has a disability which either prevents or hinders him or her from making use of educational facilities of a kind generally provided in schools, within the area of the local authority concerned for children of his or her age;
> is aged under five and falls into one of these categories or is likely to later if special educational provision is not made.

Special educational provision

For children under two years of age this means *any* educational provision but for children over the age of two it means educational provision which is *additional to or otherwise different from* the educational provision made generally for children of his or her age in schools maintained by the local education authority concerned.

Special educational needs

A pupil has special educational needs if he or she has a learning difficulty which calls for special educational provision to be made. This definition of special educational needs and special educational provision encompasses the needs of the estimated 18 per cent of pupils with less severe special needs where these may be provided for within mainstream schools. Also, approximately 2 per cent of pupils who have more complex needs and may be given statements following an assessment using statutory procedures laid down by the 1981 Education Act. The threshold at which the decision to issue a statement is made will depend upon local factors such as the availability of resources to help children in mainstream schools, as well as the local authorities' policies about the types of provision to be allocated through statements.

In the case of pupils whose needs are such as to require the local authority to determine the special educational provision to be made, the 1981 Act lays down procedures to be followed. The procedures require an assessment of the pupil's needs to be made, following which the LEA will decide whether to issue a statement. The procedures are designed to allow parents access to the advice upon which decisions are made, and to give their own views.

The assessment has to include, at a minimum, advice from the pupil's head-teacher, an educational psychologist and a doctor. The social services department is informed if a child is being assessed and asked if they have any information to offer. Other professionals who may be working with a child, such as a speech therapist or a child psychiatrist, should be asked to contribute advice for the assessment. After considering the advice, the education authority may decide to issue a statement. The statement should reflect the advice given and should give details of the child's special educational needs, of the special educational provision to be made to meet the needs, the name of the school at which the pupil will be educated, and details of any other non-educational provision to be made.

If parents are not satisfied that the provision offered will meet their child's needs, they can appeal to a local appeal committee. The findings of this committee are not binding on the LEA. Parents can ultimately appeal to the Secretary of State if they are still not satisfied following a local appeal.

Pupils with statements must have their progress reviewed at least annually. Between the ages of 12 years 6 months and 14 years 6 months they have to be re-assessed using the procedures outlined above. At the annual review and at the re-assessment, consideration should be given to whether a pupil in a segregated setting could be moved into a more integrated setting.

The 1981 Education Act places upon local authorities a duty to integrate pupils with special educational needs, including those with statements, into ordinary schools. The conditions attached to this duty are that:

The parents' views must be taken into account;
The child receives the special educational provision he or she requires;
It is compatible with the efficient education of other children in the school;
It is an efficient use of resources.

It has been said that these conditions will allow local authorities to continue to segregate pupils. This will depend upon local authorities' willingness to take account of parental wishes, and to make extra resources available in mainstream schools to enable pupils to succeed.

Circular 1/83 (Department of Education and Science, 1987) which followed the 1981 Act gives details of the ways in which the duties and responsibilities laid on LEAs, DHAs and SSDs should be carried out. It stresses the role given to parents, calling for 'frankness and openness' in the LEAs' and other agencies' dealings with parents. It also calls for greater inter-service cooperation and collaboration in meeting the needs of children.

Some of the Warnock Report's proposals were not brought into effect by the Act. For example, the concept of the 'named person' as an independent supporter of parents was not mentioned. The Report also called for an advisory committee to monitor developments on special education, to review current practices and inform policy-making. This was not set up.

Research into the implementation of the 1981 Education Act

The Department of Education and Science funded a research programme following the implementation of the 1981 Education Act consisting of three research projects: based at the National Foundation for Educational Research (Hegarty, 1988); the Hester Adrian Research Centre, Manchester and Huddersfield Polytechnic; and London University (Goacher *et al.*, 1988). The NFER project looked at local authority support services, links between ordinary and special schools, and in-service training. The Manchester/Huddersfield project had three inter-related themes: the development and evaluation of a modular diploma in special educational needs; the development of short school-focused courses for teachers; and a follow-up evaluation of the EDY (Education of the Developmentally Young) training package. The third project, the results of which are reported in this chapter, was the Policy and Provision for Special Educational Needs project, based at the University of London Institute of Education. This project undertook a study of developments in policies, practices and provision for children with special educational needs between 1983 and 1986, following the implementation of the 1981 Act.

Methodology

The research, which was partly based on a previous DES pilot study by the research team directors (Welton *et al.*, 1982) was carried out in three phases. Firstly, preliminary discussions were held with a wide range of personnel in health, education and social services departments in a total of thirty-seven locations in England and Wales. This initial phase allowed the project team to explore a wide range of issues concerned with the 1981 Education Act with those who were centrally involved in its implementation. The discussions took the form of group interviews with representatives of the education, health and social services in the local area concerned. The agenda was fairly broad, covering a range of issues which the team thought were likely to be relevant to implementation. These initial discussions resulted in the development by the team of a conceptual framework within which to gather data during the main phase of the project.

Secondly, detailed studies of implementation in five English LEAs, and their associated social services departments and district health authorities, were carried out using the conceptual framework developed as a result of the findings of phase one. The LEAs were chosen because of their differences in geographical area, size, social and economic circumstances, and organization of special education services. A qualitative methodology was adopted, using semi-structured interviews, documentary analysis and observation to gain an insight into the processes involved in implementing legislation. This methodology was supplemented by the findings from a national questionnaire survey, which had a 79 per cent response rate, and which provided data on changes in special needs provision, funding policies and the implementation of the statutory assessment procedures. The third phase consisted of:

1. A questionnaire survey of all LEAs in England, concerned with administrative aspects of the 1981 Education Act;
2. A series of special studies, including: (a) the role of the administrator in the provision of services for special educational needs, (b) the delivery of services in sparsely populated areas, and, (c) the views of parents about their experience of the statutory assessment procedures.

The development of a conceptual framework

The conceptual framework, developed as a result of the findings of the initial phase of the research, indicated that the process of implementation was extremely complex and that it involved a consideration, not only of the immediate consequences of legislation, but also of other factors which were influencing special education policy-making.

Policy implementation was seen, not as a simple linear process which stemmed from the passage of the legislation, but as a complex series of negotiations between different interests which both precede and follow legislation. The publication of the Warnock Report and the negotiations and consultations which occurred, both before and after its publication, show one way in which policy is formed. The feedback which the DES received during and after the passage of the legislation is another. Articles and letters in professional journals, conferences, and other forums for discussion and debate are all part of the implementation process, during which groups affected by legislation seek to influence the way in which it is implemented.

Structural and organizational factors will also influence the way in which legislation can be put into operation locally. The local authorities, of which the education and social services are parts, have different structures, funding mechanisms and systems of accountability from the health authorities. The organizational system which had to implement the 1981 Act is loosely-coupled. That is to say, it consists of many autonomous groups which have no overall command structure which can control implementation. Within such a structure, agreement can only be reached by negotiation and, if cooperation is not forthcoming, there is nothing that can be done to ensure it. The conceptual framework which we developed to study the implementation of the Act took into account all these factors (Welton and Evans, 1986).

The research findings

The research findings are presented under the following headings:

1. Working with the new concept of special educational needs.

2. Attitudes and practices with regard to integration.
3. The operation of the statutory assessment procedures.
4. Inter-service cooperation.
5. Parental involvement in decision-making.
6. Policy implementation and managing change.
7. Planning and resource allocation.

1. *Working with the new concept of special educational needs*

The research found that the abolition of categories was generally welcomed by those working with children with special needs. There was a recognition that the old system did not adequately reflect the complexity of children's needs. However, there were difficulties in moving away from labelling towards considering each child's needs individually. There were several inter-related problems which contributed towards this.

Professionals concerned with writing advice for statements still tended to concentrate on the child's difficulties, rather than considering the 'child's strengths and weaknesses and his or her relationship to the environment, at home and at school', as suggested in Circular 1/83. Statements, therefore, usually became mechanisms for removing a child from mainstream education, rather than for considering whether extra resources could be made available in the child's present setting to enable his or her needs to be met there.

There is a wide variation in practice, both between and within LEAs, in the proportions of children who are given statements and the types of need which are considered eligible. The criterion for issuing a statement is that a child has a learning difficulty which cannot be met within generally available provision. The interpretation of the term 'generally available' varied widely between authorities. Some LEAs consider that anything extra must be the subject of a statement. Others, that anything extra that is provided in mainstream schools is 'generally available' and therefore does not warrant a statement. Such inconsistency results in widely varying proportions of children being given statements in different LEAs.

This situation is further complicated by the fact that some LEAs have evolved policies about which types of extra provision are tied to statements and which are not. Therefore, the criterion for issuing a statement is not whether a child's needs can be met within available resources, but whether the child's needs fall within one of the categories specified by the LEA for which provision is made available through the issue of a statement.

Many working in LEAs, DHAs and SSDs were unclear about which children should be included in the population of children having special educational needs. The Warnock Report referred to a continuum of need, and the 1981 Education Act has followed this by offering a general definition of special educational needs. However, the 1981 Act makes a distinction between children whose needs can be met within generally available provision, and those whose needs are such that they require 'additional or different' provision to be determined by the LEA.

It appeared that the allocation of resources to children through statements had diverted attention away from those children with special educational needs who do not have statements. Much time, energy and resources were being allocated to the statutory assessment procedures, and to making provision for children with statements. The proportion of the total education budget going to special education has increased in 72 per cent of LEAs. Fears were expressed in some LEAs that this was at the expense of 'remedial' or 'special needs' departments in mainstream schools.

Planning services in response to an open-ended concept such as 'need' was seen to be a difficult task by those responsible in LEAs, DHAs, and SSDs. Demand for services was constantly increasing, but there was no firm basis upon which to base predictions of the size of the special needs population. Some LEAs operated a constant monitoring of the decisions made about allocation of provision through statements, in cooperation with their colleagues in health and social services departments. Such mechanisms created an opportunity to review the way in which the demand for services was developing, and provided the basis for a more rational assessment of the likely future demand upon all three services.

2. *Attitudes and practices with regard to integration*

The research indicated that LEAs were becoming more flexible in their approach to meeting special educational needs in mainstream schools. Some 76 per cent of LEAs reported that they were placing more children with special educational needs in mainstream primary and secondary schools since the 1981 Act had been passed. But, on the whole, children with statements are placed in segregated provision. Only a quarter of LEAs place more than a quarter of their children with statements in mainstream schools. There is, however, an increasing use of unit provision by LEAs, and this may lead to greater mixing of children, provided that the opportunities offered by its location in a school are taken advantage of.

One indication that integrated provision is not the first option to be considered is that, on the whole, pre-school children who are being assessed for statements are removed from their normal environment for this purpose. The research found that in the majority of cases studied young children were seen at assessment centres, or placed in special schools on assessment placements, rather than being seen in their own homes or in mainstream nursery or infant classes.

One of the problems that the research team found was that where LEAs did not consider integration as the first option for children who were given statements, if parents insisted on mainstream placement, the children were not given adequate resources to enable the placement to succeed. For example, children who needed speech therapy might have it made available in the special school, but not in the mainstream school.

3. *The operation of the statutory assessment procedures*

The administrative decision to initiate the statutory procedures is most likely to be taken by an LEA administrator on referral. This was the case in 56 per cent of LEAs surveyed by the research team. Normally, such a decision would presumably be made on the professional advice, for example, of the educational psychologist. Indeed, in 16 per cent of LEAs the educational psychologist was in fact charged with the administrative decision as well. Health and social services staff were rarely involved in the decision to initiate the procedures — a panel decision occurred only in 25 per cent of cases, and there was no indication whether this was a multi-service panel. Similarly, at all stages of the statement process, key administrative decisions appear to be taken predominantly by education officers without any role given to agencies outside the education service. It may be that in some LEAs there are informal consultations between education, health and social services personnel about particular children, but there does not appear to be any formal mechanism for such dialogue. The assessment, therefore, appears to be seen, on the whole, as a bureaucratic process within the education department, rather than as a way of consulting with professionals in all three services to come to an understanding of children's needs.

The process of assessment varied in its efficiency and sensitivity between authorities. One of the main concerns which parents had was that there were long delays between the start of the procedures and the completion of statements. During this time parents were not informed of the reasons for delay or given an estimate of the length of time they should expect to wait. There was also evidence of lack of feedback to other departments and services about the outcome of assessments. Health authorities and social services departments were not always told of the decisions made about the children on whom they had been asked to give advice.

The research found that statements tend to be worded in vague and generalized terms. This means that children do not have their needs described precisely, that the aims of any intervention are not specified, and that the resources offered to achieve the aims are not related in any specific way to the needs or the aims. Under these circumstances, it is difficult for any parent to challenge the provision offered to the child. Therefore, the rights of children and parents to a voice in decision-making are, to an extent, being undermined. Furthermore, the vagueness of descriptions of need tends to mask any discrepancies between the needs and the provision offered so that there is no way of monitoring the demand for services or for forward planning to meet emerging needs. This tendency to mask the extent of the problems of resourcing faced by LEAs, DHAs and SSDs, will have serious long-term consequences for the development of services, unless some mechanism for recording and planning to meet shortfalls in provision is available.

Parents who are not satisfied with an LEA's decision about their child's special educational needs have a right to appeal. Appeals can be directly to the Secretary of State, for cases where an authority decides not to issue a statement, or to a local appeal committee, if parents are not satisfied with the provision specified for their child on a statement. In such cases parents also have the right of appeal to the Secretary of State if they are not satisfied with the outcome of a local appeal. It appears from the research findings that those working in local authorities tried to avoid appeals whenever possible, since they were very time-consuming and stressful, even if they felt that, as a result, the child would not be given the optimum placement. Where appeals had taken place the outcomes were likely to be in favour of the LEA: 73 per cent of local appeals were decided in favour of the LEA. Of those that went to the Secretary of State some 25 per cent had been decided in favour of the parents. It may be that the appeals system as presently constituted does not provide an effective mechanism for reviewing LEAs' decisions.

A mandatory re-assessment takes place for children with statements between the ages of 12 years 6 months and 14 years 6 months. There has been some criticism of the timing of this re-assessment, as being either too early in a child's school career, or too late. There seems to be some misunderstanding of the function of this assessment which is to take a prospective view of the child's post-school needs. Under the Disabled Persons (Consultation and Representation) Act 1986 this re-assessment will play an important part in establishing liaison between education and social services departments in respect of children who will need further help after leaving full-time education. At the time of this research social services departments were not routinely involved in re-assessments in many areas.

4. Inter-service cooperation

The research found that there had been very little joint planning between education, health and social services for the implementation of the 1981 Education Act. Some LEAs had set up working parties with representatives from each of the services, but the more common pattern was for the Education Department to decide on its procedures, and then to call a meeting with the Health Authority and, less often, with the Social Services Department to inform them of what was required. Many of the later problems of collaboration and coordination could be traced back to this initial failure to consult.

The failure to consult widely seems to reflect a lack of consultation and joint planning for children with special needs at a strategic level in local authorities and health authorities. There is collaboration and cooperation for individual *ad hoc* initiatives and for individual children, but this is not systematized, and is often unofficial. Responses to the questionnaire indicate that the majority of LEAs are not making full use of joint-funding arrangements at the present time, nor are they engaged in major strategic joint planning initiatives with DHAs.

Within the Statutory procedures, new roles had been given to education, health and social services personnel. There were often difficulties in adapting to the new roles. For example, the research reported that doctors, and others working with children with special educational needs, found it difficult to avoid discussing particular schools with parents, even though LEAs had made it clear that this was no longer acceptable.

Social workers had no clear idea of their role within the procedures, nor the type of advice which the LEA considered relevant. There were often no clear guidelines given by LEAs to social services departments about how they were expected to respond to a notification from the LEA that they were proposing to assess a child. Social services departments, for their part, often did not have one person as a clearly identifiable link person with the LEA. In one area which the research studied, many of these problems had been overcome by the establishment of a multi-service panel which met to assess the advice and to discuss the draft statement. This meant that all the key people involved were known to each other and met on a regular basis.

5. Parental involvement in decision-making

The greater involvement of parents in the assessment procedures was broadly welcomed by those working in education, health and social services departments. It was, however, sometimes difficult to put into practice.

The 1981 Education Act requires LEAs to provide information for the parents about the statutory procedures and about their rights. LEAs have produced booklets for parents containing this information. They have also produced carefully worded letters for each stage of the process to inform parents of decisions at each stage. Some of the booklets and letters are clear, concise and sympathetic in their presentation. However, both the research and a study by CSIE (Rogers, 1986) found that many of the parents' booklets contained misleading, incomplete or incomprehensible information. They did not encourage parents to become active participants in the assessment process.

The 1981 Act provides for the parents to be given the name of an 'officer' from whom they can obtain further information about the procedures. Once a statement is written parents are given the name of a person to whom they can go for information and advice about their child's special educational needs. Both of these appear to be an attempt to provide a 'named person', as suggested in the Warnock Report. However, the research found that parents rarely contacted the named officer if they had queries about the procedures; they preferred to use someone they already knew, such as a head-teacher or educational psychologist. Many parents felt isolated and unsupported during the procedures, particularly if there were delays. The role of the named person, as the Warnock Report envisaged it, does not appear to be fulfilled adequately under present arrangements.

The involvement of parents in decision-making about a child's needs will also involve discussions about provision. If LEAs have a limited range of provision there is often little choice about the final placement of a child. Parents interviewed by the research team noted that they had felt that LEA officers had often not been frank with them about the limitations on provision, and had instead attempted to manipulate or coerce parents into accepting provision for their child which they thought was unsuitable. The lack of a real choice and of an active role in decision-making, and the sense of being manipulated by officials, were recurring themes in the parental interviews.

In Circular 1/83 it is suggested that voluntary organizations could have a role to play in informing and supporting parents. Health Authorities are charged with the responsibility of informing parents of children under five if they feel that a particular voluntary organization could be of help. The research found that parents were turning to voluntary organizations for help but only when relations between them and the LEA had become strained. This was forcing voluntary organizations into confrontations with LEAs, which the former regretted. Representatives of the voluntary organizations interviewed by the London University team felt that such problems could be avoided if they were put in touch with parents at an early stage in the assessment procedures.

The research found that parents were not unduly worried about the formality or the bureaucracy of the procedures. This was what they expected in their dealings with officialdom. They were more concerned about the quality of the interactions which they had with the various LEA and DHA personnel, with whom they had to deal on behalf of their child. Although it was apparent from interviews with LEA and DHA staff that they were more aware of their duty to involve and inform parents, and that they considered that it was a good thing to do, it was difficult for both sides to achieve the partnership envisaged by the 1981 Act. Parents were inhibited by their lack of knowledge and support; officers and professionals by their lack of time and resources.

6. *Policy implementation and managing change*

The research indicates that there was a lack of a clear model for policy implementation. LEAs, DHAs and SSDs in different parts of the country adopted widely differing methods of implementing the new legislation. In some LEAs there was a collaborative approach and detailed involvement of colleagues in DHAs and SSDs in the preparations for the 1981 Act. In other areas, there was little consultation, and the other services were presented with a *fait accompli* by the LEA. In those areas where there was limited involvement of DHAs and SSDs in policy formulation for the 1981 Act, it was more difficult for their professionals to get information about what was required. Although there was a positive attitude towards the legislation and a desire to cooperate, there was little knowledge about the roles of the various professionals involved. This appeared to be especially true of social services personnel. Both the research reported here and a study by Wingham (1986) indicate that social workers know very little about the 1981 Education Act.

Policy-making for special educational needs appeared to be *ad hoc* and incremental in many LEAs. The research found that in some policy areas there were inconsistencies and competing initiatives. For example, in the area of post-16 provision, new courses were being developed in both special schools and FE colleges, who were competing for the same clientele. Consultation of those who were to be affected by policy changes did not always take place. There appeared to be a lack of clear, authoritative policy statements about crucial issues, such as integration.

One of the crucial elements in the implementation of any new policy is training, or at the least, the giving of information to those who will be affected. The research found that the majority of LEAs had given *information* about the 1981 Act to governors, headteachers, some parents and some professional groups. However, rather fewer had offered *training* to those who would be directly involved in the operation of the 1981 Act. No LEA answering the London University research questionnaire reported providing training for governors, for example, and only 38 per cent had provided training for DHA personnel. Some 80 per cent had given training to headteachers of mainstream schools but only 49 per cent to heads of special schools. Only 11 per cent of LEAs gave training or information to voluntary organizations.

Administrators felt that they were under so much pressure just to keep the system functioning that they had very little time to stand back and evaluate the service as a whole. Therefore much of the change and development apparent in LEAs was incremental rather than managed, although some LEAs such as the ILEA (1985) had undertaken major reviews of their services.

7. *Planning and resource allocation*

A key theme running through many of the problems highlighted by the research was the lack of resources available to implement the 1981 Act. Change itself costs money and the Government's level of commitment to the 1981 Act was reflected in the fact that no specific funds were made available for implementation.

Despite the fact that no government money was made available, the majority of LEAs surveyed by the research team had increased their spending on services for children with special educational needs in real terms. They had also increased the proportion of their total education budget going to this area. LEAs have, therefore, both increased funding and re-allocated resources to special education. However, the wider definition of special educational needs and the increased awareness of special needs among both parents and teachers have meant that demand has increased also, so that LEAs and their partners in DHAs and SSDs are facing ever-increasing demands for services.

The increased demands for therapies from the health service, particularly for speech therapy, has created problems for health authorities. Their budgets are subject to different constraints from those of education authorities, and are less flexible. They would have to be able to make a good case for the need for extra speech therapy in the face of demands for other health service priorities. These shortages have led to difficulties for LEAs in making statements. They cannot specify speech therapy under 'non-educational provision' unless they are satisfied that the health authority is able to provide it. The problem seems to reside in the fact that, although the education authorities have the ultimate responsibility for meeting children's special educational needs, they sometimes have to rely on resources which they cannot command. By the same token, health authorities have found themselves under pressure to provide resources under circumstances which they cannot control, that it, the increasing demand from education authorities.

There appears to be very little joint planning or monitoring of demands for services for this client group at the strategic level between education and health authorities. Therefore, it is not possible for health authorities to respond to emerging needs. In many cases, the demand for services is hidden, as those at the grass roots level 'make do', or are specifically discouraged from revealing the extent or nature of a pupil's needs. This means that shortfalls in services are hidden, and do not feed into the planning process in any systematic way.

Resource limitations have undoubtedly led to frustration and cynicism among those attempting to bring about change in local authorities and health authorities. There has been some movement to re-allocate resources, but this has been against a background of increasing constraints on spending. Any goodwill and movement towards inter-service cooperation is in danger of being under-mined because the amount of effort required to act collaboratively is not rewarded by increased benefits in terms of extra resources being allocated to services for pupils with special educational needs.

Conclusion

The research reported here indicates that the implementation of policy changes brought about by legislation is a complex and lengthy process. Legislation, of itself, may not directly change policies, practices or attitudes. In fact, it could be argued that legislation is an outcome of these changes and merely gives them recognition. The implementation of changes in policies and practices is a *process* of which legislation is a part. The variability of the service provided, both in terms of provision and practice, is a reflection of the diversity of local authorities.

The 1981 Education Act has undoubtedly been a stimulus for changes in the services for children with special educational needs and their parents. More consideration is given to parental involvement in decision-making; more efforts are made to educate children with special needs in the least restrictive environment; more resources are being put into services for children with special educational needs. However, the base from which the service starts will be a major influence on the quality of services which can be provided. Central government saw the 1981 Education Act as

> a new legal framework to cause everyone with responsibility for special educational needs to look at their practices and to be a starting point for all LEAs to match the practice of the best.

The findings from the research programme indicate that further development is needed in order to increase the effectiveness of the operation of the 1981

Education Act in local areas. The DES and DHSS have, therefore, jointly funded a development project, based at the University of London Institute of Education, which is developing a training strategy and supporting materials to enhance the service offered by the three agencies (Evans *et al.*, 1989). The project team is aiming to build on good practice which already exists and to work with LEAs, DHAs and SSDs to help them to identify areas for development. The team, which consists of a senior development officer, an assistant, two directors and a number of consultants with a range of management training experience both in industry and in the public sector, is developing and piloting materials along with personnel from the education, health and social services in three areas of the country. The team's strategy is to develop the *whole system* concerned with services for children with special educational needs. This involves working with decision-makers at all levels in each agency, including senior officers and elected members in LEAs, and managers and members of the DHAs, in a multi-disciplinary setting.

References

DEPARTMENT OF EDUCATION AND SCIENCE (1975) *The Discovery of Children Requiring Special Education and the Assessment of Their Needs*, Circular 2/75, London, DES.

DEPARTMENT OF EDUCATION AND SCIENCE (1978) *Special Educational Needs: Report of a Committee of Enquiry into the Education of Handicapped Children and Young People*, The Warnock Report, London, HMSO.

DEPARTMENT OF EDUCATION AND SCIENCE (1983) *Assessments and Statements of Special Educational Needs*, Circular 1/83, Joint Circular with DHSS HC (83) 3, London, ILEA.

EVANS, J., EVERARD, T., FRIEND, J., GLASER, A., NORWICH, B. and WELTON, J. (1989) *Decision-making for Special Educational Needs: An Inter-service Resource Pack*, (forthcoming).

GOACHER, B., EVANS, J., WELTON, J. and WEDELL, K. (1988) *Policy and Provision for Special Educational Needs: Implementing the 1981 Education Act*, London, Cassell.

INNER LONDON EDUCATION AUTHORITY (1985) *Educational Opportunities for All?* Report of the Fish Committee, London, ILEA.

ROGERS, R. (1986) *Caught in the Act*, London, Spastics Society.

WELTON, J. and EVANS, J. (1986) 'The development and implication of special education policy; Where did the 1981 Act fit in?' *Public Administration, 64*, Number 2.

WELTON, J., WEDELL, K. and VORHAUS, G. (1982) *Meeting Special Educational Needs: the 1981 Act and its Implications*, Bedford Way Papers No. 12, London, Heinemann.

WINGHAM, G. (1986) *Closed Worlds? A Study of the Relationship between Social Workers and the Special Education System*, M.Sc. Dissertation, Polytechnic of the South Bank, London.

4
The Centre for Studies on Integration in Education

Mark Vaughan and Alison Wertheimer

Introduction

The Centre for Studies on Integration in Education was established some nine months after the 1981 Education Act was passed and a year before it came into force in 1983. With the advent of the 1981 Act the Advisory Centre for Education (ACE) had set up a coordinating committee on integration. This represented organizations who were committed to campaigning for integrated education for children with disabilities, or those with learning difficulties. Inevitably integration was, for these organizations, just one of many issues with which they were concerned. From a heavily over-subscribed conference on integration, run jointly by ACE and the Spastics Society in 1982, it was clear that there was a need for a campaign to provide a focus, and a voice for individuals and organizations, wanting to campaign for more integrated educational provision. The Spastics Society supported the view that no child should be educated in a special school if its educational, physical and social needs could be satisfactorily met in an ordinary school. At the same time the Spastics Society was running its own network of special schools, so the decision to establish CSIE within the organization was a courageous and far-sighted act by Tim Yeo, the then Director of the Society.

The Centre began in 1982 as a semi-autonomous body within the Spastics Society, and its staff established the brief of working with the voluntary sector, with education authorities and with parents. The Centre was to concern itself not only with the needs of children with cerebral palsy but with all children with special needs — a generous gesture on the part of a single disability organization.

Aims and objectives — the philosophy

The Centre was established with the following aims:

To raise public, professional and political awareness of the issue of integration;

To promote good practice;
To encourage education authorities, individual schools, parents, profession-als and governors in the implementation of effective integration of children with special needs into ordinary schools and colleges;
To work with all children with special needs.

One of the major strengths of the work of the Centre has been its clearly stated belief that all children with special needs can and should be educated within the ordinary school system. This belief, because it is uncompromising, at times has led to the work of the Centre being described as idealistic or unrealistic. There is often a tendency to want to set limits. To agree to integration for most, but not all children, is a position which leads to the exclusion of children with more severe handicaps from ordinary schools. By declaring that integration is both desirable and possible for all children with special needs, the staff of the Centre are demanding major changes, not only making things a little bit better, but seeking radical and far-reaching changes in educational provision.

Within a framework of explicitly stated values, the Centre staff have set out to challenge the beliefs of many people working in the field of education. They believe that it is simply not good enough for professionals to justify their belief in segregation on the basis of professional judgment or expertise. Integration is about value judgments and personal beliefs, and professional judgments and practice cannot be separated.

Integration

This does not mean that there is a uniform view of what constitutes integration. The aim is not to promote a single model, a rigid blueprint for each child. Integration can be developed in many different ways and it is, above all, a continuing process rather than a one-off placement. For one child it may involve being in an ordinary class fulltime, for another, it may involve spending only a part of each day or week with non-disabled children. But, for the staff of the Centre, full social and physical integration remains the ultimate goal, and the processes involved should all be geared towards achieving this objective. Those working at the Centre believe that the social integration of children, with and without disabilities, is as important as the educational benefits which children may derive from being in ordinary schools. One of their earliest projects was to act as catalyst and coordinator for a joint holiday at an outdoor activities centre shared by children from a North London special school and the neighbouring comprehen-sive school. Ending the segregation of children with special needs in pre-school and school services is a necessary prerequisite for people with disabilities and those with learning difficulties being successfully integrated into the community as adults. Social integration also highlights the fact that it is a two-way process and has mutual benefits. Children who do not have disabilities can benefit from growing up alongside their disabled peers.

Opponents of integration have frequently argued that integrating children with special needs into mainstream schooling will, in some way, damage or undermine ordinary schools. The Centre staff believe that integration enhances and strengthens the comprehensive system at pre-school, school and college levels. In evidence to the Parliamentary Education, Science and Arts Select Committee's investigation into the workings of the 1981 Act, it was stressed that integration was part of an overall move towards the establishment of comprehensive locally-based education services. Comprehensiveness is not about sameness, or establishing a total uniformity. It is about including everyone in the system and not hiving off some children into separate provision who have been identified by attributes beyond their control. Integration must be *part* of the overall development of the educational system — not something which comes *after* we have 'got everything else right'. The argument put forward by some professionals and politicians, that integration can only take place *after* all the resources are available, is not acceptable. First establish the commitment and will to pursue integration; the resources will follow.

Parents and professionals

Although the Centre has never addressed itself solely to one particular group of pupils, it does have a particular role in advocating for, and working with, the parents of children with disabilities or those with learning difficulties. The staff of the Centre try to articulate the concerns and wishes of parents who, it is thought, have a much undervalued expertise whereby they are not facilitated an equal share in decision-making. Staff have also worked alongside those involved in segregated special education. This is in recognition that special educators have much to offer those in ordinary schools who are attempting to integrate pupils with special needs. When a special school head works hard to integrate pupils, staff, resources, and equipment, for example, into local mainstream placements, then the commitment to integration is believable.

It is the separate buildings as well as separate administrative and career structures that CSIE wants to see dismantled, not the concept of special educational provision.

The achievements of the centre

Whereas many organizations concerned with disabilities have, of necessity, to focus on a range of very different issues, as a single-issue campaign, the work of the Centre has been to invest all its resources into pursuing a single objective, the de-segregation of all special educational provision. After six years, the Centre is seen by many parents and professionals as a unique source of expertise, advice and information about all aspects of integration and related issues. The Centre has contributed significantly to an informed debate about the best way to proceed with developing more opportunities for integrating children with special needs in ordinary schools. Although primarily representing the interests and aspirations of parents, the Centre has also been able to offer through its variety of activities a middle ground — a forum where parents and professionals can discuss and debate the issues relating to integration.

Information and advocacy

The collection and dissemination of a wide range of information about integration has been a major focus of the Centre's work and one of its greatest achievements. After six years, it has a unique information resource, gathered from parents, schools, education authorities, voluntary organizations, academic institutions, newspaper cuttings, books and journals. The organization is strongly committed to getting information out to people who are not generally recipients of this sort of material; parent groups and individual parents have been a major target, and the Centre has a deliberate policy of offering publications either free or at minimal cost so that no one will be debarred from finding out about integration on grounds of cost. At its three most recent day conferences, all parents attended free of charge. As an organization whose permanent staffing has never risen beyond two full-timers, producing and disseminating information in written form has also been a necessary and useful way of communicating to a greater number of people than the staff could possibly work with directly. Outside commissions and freelance work have helped it cover such a wide field. There are now over thirty publications available, including: a series of attractive illustrated fact sheets and reports on integration in practice; easy-to-read guides to the 1981 Education Act; arguments in favour of integration; information on provision for 16–19 year olds; LEA survey reports; and reports of day conferences written in a lively and illustrated style. The single most popular publication has been the leaflet 'A class apart', written for BBC Radio 4 who paid the production costs. This clear and readable guide to the somewhat complex provisions of the 1981 Education Act has already gone through several reprints, and over 50,000 copies have been distributed. The Centre also offers a free advice service to anyone by telephone, letter or, to a lesser degree, by visiting the office and a very large number of parents and professionals have taken advantage of this facility. Spending time talking with visitors to the office is a regular part of the Centre's work, and parents and educators from many parts of the world have come to the Centre to learn about developments in integration in Britain. Students of education, looking at aspects of integration, are heavy users of the information service.

The Centre's opportunity to act as advocates for individual families is clearly restricted by its slender staffing resources, though over the years the workers have been able to support a small number of families seeking to obtain integrated schooling for their child with special needs. This small group of families is selected on the basis that their case has a wider applicability which may help other parents who are fighting similar battles. The task is to work closely with these families and formal advocacy may involve, for example, representing the family at appeals to the LEAs or to the Department of Education and Science. Although there is a limit to this extremely time-consuming advocacy work, it has wider benefits beyond the family concerned. The Centre's six-year involvement with Kirsty Arondelle, who has Down's syndrome, and her family, for example, has resulted in three publications, charting Kirsty's progress through integrated pre-school and school services, and describing the many difficulties her family have had to surmount in order to secure integrated provision for their daughter. The family, in turn, have passed on the benefit of their experiences to hundreds of other families.

Training activities

Since it was established the Centre has organized training events comprising workshops, conferences and seminars. The workshops, or training days have been particularly important events. Between 1984 and 1986, the Centre and the Children's Legal Centre jointly ran ten of these days on the 1981 Education Act which were attended by a total of 1200 people in different venues in England and Wales. These events, all of which were oversubscribed, were important for a number of different reasons. Firstly, they enabled the Centre and the Children's Legal Centre to disseminate information and commentaries on the new legislation based on their own progressive interpretation of the 1981 Act. Speakers at these events all stressed the fact that the new legislation provided, at the best, only a weak framework for integration, which would need to be exploited as fully as possible. Secondly, they provided a meeting place for parents and professionals to discuss integration issues on an equal footing; towards the end of the series, parents and professionals were attending the workshops in equal numbers, which helped this process. Thirdly, the workshops had a catalytic effect; in some areas, local people went on to organize their own training events, using the knowledge and experience gained at the workshops and training days.

As well as providing a forum for debate, the training days were also an opportunity for delegates to obtain a great deal of practical information. Presentations, which were backed up by the provision of information packs, focused on the philosophy of the 1981 Act, on the legal rights involved, on the new role envisaged for parents of children with special needs, and on the necessary change in attitude that was needed on the part of professionals and administrators. There were also workshop sessions, which developed the themes raised in the plenary presentations. These looked in more detail at such issues as assessments, statements, and appeals, definitions in the 1981 Act, pre-school and post-16 provision, integration, and support for parents.

In addition, four national conferences have also been held. The most recent, in May 1986, was attended by over 120 parents, and was the springboard for launching '81 Action' — a national parents' network which initially was developed under the aegis of the Centre and has recently become an independent organization.

Networking

The Centre has played a key role in linking up both individual parents and parent groups with one another — bringing together those who want to secure integrated schooling for their children with parents whose children are already in ordinary schools. When, in most parts of the country, integration is still the exception rather than the norm for special needs children, with a one in five chance of achieving it, giving parents information about successful schemes which are 'up and running' can be powerful ammunition in their own battles.

The Centre's descriptions of integration in practice have been amongst CSIE's bestselling publications. The careful descriptions of the processes involved in securing integrated education have helped to put across the message that good practice in integration is not something which can be achieved overnight; it requires considerable time, effort and commitment if it is to work properly. The stories of individual children in integrated schooling have also been a powerful means of convincing those who doubt that integration can be achieved. The published accounts are living proof of this.

Discussing and debating the issues with others, has enabled the staff at the Centre to develop its own thinking. It has strengthened the conviction that children with special needs can have an experience of schooling which is not just marginally better than that which they are receiving in special schools; the future can be radically different and it is worth pursuing.

The Centre has also worked collaboratively with other organizations, pooling its resources with groups who are pursuing the same objectives. As well as the work with ACE and the Children's Legal Centre mentioned above, the Centre staff have worked with a number of 'disability' organizations including the Royal National Institute for the Blind, the Campaign for People with Mental Handicaps and the Greater London Association for the Disabled, as well as with the Open University with whom it has run two seminars.

The Centre has developed a good working relationship with the press and media and acted as consultant on numerous occasions to radio and television programme-makers who have often asked for a new Centre factsheet as back-up material sent out to listeners and viewers after the programme.

Monitoring current practice

While the Centre does not claim to be primarily a research organization, it has undertaken three major surveys of aspects of the workings of the 1981 Act, all of which have been well received and widely quoted. Together they form a unique national picture of the implementation of the 1981 Education Act and have provided accurate thumb-nail sketches of the national position.

The first of these surveys, *Caught in the Act* (1986), was an inquiry into what individual LEAs were telling parents, given their new legal duties to provide information for parents about the 1981 Act, and in particular, their policies and practices relating to identification, assessment, statementing, and appeals procedures. On the basis of information received from 63 per cent of LEAs, it was clear that many authorities were reluctant to spell out their new duties regarding assessment and provision. Only 11 per cent of LEAs mentioned to parents their duty to pursue integration! Only 6 per cent listed parents' duties under the 1981 Act and only 8 per cent gave parents a comprehensive account of the assessment process. Nearly half gave insufficient information about parental rights under the legislation. Indeed only a minority, the report concluded, even 'saw parents as partners'. These kinds of findings have been the hard evidence used by the Centre in its campaigning for better information for parents and a more responsive and flexible service for children and young people.

Also in 1986 the Centre published *Guiding the Professionals* which reported on the guidelines that LEAs were providing for the various professionals involved in implementing the 1981 Act, such as teaching staff and educational psychologists, for example. With a similar response rate of nearly two-thirds of all LEAs, it was found that over a third did not spell out the authority's general duties and only about a half explained in any detail the various parental rights. The survey revealed that many LEAs expected their professionals to fall in with blanket policy decisions and much of the advice they were given ran contrary to the consumer-oriented approach of the 1981 Act. This second survey also revealed that only 50 per cent of LEAs informed their own professionals about the new duty to integrate children with special needs.

The most recent survey, *Duty to Review* (1987), reported on how, three to four years after the 1981 Act came into force, LEAs were responding to their duty under the 1981 Act to *review* their special educational provision. As with the two previous surveys, the exercise revealed considerable discrepancies between individual authorities. Some LEAs had made careful in-depth responses to the legislation and considered how their special needs policies and practice might be welded into their overall strategy. Others had adopted a much more *ad hoc* and uncoordinated response. But the survey showed considerable variations in the way in which LEAs undertook consultation with other bodies as part of their policy development work.

Campaigning and lobbying

The Centre has undertaken a limited amount of direct lobbying with central and local government, and has twice given evidence to the Parliamentary Select Committee for Education, as well as to the Fish Committee set up by the Inner London Education Authority. It has also taken part in fringe meetings at the annual political party conferences. The staff of the Centre have been invited to brief Opposition spokesmen on the 1981 Education Act and on the issues surrounding integration in education.

Its detailed knowledge of the workings of the 1981 Education Act enabled the Centre to put forward to the Select Committee for Education a series of detailed proposed amendments to how the legislation was being implemented. For example, the view of the Centre staff is that assessment and statementing processes should be completed within a legally stipulated time-limit of three months.

Talks and lectures at conferences, workshops, and a range of other training events have provided further opportunities for the Centre to state its case for integration, and staff have given over 100 such presentations to audiences across England and Wales as well as in Belgium and Massachusetts.

Challenges for the future

In March 1988 the Centre was launched as an independent organization with its own Council, becoming an educational charity and a limited company as it moved into new premises in North London. Over the next few years, the Centre will be seeking to further its own aims and objectives as well as facing up to the implications of proposed changes to the educational system as a whole. At the beginning of this new era of independence, CSIE has set as its central aim, an end to all segregated special educational provision.

Although the impact of the 1988 Education Reform Act is not yet clear, there is concern that the proposals related to establishing a national curriculum and to opting-out by individual schools will threaten current and proposed integrated provision. The proposed national curriculum, in particular, may create problems in schools that have been developing whole school policies with a 'curriculum for all' approach which can enable them more easily to integrate pupils with disabilities and those with learning difficulties. The Centre, however, will continue to press for amendments and 'fine-tuning' of the 1981 Act.

The Centre will also be pressing LEAs to adopt more radical policies regarding integration. Particularly, the Centre would like to see education authorities being generally more explicit about how they intend to implement Section 2 of the 1981 Act, particularly in light of the 1988 Education Act. Using the information gained through the three surveys discussed above, the Centre is strongly placed to continue contributing to an informed debate with LEAs.

Some authorities have adopted policy statements that their educational services will not discriminate against individual children on the grounds of race, gender or class. The Centre would like to see them add *disability* to those statements of intent.

The Centre will also be campaigning for the introduction of disability awareness programmes in all schools, regardless of whether or not they are integrating pupils with disabilities or learning difficulties.

The Centre will continue to pursue its commitment to offering advice and information to more people and in more accessible forms. Training days, conferences and new publications will all play a part in meeting this objective.

There are plans to launch a major initiative on pre-school provision for children with special needs. The campaigning project will be pressing for a *comprehensive* pre-school service offering a *variety* of provision in de-segregated settings. The project has two stages; the first will involve an 'audit' consisting of surveys of current provision, case studies, and general information-gathering plus conferences; the second stage will be a campaign for legislative changes and will involve campaigning at local and national level together with new publications. The Centre staff see this as a priority for future action since the achievement of totally integrated pre-school provision should offer a firm foundation from which children with special needs can proceed to ordinary schools.

At the other end of the age range, the Centre will be campaigning to change the law so that students with disabilities or those with learning difficulties, would have a guaranteed right to full-time education up to the age of 23 years. This would bring Britain into line with current practice in many other countries including America.

The fact that the Centre has collaborated extensively with parents has been one of its great strengths, and over the next few years it hopes to continue supporting the growing number of parent groups, helping them to be more informed and effective advocates for their own children.

The Centre will also be lobbying for LEAs to set their own time-limits — say, ten years — after which all children with disabilities or learning difficulties would be included in mainstream education. This is in the certain belief that it is only time-limits of this kind that will bring about an end, once and for all, to segregated educational provision. The address of the Centre is as follows:

Centre for Studies on Integration in Education, 4th Floor, 415 Edgware Road, London NW2 6NB. Tel. 01 452 8642.

Part Two
Learning and Parents

5:
Parents as Reading Tutors for Children with Special Needs

Keith Topping

Introduction

Parental involvement has been a fashionable catchphrase in education in recent years, but in the special educational needs field there are considerable organizational difficulties in translating this concept into practice. For example, special schools and special units often have large catchment areas for their pupils and this militates against frequent contact between the school or unit and parents. The involvement of parents in their children's education on any widespread basis is a relatively new phenomenon. In the late eighteenth and early nineteenth centuries a rising professionalization developed amongst the teaching fraternity, whereby teachers increasingly distanced themselves from parents. This process had occurred in other professions like medicine.

One result of this was to make parents feel unskilled in helping their children in their education. This brought about a lack of confidence in parents, and between parents and teachers, with parents becoming uncertain whether they were helping or hindering what was happening at school. After the Second World War parents began again to take interest and be encouraged to participate in the activities of their children in relation to schooling. Schools began to have more open evenings, and developed arrangements for contact with parents prior to a child's admittance. Parents then began to be invited into school and now most schools make use of parent helpers on outside visits, while the majority of schools claim to use volunteer parent helpers with art and craft, sewing and baking activities within school hours. A smaller number of schools, however, have involved parents in more cognitive aspects of the curriculum, and fewer have regularly supported parents in educating their children at home.

The process of involving parents in school activities has a number of aspects. Clearly, parents cannot become involved if procedures for information exchange between home and school are not well developed. The 1980 Education Act requires schools to produce a brochure for parents, but the evidence so far seems to suggest that less than half of schools are meeting their statutory obligation in this respect. Parents have been involved in legal procedures, as in the 1981 Education Act, but a recent study by Sandow *et al.* (1987) shows that parents have not, on the whole, found the bureaucratic paraphernalia of the 1981 Act very useful as a means of providing more practical help for their children. Another area of parental involvement is where parents are represented on governing bodies.

Evaluative research on the effect of parental involvement on pupil achievement in nursery schools and classes is encouraging. The situation is less clear for primary schools, where many studies have not separated out the effect on pupil learning resulting from parent involvement. The deploying of parents as teaching aides certainly seems to raise the level of children's skills independent of the effect of the extra attention. Parent involvement at secondary school level is not so prevalent as in the primary schools (Topping, 1986a).

Merely establishing closer communication between the home and school, through the use of some form of home/school book, provides a valuable link between parents and teachers. Teachers can report on events happening during the school day, thus providing parents with the opportunity to respond, and vice versa. Where schools have an established pattern of homework, the evidence suggests that this raises pupil attainment, but in too many cases homework is given to pupils in a random and *ad hoc* manner. Just providing homework does not ensure the involvement of parents.

Behavioural home/school reporting is an easily delivered intervention, widely acceptable to parents on account of its simplicity, and is usually cost-effective. Parents who are not very well organized, or indeed cooperative with school, usually manage successfully to operate a well structured home/school scheme. However, the most potent thrust of the parental involvement movement has been the encouragement of parents in the role of direct educators of their own children in the home setting. There is now no doubt whatsoever that this 'works', in the sense of raising child attainment levels. This seems to be true for a wide range of curricular areas and for a wide range of child ability.

Many ordinary primary schools would claim to have a policy of sending reading books home, so that children can read to their parents. Surveys indicate however that practices even within one school often vary between classteachers. Sometimes little guidance is given to parents as to what they are actually expected to do with the reading material the child has brought home.

In 1980 Hewison and Tizard reported research in a disadvantaged area of Inner London, which demonstrated that one of the largest factors in children's reading attainment was whether they read with their parents at home, irrespective of any formal parental involvement scheme. This research was followed up by a direct intervention wherein teachers encouraged parents to hear their children read at home (Tizard *et al.*, 1982). In this project the attainment of the children rose substantially in comparison to control groups and also to a group which received extra remedial help from qualified teachers. These differences were maintained at long term follow-up (Hewison, 1987). It became clear from this research that it was cost-effective for teachers to spend some time encouraging and organizing the involvement of parents in their own children's reading development, rather than directly teaching reading wholly by themselves.

The early 1980s saw a rapid expansion in involving parents in their children's reading development. In Inner London the PACT Scheme was developed and in South Wales the CAPER Project expanded. More structured approaches for parents grew in popularity, particularly the scheme known as *Paired Reading*. In a very short time a whole range of methods and approaches were in use in many schools throughout the country. The special needs sector, however, was not particularly swift in taking up these developments.

The question soon arose as to what parents could offer that teachers could not. Earlier research had indicated that a large proportion of the variance in pupil attainment could be attributed to differences in home circumstances. There had been recognition that the home plays a major part in a child's learning, but research had focused on what a handicap parents could be to their children, a kind of deficit model of parenthood. Now there was a change in thinking to how parents could make a positive and useful contribution. It began to become clear that parents had a great deal to offer.

Firstly, children who read at home regularly simply get more practice at reading than those who do not. It is well established that practice consolidates a skill, promotes fluency, and minimises forgetting. It is important, however, to note that it is successful reading practice that leads to consolidating and promoting the skill of reading. The parent, in a one-to-one situation, can provide the child with immediate feedback and thus prevent the compounding of errors. Detailed guidance about the nature of parental feedback, particularly in relation to errors, is incorporated in all good parental involvement reading schemes. Poor readers by definition experience little success because they generate few opportunities for the teacher to give meaningful praise. Teachers do not always praise children as often as they would like to think they do and the evidence suggests that natural rates of parental praise are a little lower than those of teachers. In a parental involvement project great attention is given to the development and application of parental praise, which has the added advantage of being offered by someone who is a major figure in the child's life.

The fourth advantage of the parent as reading tutor is the greater scope for demonstrating required behaviour. It is normal for children to want to be liked, and this is particularly so from the most significant grown-up people in their lives, their parents. Where parents can demonstrate enthusiasm for books, the effect on the child is considerably more profound than encouragement in a classroom. In this respect the father's role can be particularly crucial for boys. Thus, parental involvement includes powerful modelling and reinforcement for a child learning to read, with feedback immediate and the opportunity for practice regular. It is not unusual for parents to report that where there has been a parent involvement project in operation, the children have shown improvement in their behaviour, have gained greater confidence in relation to other areas of curriculum, and this has had a spin-off in relation to social skills.

Current status of the field

As the field has developed, a variety of techniques for parents to use have been promoted. The simplest technique could be called *parental listening*, a more sophisticated extension of the traditional practice of encouraging parents to hear their children read. In this case 'reading scheme' books are often used, related to the child's reading level, and sometimes accompanied with a list of do's and don'ts and a demonstration of good practice. Often a simple recording system is used. The work at Belfield followed this model and subsequent projects made advice for parent more specific, (Swinson, *et al.*, in Topping and Wolfendale, 1985).

Paired Reading is a specific technique which was promoted by Roger Morgan in the 1970s. It consists of two aspects. Children choose books of high interest irrespective of readability and are supported through high readability texts by both the parent and the child reading together. Through practice the parent and child synchronize their oral reading in a context of discussion and frequent praise, and a very simple correction procedure is incorporated. On easier texts, the child signals the parent to be silent and reads alone until an error is made, when 5 seconds is allowed for self-correction before returning to reading together. A number of variants on the original paired reading technique have been developed. It is important for professional workers to be clear about the technique that they are using, since confusion usually develops in the absence of a precisely defined and shared vocabulary.

A number of different schemes are confusingly all labelled *Shared Reading*. One of these is a class based technique for use by teachers, originated by Don Holdaway, involving giant books for large group reading tuition. Some teachers use the expression 'shared reading' for almost anything parents and children do together with a book, simply because they are sharing a book. This notion of shared reading owes much to the concept of reading apprenticeship promulgated by Liz Waterland, and although this may be fine in the hands of teachers and confident and imaginative parents, other parents are likely to need clearer training and support.

There are two further meanings of the expression 'shared reading'. In the county of Cleveland the term is used for parent and child reading a book simultaneously, without the specification of any particular correction procedure. As in the reading together aspect of paired reading, a wide range of books of unrestricted readability is used. Shared reading in this version is simpler than paired reading and perhaps particularly suitable for younger children. The final version of shared reading is the South Wales variant, which consists of the parent reading the book to the child, followed by the parent reading a book to the child but stopping occasionally for the child to supply a contextually relevant word unaided, with the parent supplying any word that the child cannot.

The *Pause, Prompt and Praise* technique is another structured technique, which originates from New Zealand. It consists of the child reading aloud to the parent from texts of controlled readability, with the parent pausing at errors to allow the child to self-correct. In the absence of self-correction, the parent gives a discriminatory prompt related to the nature of the error, which can be semantic, visual or contextual. Praise is much emphasized. This techanique is specifically conceived as suitable for children with reading difficulties. It has been utilized successfully in Australia and New Zealand as well as in the United Kingdom.

The *workshop approach* typically involves parents in a series of meetings in school, with emphasis often on the use of reading games. Parents make games, observe these in use, and borrow them for use at home. There may be further modules in the workshop curriculum including specific advice on reading to and with children and hearing children read.

Token reinforcement procedures were first developed for use with children with very severe reading problems. Children read single words and/or sentences on flash cards and then receive a point or token for each success. Points are subsequently exchanged for rewards or treats according to a pre-arranged menu.

Precision teaching is an approach to evaluating the effectiveness of teaching rather than a method of teaching itself. Individualized behavioural objectives in reading are set for each child, and parents check performance on the prescribed tasks daily, charting the child's improvement in correctness and speed of response. Programmes of work are individualized for specific children.

Direct instruction procedures are also largely used with children with special needs. The most familiar commercially produced direct instruction packages in the United Kingdom are the DISTAR materials. Direct Instruction procedures are characterized by highly structured scripted materials, using a prescribed sequence of lessons, involving rapid-paced interaction and much oral responding from the children. Practice and generalization exercises are incorporated into the teaching sequence. Children are placement tested to ascertain they start at the appropriate point in the programme. Such materials are popular in special schools in the United Kingdom but are increasingly being used for children with special needs in ordinary schools. Teachers wishing to use the materials usually need some training to ensure good practice but the scheme has been extended for use by parents. In America, Direct Instruction manuals have been prepared especially for parents.

A variety of other approaches to parental involvement in reading can be identified. In some areas *family reading groups* have been established, orientated to heighten appreciation of literature, wherein parents and children meet regularly to discuss, mutually review and recommend books that they have read. Some reading schemes are structured to facilitate parental involvement. The *Puddle Lane Reading Programme* is a series of structured books designed for parental use, devised in levels so that initially the parent reads rnost of the text to the child, but as the scheme progresses children read more and more of the text which is of a controlled readability. A similar approach is taken in the *Read Along Stories*. It is possible to use a combination of methods for a particular child at the same time, or to use different methods with the same child at different ages and stages in the child's reading development, as part of a whole school approach to parental involvement in reading. Further details will be found in Topping (1986b).

Organization of service delivery

It is usual for parent listening to be offered on a mixed ability basis and this is also true of the workshop approach and those based on specific sets of materials. Any service offered on a mixed ability basis will by definition include the 20 per cent of pupils with special needs. Continuing along the dimension of special need, both *Paired Reading* and *Shared Reading* are now increasingly offered on a mixed ability basis, although they did begin life conceptualized as remedial techniques. The *Pause, Prompt and Praise* method was conceived primarily as a remedial technique, and has so far been entirely used as such. The *precision teaching* approach, the *direct instruction* method and *token reinforcement* systems are almost entirely used for children with reading difficulty in the United Kingdom. We can now look at some of the organizational issues of service delivery in general and then consider in detail those aspects which need extra attention where a project is targeted on children with special educational needs, especially if they attend a special school.

Consideration must be given to the setting in which a parental involvement reading scheme is to be initiated. One factor is whether teachers already encourage children to take home reading books and whether a number of parents already come into school to help with reading. A second factor is the ethnic composition of pupils in the school, since those families for whom English is a second language will have special needs and require extra support. Further consideration is needed of whether the proposed project will cut across the curriculum objectives and teaching approach of some, if not all, of the classteachers in a given school. To this extent it is useful to know at the beginning the availability of time and energy of staff who are concerned to be involved with the project. There is sometimes a temptation to launch a first project with a target group of pupils who have particularly severe reading problems, but it has been found wiser to begin a project by choosing a mixed group of children. It is, of course, important that parental involvement is not encouraged simply to mask the existence of fundamental problems in the teaching of reading skills in a school.

For a first project to be successful a minimum of two committed and enthusiastic members of staff are normally required. It is also useful to secure the active support of other members of staff from the school, especially any member of staff with a specific responsibility for home/school liaison. It is also necessary to cost out physical resources, for example the purchase of extra books, buying other materials such as plastic bags for safe transfer of books to homes, duplicating and photocopying, video hire, the printing of diary sheets or cards, provision of storage and shelving, materials for evaluation, and overtime and travel payments for extra hours worked by certain personnel.

Having identified a target group of children for the project, it is then necessary to consider which of the various schemes and techniques are to be employed. The criteria for choice may include evidence of proven effectiveness, compatibility with current teaching methods, likely popularity with the intended consumers, relative costliness in time and resources and whether or not a subsidiary objective is to compare different methods. Before embarking on any scheme, it is essential that all the professional personnel involved have been adequately trained in the technique, have some experience of using it themselves and understand the organization of service delivery.

In projects of this kind, the children's enthusiasm for reading increases greatly, and this can embarrass schools who thought prior to the scheme that their book stocks were adequate. If a *Paired Reading* scheme is employed, then children have free book choice, and much of the existng book stock may be perceived by the children as undesirable and irrelevant. It is necessary to review current reading resources in a school from the point of view of volume, type, current location, frequency of child access and the existing policy on which books are allowed to go home. The existing record-keeping system for books on loan may need to be reviewed because a new project might make demands that will make the record-keeping system too complex and too time consuming.

Some schools differentiate one way or the other between books which belong to the school and those that are on loan, but children often find it hard to understand such a discrimination. A decision has to be made about where the reading scheme books stand in relation to the project and whether they are the only books to go home or the only books not to go home or whether they are to be treated like any other book. The latter option becomes particularly appropriate in relation to individualized reading by colour-coded levels of reading difficulty based on a wide collection of different types of book. A special collection of books serves to raise the status of the project. A school book shop can be given a boost in the context of a project by both new and second-hand items.

A reading project sometimes provides the initiative for a greater use of the local public library or for parents to be directed towards utilizing the facility of a mobile library in the neighbourhood. Special funding to increase book stocks may be sought from the Local Education Authority, or funding from the parent/teacher association or through a sponsored read fund-raising event.

Clearly, it is important to use every opportunity for direct personal contact to introduce the project to all concerned. This allows immediate mutual feedback about the project, helps put people at ease, and lessens the risk of misunderstanding. Planning the project well in advance will often enable it to be mentioned at a parents' evening in the previous term. With younger children, parents may be seen as they leave or collect children from school. A letter home is desirable to ensure all invited parents have the same information, with a reply slip for parents to indicate likely attendance at a meeting. A final reminder about meetings is necessary and in some cases teachers have found it useful to make a home visit or talk to parents on the telephone. A supplementary hand-written invitation may be more powerful than a duplicated circular.

Where children are known to be unreliable carriers of messages, it may be worth paying for regular mailing. It has been found worthwhile to discuss the project from an early stage with the children concerned, enlisting their help in preparing and illustrating invitation letters or booklets. This allows the children to develop group enthusiasm as the date for starting the project draws nearer. Where meetings are organized for parents, the availability of a crèche or other child-minding facility is extremely helpful. The environment of the meeting should be welcoming, with comfortable chairs and refreshments.

At the meetings, relevant books and materials can be shown and parents introduced to the techniques that they might engage in. If parents and children are to practise some relevant technique or activity at these meetings, an adequate number of teachers must be on hand to ensure that every family has at least five minutes of individualized discussion, advice and help. For some techniques more than one meeting is necessary and some projects use a multi-session instructional workshop from the outset. It is important that in such cases the meetings are run as modular sessions because there are few parents who are likely to be able to attend all sessions.

The introduction to the meeting explains why the project is being initiated and how similar projects have been successful elsewhere. Some schemes include a session on the things to avoid, utilizing discussion, role-play or video. Usually parents and children will require an actual demonstration of what they are supposed to do and while this can be presented on video, a live role-play may be of greater impact.

Some form of record-keeping at home by parents and/or children is usual. A simple weekly colour-coded diary card can include a note of days when activities are completed or books read, and with whom and for how long, followed by some comments from the parent. These should be of a positive nature about the child's effort and application and the success of that session. Cards can be returned to school on a weekly basis for the child to show the coordinating teacher, who should set a good example by adding some very positive comments on the bottom, signing officially, perhaps clipping the next week's blank card to the original, and returning the accumulating diary back home for the parents to scrutinize. In this way, parents, children and teachers are kept constantly in touch and mutually accountable. Some parents run out of a variety of positive comments to put on the card. To help in this situation one local authority has produced a dictionary of praise.

As a project proceeds it is useful for there to be further meetings between teachers, parents and children. Some teachers offer the opportunity for a one-to-one consultation with parents, but parents who need support may not actually avail themselves of it unless it is offered and provided in a very structured way. It is effective to schedule support meetings, giving parents a chance to report on their experiences, good and bad, and for the group to brainstorm solutions for any problems that have arisen. Teachers have also found it useful to make a home visit while the scheme is in operation to see parents and children working in their own natural environment. Experience shows that home visits are usually well received by the vast majority of parents and children.

Some form of evaluation of the success of the project may be desirable. This may take the form of soliciting views from parents, children and teacher colleagues as to the effectiveness of the project, from verbal feedback at meetings or on the basis of some simple questionnaire. It is also useful for information to be collected on how the project is working in terms of parent attendance at meetings, levels of take-up, rates of return of diary cards, and content of diary cards, for example. Equally, it is valuable to hold a feedback meeting for parents at the end of the intensive phase of the project, to encourage parents to feel that the project was their own. Some teachers like to carry out a more detailed assessment of progress made during the project using a standardized reading test at the beginning and the end of the project, or some form of criterion-referenced reading assessment.

In some schools an attitude to reading scale has been used, or an analysis of shifts in children's reading style. The results of such tests and assessments are better fed back to the parents only as group averages. It may be possible to gather baseline data, to enable progress during the project to be compared to a similar period prior to the project, or to gather data on a control or comparison group of children who are not involved in the project. Good evidence that the technique was actually used in the home is desirable. Observations made during home visits or tape-recordings made by parents and children at home form a supplement to the very basic information recorded on diary cards.

Particular organizational difficulties may arise in the case of children with marked special needs. Such children may come from homes where there are few books available, where levels of parental ability to read English are low and where parents may lack confidence in helping their own children to read. The technique for parental involvement must be carefully chosen so as not to over-stress parents. In some circumstances it has been found necessary or useful to recruit what might be called surrogate parents, including older brothers and sisters, grandparents, aunts and uncles, or possibly even friends and neighbours. Equally, recourse can be made to the provision of a parallel experience in the school setting, perhaps using another volunteer parent or a volunteer teacher or a peer or cross-age tutor.

Some schools experiment with self-teaching packages, taken home by children as homework. Parents can give general approval even though they might not fully understand the nature of the activity in which the child is engaged. Parent volunteers may come into a school to assemble such packages, dual language texts based on the children's own community experiences, or tape-text combinations in one or more languages to accompany existing books. Where the target group of children have extremely low reading skills or are non-readers, it may be necessary for the school to produce basic materials on a language experience model.

Parents may need to be trained in more than one technique at a time. Thus *precision teaching* of basic sight vocabulary, using direct instruction correction procedures, could lead to the development of self-generated reading books on the language experience model, illustrated by photographs or the children's own drawings, which are then read and re-read at home using a technique such as *Paired Reading* in the first instance, but later developing into something less supportive such as *Pause, Prompt and Praise*. There may be great difficulties in finding sufficient real books at a low readability level, particularly in the non-fiction area.

For special needs families it may well be necessary to provide transport to meetings and this increases the cost of running the project. Reimbursing fares for public transport is helpful up to a point, but may not compensate for the stress and strain of coping with a number of small children on a two bus ride across town. Crèche facilities may be particularly relevant for such families. The larger the family, the more likely there are to be very young children who would have difficulty coping with an evening meeting. Parents with children who have severe reading difficulties are more likely to have themselves been unsuccessful at school than other parents, and it is particularly important that every care is taken to be reassuring and welcoming with these parents. Some such parents will demonstrate learnt helplessness with respect to educational activities, and when they say 'I can't', they actually mean 'I don't have the confidence'.

In a project for children with marked special needs it is essential that the training procedure is extremely well organized and delivered, allowing a great deal of time for individual discussion and tuition for all families. Strong support and early problem-solving are vital if parents are not to give up. Irrespective of any booster meetings in school, a programme of supportive home visits is almost certain to be essential. This can be made somewhat more cost-efficient by allocating home visitors to sub-groups of parents who live relatively near to each other. Where the school's catchment area is so large as to make parental attendance at meetings impossible, consideration can be given to intensive residential courses for parents, the use of self-instructional packages or the provision of parent surrogates within the school.

Evaluation research

Firstly, we can briefly consider unevaluated methods and methods on which there is a small amount of evaluation evidence but which have not been widely deployed. Evaluation research with mixed ability populations will then be considered for each of three well-evaluated and widely-used major techniques:

parent listening, Paired Reading, and *Pause, Prompt and Praise*. The evaluation research on projects which have specifically targeted pupils with special needs will then be considered.

There is no published evidence on the effectiveness or otherwise of materials-based approaches such as the *Puddle Lane* books. Descriptions of the impact of family reading groups emphasize high take-up rates and participant enthusiasm but more objective evidence is hard to find. Much the same applies to the workshop approach, where there is a great deal of evidence of high take-up rates and considerable parent and teacher enthusiasm (Weinberger, 1983). The South Wales variation of *Paired Reading* has been evaluated in one major study involving thirty children, some of whom were considered dyslexic and some of whom were considered to be standard remedial children. Twice normal rates of progress were sustained for a whole year for both groups, who benefited equally in a controlled study (Topping and Wolfendale, 1985). The *Gillham variation* on *Paired Reading* is not associated with any adequate published evidence of effectiveness. Likewise there is no published evidence on the effectiveness of the South Wales technique of *prepared reading* other than as a component of the work previously mentioned, and then only for some children. Much of this also applies to the South Wales version of *shared reading*.

The *relaxed reading* technique has been subject to a well constructed pilot study of twenty children, which indicated that *relaxed reading* could be as effective as *Paired Reading*, but replicatory research is needed (Lindsay and Evans, 1985). The original version of *Shared Reading* (reading simultaneously without a specific correction procedure) (Greening and Spenceley, 1987), has now been used in a number of schools in its home area. Evidence of substantial gains in reading accuracy is available for 125 children, the majority of whom had some degree of reading difficulty and the rest of whom were beginner readers. The technique is certainly worth considering for some special needs children, particularly those with a very limited sight vocabulary since, as the skill level of the child rises, it is easy to develop into the full method of *Paired Reading* which offers a bridge into independent reading.

Turning to the major approaches which have been more widely used and fully evaluated, the *Parent listening* approach generates variable outcomes on reading tests. Aggregating the test outcomes from many studies shows progress in reading accuracy at about 2.3 times the normal rates and the same in reading comprehension, assuming normal progress to be one month of reading age in one calendar month. There is solid evaluative evidence from control group studies, including long-term follow-up, and while there is no doubt that this approach can work well, it is clear that not everybody has made it work well.

Paired Reading in its more or less pure or original form has been the subject of a great deal of research. A recent bibliography (Topping, 1986c) listed over 130 articles on the topic. What emerges from these reports is that paired readers progress at about three times normal rates in reading accuracy and about five times normal rates in reading comprehension. These results are not confined to seminal research projects, as in the Kirklees local authority; the technique has been used widely by a large number of schools, and in a sample of 2750 children in consecutive projects run by many different schools, average gains of over three times normal rates in reading accuracy and four times normal rates in reading comprehension have been found. These aggregate results are supported by baseline and control group data.

The *Pause, Prompt and Praise* technique has registered very few poor results and the overall average gain is roughly equivalent to 2.5 times normal progress. On the other hand, there is as yet little research evidence from more widespread and less controlled dissemination, and it will be interesting to see to what extent effectiveness is sustained once the approach percolates into the fabric of everyday school life. The aggregates quoted include studies on *Pause, Prompt and Praise* with peers and cross age tutors.

A number of *parent listening* projects have been targeted on children with reading difficulties. Portsmouth *et al.* (1985) deployed *parent listening* with children attending a special school for those with moderate learning difficulties. The project children did marginally better than the control children. Knapman (in Topping and Wolfendale, 1985) reports a successful project in a smaller school which combined *parent listening* with a token *reinforcement system* linking home and school and incorporated six training sessions for parents and children. The children progressed at 2.2 times normal rates in reading accuracy and comprehension over an eighteen-week period.

The literature available on the use of *Paired Reading* in the special needs population is extensive and many reports of *Paired Reading* with children with reading difficulties in the ordinary school will be found in the bibliography in Topping (1986c). Here also are references for a number of reports on the use of *Paired Reading* with children in special schools, which will be briefly reviewed below. O'Hara (1986) outlined the parameters for the use of *Paired Reading* with children with severe learning difficulties. Dickinson (1986 and 1987) went on to report on the actual use of *Paired Reading* with children with severe learning difficulties. Dickinson (1986 and 1987) went on to report on the actual use of *Paired Reading* in this way, in combination and in parallel with other techniques. Topping and McKnight (1984) and McKnight (1985) reported on the very successful use of *Paired Reading* with children in a moderate learning difficulties special school. Holdsworth (1986) reports on the use of *Shared Reading* in combination with *direct instruction* and *precision teaching* for children on short-term contracts in a special school for those with moderate learning difficulties.

O'Hara (1985) reports on a project in a special school for physically handicapped children in which the usual substantial gains in reading ability in comparison to control groups were found, but also there were ancillary benefits in social behaviour and educational gains generally. Topping and McKnight (1984) and Topping *et al.*, (1985) report on the use of *Paired Reading* with surrogate parents in a residential school for maladjusted children.

Paired Reading has worked with adults with literacy problems, via the training of family, friends, neighbours and workmates who can offer frequent practice in the natural environment (Scoble *et al.*, 1988). It is commonly thought that *Paired Reading* is not possible for Asian families where English is a second language, but reports on projects which have successfully achieved this have been produced by Welsh and Roffe (1985), Vaughey and McDonald (1986) and Jungnitz (1985). It is also commonly believed that *Paired Reading* cannot work with children who have no basic sight vocabulary but Jungnitz *et al.*, in Topping and Wolfendale (1985), reported on the successful use of the method with non-reading children who attended a special unit in an infant school.

Ten studies of the *Pause, Prompt and Praise* technique are summarized in McNaughton *et al.*, (1987), where its use with seventy children aged 7 to 12 years with reading deficits ranging from 6 months to 5 years is described. Most of the tutors were the natural parents of the children involved. Six of the ten studies used reading tests for evaluative purposes, while five used criterion-referenced assessment approaches. In four of the studies, all the tuition took place at home, in four further studies all the tuition took place at school and in two studies tuition took place both at home and at school. Median tuition input was six to eight hours during the experimental period. The training time for a tutor was almost equally lengthy, however, and in only two studies were tutors trained in a group format. The median ratio gain was 2.6 times normal progress with reference to assessment of home reading, but the ratio gain for three studies where assessment was also conducted in school gave a rather lower figure, 2.3 times normal progress, for generalization to school reading. Where tuition occurred in school as well as at home, gains increased still further.

Further sources of information on *Pause, Prompt and Praise* are the papers by Glynn and Winter in Topping and Wolfendale, (1985). Winter trained parents in both *Pause, Prompt and Praise* and in *Paired Reading* techniques and left them to choose which method to use at home with their children. An increase in the speed of reading and a reduction in error frequency and refusals were evident, although self-corrections did not increase. Both techniques produced equally good results.

Wheldall *et al.*, (1987) reported on a parent tutoring programme with high progress among young readers aged 5 and a half to 7 and a half years. However, the *Pause, Prompt and Praise* group showed no greater gains in reading ability than another group where parents had received much more general advice. O'Connor *et al.*, (1987) trained fourteen residential child-care workers to use *Pause, Prompt and Praise* with eighteen low progress readers of primary school age in school and residential settings during a short-stay residential programme. The *Pause, Prompt and Praise* technique produced substantially superior results compared to those children receiving a practice reading approach.

Given that the essence of the precision teaching technique is the daily evaluation of individualized curriculum-based programmes, much of the evaluative data is available only on a multiple case-study basis. There are, however, strong indications of effectiveness. Belcher (1984) cites reading test gains for a group of seven non-readers. Over two years the children averaged reading age gains of 2.4 years with the help of parent-tutored *precision teaching*. A comparison group of similar children who received *precision teaching* in school from professionals averaged 1.7 years gain. Pennington (1982) had described parental involvement in precision teaching two years earlier, in a small-scale project designed to help six children with reading difficulties in the Sefton area of Liverpool. Winter gave detailed case-study information on a small sample of four children with reading difficulties in a paper published in 1983. Stewart (1984) reported a parent-powered precision teaching project for eight children with reading difficulty in the junior school, which focused on word-building skills. During a three-month period the children gained five months in reading accuracy and comprehension on the Neale test, and improved in attitude and motivation.

Jordan (1985) summarizes data on reading age gains from a much larger number of children attending a reading centre. Children made three times normal gains in reading in the short run, with continued acceleration at five month and eight month follow-up, irrespective of whether they experienced precision teaching with their parents or with qualified teachers. Children who did not experience precision teaching made lesser gains. Similar acceleration was evident in the spelling area also. Rippon *et al.* (1986) reported training parents to use the *Datapac PT* programmes to teach their own children with reading problems. Channon (1986) describes a project where five low progress readers in an infant school were involved in a precision teaching programme based on word recognition, with the words drawn from target vocabulary in the reading scheme. On a reading test the children made gains at 2.3 times normal rates over a three-month period and there were marked increases in sight vocabulary.

One of the earliest reports of the involvement of parents in the *direct instruction* technique was that of Levey and Emsley (1982). During five evening workshops for parents at a school for children with moderate learning difficulties, training was given in different skill areas of the DISTAR reading programme. Parents were introduced to the sound system, signalling and touching procedures, correction procedures and blending methods, and orthography.

Szwed and Hanson (1984) involved themselves with the parents of a group of fourteen first-year pupils in the remedial department of a high school who were following the Corrective Reading DI programme (SRA). Parents consolidated their child's learning by hearing the child read the materials covered by the Corrective Reading lesson in school that day. Over a four-month inter-test period, participating children gained nine months in reading accuracy and ten months in reading comprehension on the Neale Test, while non-participating children gained five months in reading accuracy and ten months in reading comprehension.

Holdsworth describes (in Topping and Wolfendale, 1985) the large scale involvement of parents in both *direct instruction* and *precision teaching* in a special school for children with moderate learning difficulties in a rural area. Parent training was conducted over five workshops based on the Corrective

Reading programme. The parents were themselves taught by *direct instruction* methodology, and the workshops included parents working in pairs, presenting sounds to each other with the appropriate signal. Holdsworth gives outcome data for both accuracy and comprehension on the Neale test for various groups of children: ratio gains over inter-test periods of between four and ten months range between one and five times normal progress, the mean ratio gain being two. Subjective feedback from parents and children was very positive.

Almost all schemes for parental involvement in reading lay some stress on the importance of praise from the tutor. It is now usual to confine the *token/tangible reinforcement* approach to those children for whom other approaches incorporating merely social reinforcement have been demonstrated to be ineffective. There is no doubt that the *token reinforcement* approach is effective. Up to four times normal gains in reading accuracy has been found to accrue in such projects. There are several studies with baseline and reversal data, which clearly demonstrate the effectiveness of approach in the short term. In some studies it is clear that the gains made tend not to continue where the reinforcement ends, and it may well be that insufficient attention has been given to maintaining the required reading behaviour by generalizing the impact of tangible reinforcement across to social reinforcement.

There is now an increased interest in developing and accelerating the reading skills of the mentally handicapped for both children and adults. *Paired Reading* and *Shared Reading* in the sense of simultaneous reading have been used by parent and surrogate tutors with this population, together with *token reinforcement*, *precision teaching* and *direct instruction* delivered by teachers in school or college. A quite different approach has been described by Buckley (in Topping and Wolfendale, 1985), who worked with the parents of young Down's syndrome children, teaching reading as a means of accelerating expressive language. The visual recognition capabilities of many of these children proved to be well in advance of their expressive language capabilities. Many children developed a substantial sight vocabulary relatively quickly, which then served to facilitate the elicitation of the relevant expressive language.

The future

There is now such a large number of research reports on parental involvement in reading which unequivocally demonstrate overall effectiveness that the issue is no longer in doubt. This does not mean that every project will be successful, since quality of organization and the incidence of natural disasters will vary from project to project, even those run by the same people. However, there are results positive enough to sustain the contention that the deployment of a portion of each teacher's time to support parents as reading tutors would raise professional cost-effectiveness.

The issue of the relative effectiveness of different techniques is more complex, particularly when we are concerned with special needs populations. A number of the comparative studies in existence were very small-scale research undertaken as part of a student thesis, and the work has often been carried out in a short time, with limited resources, and has not developed as part of the natural growth of the school. Some of the measures of outcome used have been highly suspect. There have been three studies directly comparing *Paired Reading* with *Pause, Prompt and Praise*. These have all found the techniques equally effective, although in two of the studies *Paired Reading* demonstrated some extra benefits which failed to reach statistical significance. Four studies have compared *Paired Reading* with *parent listening* and, of these, two studies found significant differences favouring *Paired Reading*, while the other two studies found the two techniques equally effective. Other single comparative studies have shown *Paired Reading* to be more effective than just *reinforcement*, and *Paired Reading* and *relaxed reading* to be equally effective.

There is a need for teachers to become more proficient in the whole range of techniques for parental involvement in reading which are of proven effectiveness, to enable the techniques to be deployed selectively and possibly sequentially to meet the needs of individual children. As research, dissemination and experience increase in this field, we should become clearer about which techniques are appropriate to children of different ages, developmental stages, and degrees of retardation. An overall aim would be to develop a whole-school policy on parental involvement in reading, wherein parents can be guided and supported in the use of a range of techniques which are relevant to the developmental stage of their children at any one moment in time.

Thus, in the nursery, parent involvement may revolve around the value of story, parents reading to children and access to a library of language games to use at home. In reception infants, this may extend to the development of *Shared Reading* in the sense of reading together synchronously. In middle infants, parent listening could be introduced and extended into the first year or two of the junior department. Alternatively, or in parallel, *Paired Reading* could be offered on a mixed ability basis to all children. This technique should remain relevant through to the fourth junior year. Running alongside these developments those parents with more time and/or energy could be offered the use of a library of reading games, perhaps leading on to involvement in more intensive workshops.

For those with special educational needs the involvement on general offer should be tried first as a matter of course, but for children who have not learnt to read satisfactorily in the infant department, a choice can be made between *Pause, Prompt and Praise, precision teaching, direct instruction* and *token reinforcement*, or a combination of two of these. Much the same applies to the high school age range, except the reintroduction of *Paired Reading* could be considered here. At the adult level, a combination of *Paired Reading* and *precision teaching* is likely to be the most potent and easily deliverable package, perhaps combined with some form of self-recording and/or self-reinforcement.

As a further strand in a whole-school policy on parental involvement in reading, other alternatives may need to be considered to sustain parent and child interests through the introduction of novelty, or to tailor a technique particularly suited to certain idiosyncratic individuals. Some of these may not be well researched at the moment, but if teachers use these approaches thoughtfully and methodically, evaluating their effectiveness and disseminating good practice, then more teachers and families will be helped. The role of parents coming into school to act as tutors must also be carefully considered. It may be tempting for schools to recruit a small group of middle-class trusties who are considered reliable and discreet, but it would be a pity if this impeded a wider involvement of a larger number of natural parents as educators in the home.

There seems little doubt that new techniques of paraprofessional tutoring will continue to emerge in the years to come. Those schools who have developed a whole-school policy will be able to evaluate these in the light of the research evidence on their effectiveness and also with respect to where they might fit in the hierarchy of strategies and techniques already at the teachers' fingertips. It is evident that the parental involvement movement will push relatively rapidly into other curriculum areas, particularly those related to basic skills. There is already a considerably amount of work being done on parental involvement in mathematics, especially with children in the infant department, often based on mathematical games. The extension of the *precision teaching* approach to other curriculum areas, such as spelling, writing and mathematics is already taking place. A technique for accelerating spelling ability which has many of the features of *Paired Reading* and precision teaching has been developed, known as *Cued Spelling*. Some schools have also developed parental involvement in other curriculum areas such as art, and Paired Sculpture has yielded some aesthetically impressive results.

There is a danger of increasing vagueness in nomenclature, accompanied by dilution in techniques, and perhaps most crucially, the amount of thought given to the planning and organization of initiatives. Even the most effective parental involvement in reading technique will not survive a ramshackle attempt to deliver it, wherein no one teacher takes full responsibility for coordination and the meeting of planning objectives in terms of both large issues, such as type and frequency of follow-up, and trivial issues, such as whether the television is working. Carefully planned and executed service delivery is essential if the effectiveness of initiatives is to be sustained in the long term.

References

BELCHER, M. (1984) 'Parents can be a major asset in teaching reading', *Remedial Education* 19, 4, pp. 162–4.

CHANNON, S. (1986) *Parental Involvement in a Precision Teaching Word-Recognition*

Programme for Infant School Children: A pilot study, unpublished M.Ed thesis, University College, Swansea.

GREENING, M. and SPENCELEY, J. (1987) 'Shared Reading: supporting the inexperienced reader', *Educational Psychology in Practice* 3, 1, pp. 31–7.

HEWISON, J. (1987) 'The Haringey Reading Project: long term effects of parental involvement in children's reading', *Paired Reading Bulletin* 3, pp. 50–53.

HEWISON, J. and TIZARD, J. (1980) 'Parental Involvement and reading attainment', *British Journal of Educational Psychology*, 50, pp. 209–15.

JORDAN, A. (1985) *Parental Precision Teaching Project — Summary*, unpublished report, Department of Psychology, North-East London Polytechnic.

JUNGNITZ, G., OLIVE, S. and TOPPING, K. J. (1983) 'The development and evaluation of a Paired Reading Project', *Journal of Community Education*, 2, 4, pp. 14–22.

LEVEY, B. and EMSLEY, D. (1982) 'Involvement of parents in the teaching of DISTAR reading to slow-learning children', *Occasional Papers of the Division of Educational and Child Psychology*, British Psychological Society, 6, 1, pp. 43–6.

LINDSAY, G. and EVANS, A. (1985) 'Paired Reading and Relaxed Reading: A comparison', *British Journal of Educational Psychology*, 55, 3, pp. 304–9.

McNAUGHTON, S., GLYNN, T. and ROBINSON, V. (1987) *Pause, Prompt and Praise: Effective Tutoring for Remedial Reading*, Cheltenham, Positive Products.

O'CONNOR, G., GLYNN, T. and TUCK, B. (1987) 'Contexts for remedial reading: Practice Reading and Pause, Prompt and Praise tutoring'. *Educational Psychology*, 7, 3, pp. 207–23.

O'HARA, M. (1985) 'Paired Reading in a school for the physically handicapped', *Paired Reading Bulletin*, 1, pp. 16–19.

O'HARA, M. (1986) 'Paired Reading with the mentally handicapped', *Paired Reading Bulletin*, 2, pp. 16–19.

PENNINGTON, A. (1982) 'Parental involvement in precision teaching', *Occasional Papers of the Division of Educational and Child Psychology*, British Psychological Society, 6, 1, pp. 39–42.

PORTSMOUTH, R., WILKINS, J. and AIREY, J. (1985) 'Home based reading for special school pupils', *Educational Psychology in Practice*, 1, 2, pp. 52–8.

RIPPON, C., WINN, B. and INGLEBY, S. (1986) 'Can parents teach their own children with reading problems?' *Paired Reading Bulletin* 2, pp. 76–81.

SANDOW, S., STAFFORD, D. and STAFFORD, P. (1987) *An Agreed Understanding? — Parent-professional Communication and the 1981 Education Act*, Windsor. NFER-Nelson.

SCOBLE, J., TOPPING, K. and WIGGLESWORTH, C. (1988) 'Training family and friends as adult literacy tutors', *Journal of Reading* (International Reading Association) 31, 5, pp. 410–17.

STEWART, F. (1984) Report on the Parental Involvement in Reading Project at Reaside School, unpublished report, Frankley Urban Programme Project.

SZWED, C. and HANSON, B. (1984) Report on the Parental Involvement Home Reading Project at Frankley Community High School, unpublished report, Frankley Urban Programme Project.

TIZARD, J., SCHOFIELD, W. N. and HEWISON, J. (1982) 'Collaboration between teachers and parents in assisting children's reading', *British Journal of Educational Psychology*, 52, pp. 1–15.

TOPPING, K. J. (1986a) *Parents as Educators: Training Parents to Teach their Children*, London, Croom Helm: Cambridge, Massachusetts, Brookline Books.

TOPPING, K. J. (1986b) 'WHICH parental involvement in reading scheme? A guide for practitioners', *Reading* (UKRA) 20, 3, pp. 148–156.

TOPPING, K. J. (1986c) *The Kirklees Paired Reading Pack*, 2nd ed. Huddersfield, Kirklees Psychological Service.

TOPPING, K. J. and WOLFENDALE, S. (eds.) (1985) *Parental Involvement in Children's Reading*, London, Croom Helm: New York, Nichols.

VAUGHEY, S. and MCDONALD, J. (1986) 'Paired Reading Projects with Asian families', *Paired Reading Bulletin*, 2, pp. 6–9.

WEINBERGER, J. (1983) *Fox Hill Reading Workshop*, London, Family Service Units.

WELSH, M. and ROFFE, M. (1985) 'Paired Reading Projects with Asian families', *Paired Reading Bulletin*, 1, pp. 34–7.

WHELDALL, K., MERRETT, F. and COLMAR, S. (1987) 'Pause, Prompt and Praise' for parents and peers: Effective tutoring of low progress readers', *Support for Learning* 2, 1, pp. 5–12.

WINTER, S. (1983) 'Precision teaching in mainstream schools: A role for parents?', *Behavioural Approaches with Children* 7, 3, pp. 26–37.

Resources

A fuller list of practical resources will be found in Topping and Wolfendale (1985). Some of the more useful items have been selected for inclusion here.

Parent Listening

BRANSTON, P. and PROVIS, M. (1986) *Children and Parents Enjoying Reading: a handbook for teachers*, London, Hodder and Stoughton.

Partners in Reading (1984) (colour video, 23 minutes), Chiltern Consortium, Wall Hall, Aldenham, Watford WD2 8AT.

Workshops

SMITH, H. and MARSH, M. *Have You a Minute? the Fox Hill Reading Project*, from Fox Hill First and Nursery School, Keats Road, Sheffield S6 1AZ.

BAKER, C. (1980) *Reading through Play*, London, MacDonald Education.

Shared Reading (Reading Simultaneously)

Pamphlets and video available via County Psychological Service, 5 Turner Street, Redcar, TS10 1AY, Cleveland.

Paired Reading

The Kirklees Paired Reading Training Park contains both written and video material, available separately or together, and covers peer as well as parent tutoring. Adult Literacy and Cured Spelling Training Packs and Paired Reading Bulletins also available. Details from: Paired Reading Project, Oastler Centre, 103 New Street, Huddersfield HD1 2UA.
Also see:
MORGAN, R. (1986) *Helping Children Read: the Paired Reading Handbook*, London, Methuen.

Pause, Prompt and Praise

Video, professional handbook and parent handbook available from Positive Products, P.O. Box 45, Cheltenham, Gloucestershire.

Precision Teaching

The Walsall PAIRS Project is largely based on Precision Teaching methodology which is simply explained in a series of ten booklets for parents. These are available from Walsall Psychological Service, Lime House, Littleton Street West, Walsall WS2 8EN.

Direct Instruction

ENGELMANN, S., HADDOX, P. and BRUNER, E. (1983) *Teach Your Child to Read in 100 Easy Lessons*, New York, Simon and Schuster.
HARRISON, GRANT VON, *Teach Your Child to Read* (for 3–5 year olds); *Improve Your Child's Reading Ability* (for 6–16 year olds), both available in the UK from: Education Training and Technology Consultants, 1 Beechwood Avenue, Ryton, Tyne and Wear NE40 3LX.

Other

OBRIST, C. (1978) *How to Run Family Reading Groups*, Edge Hill College, Ormskirk, United Kingdom Reading Association.

BUCKLEY, S. (1984) *Reading and Language Development in Children with Down's Syndrome: a guide for parents and teachers* (with accompanying video) Department of Psychology, Portsmouth Polytechnic, King Charles Street, Portsmouth PO1 2ER, Hampshire.

6
Teaching Parents to Teach Children: The Portage Approach to Special Needs

Robert Cameron

Introduction

During the past three decades two consistent findings have reoccurred in educational and social research. The first of these is the well documented relationship between home background and early learning and the second relates to the stresses which the birth of a handicapped child can place on family relationships. Both these findings have had a marked effect on the nature of the support and help which are provided for families who have a young child with special needs.

In general, administrators and policy makers in local and health authorities have tended to respond to this research data by setting up centres of excellence designed to provide support for families with a young handicapped child. In centres like nursery schools, opportunity centres, diagnostic and paediatric units, professionals like teachers, care staff and therapists, as well as visiting professionals like advisers, psychologists, health visitors, social workers and doctors, can assess needs and coordinate necessary services.

Centres of excellence have a number of obvious advantages: they are familiar and long established work contexts for educational, health and social services professionals; a wide variety of multi-agency expertise and back-up is often available and specialist skills and services can be developed. Since groups of handicapped children can be catered for under the same roof, schools, units and centres also possess obvious administrative appeal. All of these advantages are likely to ensure continued growth for the centre of excellence model throughout the 1980s. Since centres of excellence have so many assets, it might seem almost impertinent to question the benefits of this particular service model. However, the model does have two important hidden drawbacks: it takes children out of their homes to help them and it reinforces a widely-held view that helping handicapped children is a job which is best left to 'the experts'.

The importance of parents

There are many reasons why all parents occupy a centre-stage role in the care, upbringing and education of young children. Even when a child attends a centre of excellence provision, only a relatively small percentage of their waking time is spent outside the home. Similarly, the Headstart studies in the United States have shown that early intervention is almost valueless unless it embraces the total environment of the child, the largest portion of which includes the time spent at home.

A number of national policy groups involved in planning services for handicapped children have drawn inspiration from the conclusion that parental involvement programmes have been clearly impressive in terms of productivity, permanence and practicability. The Court Committee on Child Health Services (1976) concluded: 'we have found no better way to raise a child than to reinforce the ability of parents ...' The National Development Group for the Mentally Handicapped reporting in 1978 urged that 'the detailed treatment of mental handicap should largely take place in a child's home in the first few years and gradually others (particularly teachers) should become involved ...'

The Warnock Committee (1978), which examined educational provisions for children and young people who had special educational needs, chose as their area of first priority the provision of services for children under five. Warnock committee members unanimously agreed that it should be the parents who were the primary educators of their children in the early years and the services provided by supporting professionals should be orientated towards helping parents in this important task. The Committee recommended 'greater recognition and involvement of parents as the main educators of their children during the early years'.

Recent legislation, especially the 1981 Education Act, has ensured that parents, particularly those who have children with special educational needs, now take a major role in the selection and planning of special educational programmes and provisions for their children. In short, parents are at last recognized as the crucial element in the early intervention equation!

With the argument for the home as an effective learning environment proved almost conclusively and with the case for parental involvement receiving strong support from every national policy-making group in the last decade, it would be reasonable to assume that services for preschoolers with moderate or severe learning difficulties would be planned, or perhaps re-planned, around parents and the home. Sadly, this has rarely been the case, since recommendations at a national level have challenged but apparently not changed many of the strongly held assumptions among policy makers and professional workers in the caring services. Indeed, in the past, within-family variables appear to have been considered relatively unimportant by caring professionals and were largely ignored by social science researchers. It has been left to more recent investigators like Tizard and Hughes (1984) to highlight the complexities of the parent-child interface and to demonstrate how difficult it is to replicate some of these subtle factors in centre-based provisions.

A summary of the current situation would be that despite the established importance of the family as the major factor in any child's development, surprisingly few parent-based services have been developed. Yet, services which do involve parents in a major service role are not simply stop-gap approaches, but offer some very distinctive advantages: they allow the earliest possible intervention; help parents to enhance their already considerable repertoire of child-rearing skills and can prevent any undermining of parents' self confidence. However, as the research evidence indicates, the overwhelming advantage of parent-based services is the possibility of substantial support and enduring benefit to the children and their families. A review of current initiatives involving young severely handicapped children and their families has been made by Blacher (1984).

A different type of service

A more detailed look at the home environment has revealed two priority problems which are faced by parents of handicapped children: teaching the child new and important everyday skills and managing any disruptive behaviour which the handicapped child may have acquired. What most families appear to want is practical advice on how to help their child become as full a member of the family as possible.

The Portage home visiting scheme seeks to introduce powerful teaching and management techniques drawn from applied psychology to parents of preschool children with special educational needs. The project was first set up in 1969 in Portage, a small town in Wisconsin, and was designed to 'directly involve parents in the education of their children by teaching parents what to teach, what to reinforce and how to observe and record behaviour' (Shearer and Shearer, 1972). Early success ensured that the Portage model became one of a tiny number of research projects which were recommended by the US Office of Special Education in 1975 as being 'exemplary services for handicapped preschoolers'.

During the 1970s, the Portage home teaching model was replicated extensively and by the mid-1980s there were over 140 projects in the United States and Canada (Jesien, 1984). In the interim period, successful Portage schemes had also been developed in a number of South American, Asian, African and European countries.

The first UK project, the Wessex Portage Research Project, was set up by the Wessex Health Care Evaluation Research Team in 1976 in Winchester, Hampshire. The pilot scheme had thirteen families, three home teachers, a supervisor and a small management team. Once again the early results in the UK setting were encouraging (see Smith *et al.*, 1977 for detailed results of the first six months of this scheme). Similarly encouraging results were also obtained on a sister research project in South Glamorgan (Revill and Blunden, 1979) and from these somewhat modest beginnings, Portage schemes began to spread throughout the United Kingdom. The number of services passed the three hundred mark some time in 1988 (see Figure 6.1 for details of some of the major milestones).

The Portage approach is designed to help parents with special needs to teach their own children in their own homes. This objective is achieved by home teachers from a variety of supporting professional groups including teachers, health visitors, community nurses, family service workers, therapists and volunteers, who visit each family weekly and teach parents how to use carefully planned, direct instructional techniques with their children. The resulting activity programme is not only designed to meet the educational needs of the individual child in a particular home setting but also provides an ongoing record of the child's progress.

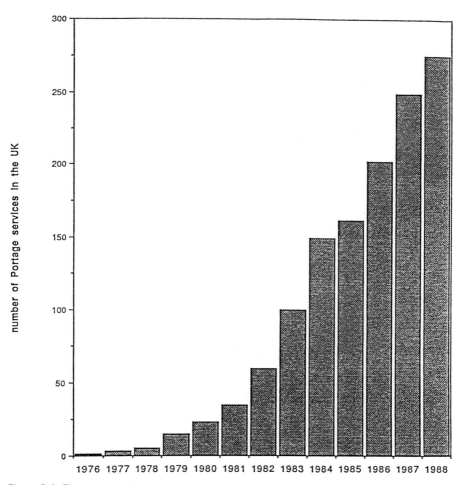

Figure 6.1: The growth of Portage Services in the UK from 1976 to 1988.

Home teaching

The central feature of Portage is the home teaching process. On weekly visits, home teachers and parents identify and agree new skills which they would like to see the developmentally delayed child acquire and working closely together they arrive at interventions for teaching these skills. These teaching strategies are not only clearly written down but demonstrated by the home teacher, then tried out by the parent while the home teacher is still present to give advice if necessary. Such carefully worked out procedures ensure that the parent is familiar with the teaching task before the home teacher leaves the home. The parent continues the teaching programme throughout the week until the home teacher's next visit when the progress of the child is monitored and new weekly teaching activities are agreed. Home teaching continues on a weekly basis until the child goes to school.

Although the Portage home visit has a carefully worked out structure (see Table 6.1 for a summary) this structure is flexible enough to be able to respond to the idiosyncratic needs of the individual child within an individual family. These major components of the home visit are as follows:

1. *Assessment is made of the child's existing skills.* However delayed in development the child may be, the emphasis from the outset is positive. Parents and home visitors put together a profile of the child's skill using the Portage Checklist (see Figure 6.2). This checklist has over 600 important developmental milestones in five areas of self-help, motor, language, social and cognitive development. The parent and home visitor fill in the details of those checklist behaviours which the child has already acquired and since this procedure is one where a knowledge of the child's existing skill repertoire is as important as an awareness of the child's future needs, it gives both parents and home teachers the opportunity to make reciprocal contributions.

Table 6.1   (taken from the Code of Practice of the National Portage Association, 1986).

The home visit
1   Families are visited regularly by a home visitor at a regular agreed time.
2   A developmental checklist is used for initial and ongoing assessment.
3   Long-term goals are selected in response to checklist information, parents' suggestions and advice from associated professionals.
4   An activity chart consisting of instructions agreed with the parents on what to teach, how to teach it and what to record, is left with them each week for each of the skills being taught.
5   The agreed teaching procedure is demonstrated by the home visitor.
6   The home visitor observes the parents carrying out the procedure and offers advice and/or agrees amendments to it.
7   The child's level of skill in the area concerned is recorded both before teaching and a week after teaching so that improvements can be measured and celebrated.
8   Opportunities are planned which enable the child to enjoy the practice of newly acquired skills during everyday activities.
9   Time is made available for listening to and sharing other relevant information offered by a parent.
10 Practical support is offered and visits are facilitated with other parents, neighbourhood resources and other agencies as appropriate.

Level Two: Age Level 1 – 2

CARD		BEHAVIOUR	ENTRY BEHAVIOUR	DATE ACHIEVED	COMMENTS
Lan 17	L48	Responds to rhymes and jingles		/ /	
Lan 18	L49	Says 5 different words (may use same word to refer to different objects)		/ /	
Lan 19	L50	Jabbers conversationally		/ /	
Lan 20	L51	Looks for hidden sound, e.g. bell in a box, clock under a cushion		/ /	
Lan 21	L52	Uses gestures to indicate desire for more		/ /	
Lan 22	L53	Responds to 'all gone'		/ /	
Lan 23	L54	Imitates use of common objects, e.g. cup, spoon, brush		/ /	
Lan 24	L55	Looks for source of sound outside room, e.g. doorbell, motorbike, children calling		/ /	
Lan 25	L56	Produces animal sound or uses sound for animal name		/ /	
Lan 26	L57	Follows 3 different one step directions without gestures		/ /	
Lan 27	L58	Responds to 6 named familiar objects by looking or touching		/ /	
Lan 28	L59	Points to/touches 3 pictures in a book when named		/ /	
Lan 29	L60	Points to 3 body parts on self		/ /	
Lan 30	L61	10 words		/ /	
Lan 31	L62	Says own name or nickname on request		/ /	
Lan 32	L63	Answers question 'what's this?' in response to familiar object		/ /	
Lan 33	L64	Asks for 'more'		/ /	
Lan 34	L65	Says 'gone' or 'all gone'		/ /	
Lan 35	L66	Can 'give me' or 'show me' on request		/ /	
Lan 36	L67	Responds to 'up' and 'down' by moving body appropriately		/ /	
Soc 28	L68	Imitates movements of another child at play		/ /	
Soc 29	L69	Imitates adult in simple task (shakes clothes, pulls at bedding, holds cutlery)		/ /	
Cog 20	L70	Points to self when asked 'Where's (name)?'		/ /	
Soc 30	L71	Plays with one other child, each doing separate activity		/ /	
Lan 37	L72	Combines use of words and gestures to make wants known		/ /	
Lan 38	L73	Knows what to do in familiar situations (going out, mealtimes, bedtimes)		/ /	
Lan 39	L74	Names 5 other family members including pets		/ /	
Lan 40	L75	Points to 12 familiar objects when named		/ /	
Soc 31	L76	Takes part in game, pushing car, rolling ball		/ /	
Lan 41	L77	Vocalizes during play with toys in response to adult speech		/ /	
Soc 35	L78	Hugs or carries doll or soft toy		/ /	
Soc 36	L79	Repeats actions that produce laughter and attention		/ /	
Lan 42	L80	Names 4 toys		/ /	
Lan 43	L81	Asks for some common food items by name when shown (e.g. milk, biscuit)		/ /	
Lan 44	L82	Names 3 body parts on doll or other person		/ /	
Soc 37	L83	Hands book to adult to read or share		/ /	
Cog 22	L84	Matches object with picture of same object		/ /	
Cog 24	L85	Turns pages of book 2 to 3 at a time to find named picture		/ /	
Soc 38	L86	Pulls at another person to show them action or object		/ /	
Soc 39	L87	Withdraws hand, says 'no! no!' when near forbidden object (with reminders)		/ /	
Lan 45	L88	Asks questions by rising intonation at end word		/ /	
Lan 46	L89	Answers yes/no questions with affirmative or negative reply		/ /	
Soc 41	L90	Plays with 2 or 3 peers		/ /	
Soc 43	L91	Greets peers and familiar adults when reminded		/ /	
Cog 25	L92	Finds specific book on request		/ /	
Cog 27	L93	Names common pictures		/ /	
Lan 47	L94	Names common objects in variety of everyday situations, e.g. in the park, garden, shops, home		/ /	

Figure 6.2: A page from the Language Section of the Portage Checklist. Item no. L93 is starred as it corresponds to the card shown in Figure 6.3 and the activity chart in Figure 6.4.

2. Teaching objectives are selected which build on the child's current skills. Parents and home visitors discuss together all skills which are priorities within the family. For example, the family may be anxious for the child to learn to feed independently and the home visitor may recommend teaching the child to concentrate for an extended period of time. These skills then become part of the teaching programme for that child. It is at this point when supporting professionals working with the family, for example a therapist, may also contribute to the choice of teaching objectives. Each item on the Portage checklist is accompanied by a teaching card. This card file provides specific teaching instructions for each of the 600 items on the Portage checklist (see Figure 6.3 for an example of a Portage teaching card). The cards have two main functions — providing useful teaching hints particularly for new or inexperienced home teachers and parents and providing suggestions on different ways of teaching the same skill, thus enabling the child to generalize and adapt the skill being taught.

3. Teaching activities are individualized. The Portage activity chart (see Figure 6.4) is a carefully designed procedure which allows parents to teach their child and to record the results of their teaching efforts. Although each activity chart is written to a carefully worked out formula which specifies what is to be taught, how it is to be taught, what level of success and how progress will be recorded, it is flexible enough to ensure that the completed activity chart is tailor-made for the individual child's needs, as the completed chart for Darren clearly illustrates. Although it appears at first sight to be very simple, educationalists will recognize

Level 2/L 93   **cognitive 27**

AGE 2 – 3

TITLE: Names common pictures

WHAT TO DO:

1. Begin by getting the child to name common household items using real objects. Cut out pictures of food, table, chairs, TV, bed, etc., out of magazines. Place pictures next to the real objects and get the child to name the pictures. Present the pictures alone for the child to name. Praise each correct response.
2. Encourage the child to look through simple picture books and name the pictures.
3. Look at picture books with child and name pictures he does not know for him.
4. Use photographs of real items in the child's environment.

 **Portage**

© 1976 Cooperative Educational Service Agency 5

Figure 6.3: The card from the Portage Teaching Cards which corresponds with the teaching objective: 'name common pictures' (cognitive item no. 27 and Language item no. 93 from the Portage Checklist).

Portage
Activity Chart

NFER-NELSON

Week no. **50**	Chart no. **41**	Attained Y/N
Parent activity Y/N		Continued Y/N

Child's name: *Darren*

Home visitor's name: *MW*

Week of: *16th April*

Long-term objective: *Names common pictures (item no. 93 in the language section of Portage checklist*

Teaching objective:

Darren will name four pictures in his book when his dad points to these.

Success criterion: **3** out of **4** daily

How often to practise and record:

once each evening, before bed.

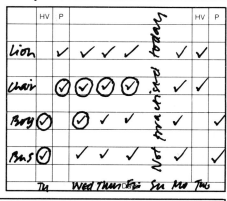

	HV	P						HV	P
Lion	✓	✓	✓	✓	✓		✓	✓	
Chair	Ⓥ	Ⓥ	Ⓥ	Ⓥ			✓	✓	
Boy	Ⓥ		Ⓥ	✓	✓		✓		✓
Bus	Ⓥ	✓	✓	✓			✓		✓

Not practised today

Tu   Wed Thurs Fri Su Mo Tue

Days

Directions: include

Materials:

Darren's new storybook.

Presentation:

Open the new picture book and point to the first page.
Say: " Darren, What's this ? "

Teaching context: *Sit Darren on your knee for this exercise.*

Success procedure: *If Darren names the picture correctly, say "Good Boy, Darren thats the... Lion/Chair/Boy/Bus."*

Teaching procedure: offering help

If Darren does not answer or names the picture incorrectly, gently take his hand and help him point to the correct picture.

Method of recording: *If Darren names the picture correctly mark ✓*
If Darren needs help mark a Ⓥ

13

Figure 6.4: Darren's completed activity chart.

that the Portage activity chart is a highly sophisticated teaching method which includes all the major ingredients for ensuring a successful teaching outcome.

4. *The home teaching service is carefully monitored.* Within the Portage model there is one final, important, and educationally untypical component — positive monitoring. The positive monitoring component has been built in to the Portage model to allow service supervisors to receive detailed reports from the home teachers on the teaching carried out by parents. At a weekly or fortnightly staff meeting, the results of successful teaching are shared and any problems relating to the acquisition of agreed targets, educational problems, difficulties which have arisen within the family, or problems which involve other supporting professionals who supply services to the family, may be clarified and interventions to these agreed and carefully monitored. The top tier of this monitoring structure is the three monthly management team meeting where representatives from health, social services, education, the voluntary sector and the Portage parents meet to hear a report prepared by the supervisor. This report lists the services successfully provided by home teachers to parents and allows members of the management team to suggest interventions to problems which may have occurred, especially those requiring solutions which can only be implemented at higher levels of management. Forward planning and policy making are also carried out by the management team.

In summary, the Portage Home Teaching Model has three key features:

1. It uses direct contact people (especially parents) to teach children who have special needs;
2. It uses an individualized educational programme accompanied by direct instructional methods;
3. It utilizes positive monitoring and recording procedures. One of the highly successful features of the Portage Model is the way in which it can allow information to travel to and from parents and supporting professionals and allow everyone to respond to carefully collected data about the progress of children on the receiving end of the service. The regularity of the visit also provides an opportunity for the development of a warm and close relationship between the family and the home visitor. For many families this element of the visit is as important as the teaching. Sharing their concern for the child, their personal anxieties and their joys is a necessary experience for any parent. Portage parents are often isolated from these experiences because their child is seen as different. The role of the home visitor allows these experiences to be shared, sometimes for the first time.

Training for Portage

To become part of this comprehensive service, home teachers, supervisors and service administrators attend a basic Portage workshop which includes the following topics:

— working within the home, e.g., introducing a service, establishing a relationship with the care giver, the involvement of other family members, establishing a home visiting routine, for example;
— a description of the Portage approach to families with young children who have special educational needs;
— using the Portage Checklist to ascertain the child's existing skill level and as a guide for future teaching;
— selecting appropriate curriculum objectives and planning a teaching programme;
— involving other support professionals outside the Portage programme;
— designing an activity chart;
— designing strategies which ensure that taught skills are maintained and can be generalized and adapted by the child;
— record-keeping and evaluation;
— helping parents to manage disruptive behaviour.

All of these are brought together in a very intensive three-day workshop where a variety of teaching formats is employed including lectures, group assignments, individual homework assignments, video-tape presentations and role play. Techniques employed during these three days also highlight the hidden curriculum of the Portage model, for example, working with other people, obtaining cooperation and agreement, using the expertise of others, sharing both successes and problems, and evaluating service delivery. (A description of the Portage workshop topics is provided in the Portage manual, see White and Cameron, 1987.)

Portage training does not, however, end with the three-day workshop. The positive monitoring component ensures continuing supervision and support, ongoing in-service training programmes are provided by many schemes and for experienced Portage home teachers, supervisors and parents, there is now an advanced Portage workshop which includes some of the more complex aspects of helping families who have a child with special needs.

Evaluation: so what?

Since the early 1970s, a number of researchers have attempted to answer the question 'to what extent does the Portage model succeed in its objectives?' Some answers have resulted from looking at the effect of a Portage service on both children and parents.

The effect on children

Techniques employed to gauge the effectiveness of a Portage home teaching service have included using standardized tests to measure the progress of children over time; comparing the progress of children on a Portage service with children who receive a different form of help; using multi-base line comparisons to examine the increase in the child's progress after receiving a Portage service, and using objectives-based evaluation to clarify the objectives of a Portage service and to see how easily these can be implemented within existing local authority and health provisions. It has been gratifying to note that all four types of evaluation have produced encouraging results for the Portage approach. These research data have been reviewed by Cameron (1986) and Topping (1986) and both texts are recommended to readers wishing to obtain a more detailed overview.

The effect on parents

In general, most research efforts have tended to focus on the outcomes of early intervention for children who have special needs and little is still known about the effects of early intervention programmes on parents. A small amount of work in this area has been done in evaluating the Portage home teaching scheme and so far results have indicated that a Portage service can (a) encourage the development of more positive attitudes to the problems of bringing up a handicapped child, and (b) decrease the feelings of depression and anxiety and increase parental confidence and child rearing skills. A summary of this research can be found in either Cameron (1986) or White and Cameron (1987) and, although this is an area where much additional research could and should be carried out, early results are again encouraging.

Portage into schools

Although originally designed as a home teaching programme which aimed to teach parents to work effectively with their children the assets of the Portage Home Teaching Model were soon appreciated by staff working in schools and other centre-based settings. Not surprisingly, the more tangible features of the Portage model were the first to be spotted by teachers. The Portage Checklist, arguably one of the most detailed of criterion-referenced procedures was seen as a useful assessment tool particularly by teachers working with pupils who had moderate and severe learning difficulties.

It has to be remembered that when the Portage scheme was first introduced into the United Kingdom, barely six years had elapsed since pupils with severe learning difficulties were deemed 'educable' and brought into the educational fold as a result of the 1970 Education (Handicapped Children) Act. By the time the first Portage workshops began, most teachers working in special schools had discovered that diluted versions of a normal school curriculum and scaled down discovery teaching methods were not wholly appropriate for children who had pronounced learning difficulties. Many components of the Portage workshop were rapidly taken up and adapted by teachers whose earlier professional training had often left them ill-equipped to deal with the everyday problems of children in special schools. Particular workshop components such as planning long and short term curriculum objectives, success and teaching procedures, daily practice and fluency building, and detailed ongoing recording procedures were soon pressed into service in classrooms.

School-based schemes based on the Portage model have tended to fall under two major headings:

1. School adaptations of the Portage teaching approach;
2. Using the Portage service model.

School adaptations of the Portage teaching approach

Teachers involved with the selection of curriculum objectives for children with special needs either in a special school or mainstream setting have recognized that different levels of specificity in curriculum planning are needed. In mainstream schools most curricula are written in teacher management objectives. However these broad statements of teacher intent usually need to be re-written in more precise pupil objectives before they can be used with pupils who have moderate or severe learning difficulties. Writing detailed curriculum objectives for special needs pupils can be a time and energy consuming exercise. Fortunately, the Portage Checklist can act as a starting point for designing a core curriculum in schools.

The Portage teaching model has also been adapted for use in schools. In most instances, this has meant that objectives in priority areas of need have been selected for individual children and Portage activity charts have been used to teach these objectives. In some schools Portage activity charts designed by the teacher have been carried out by classroom aides in school and/or by parents at home. Such continuity ensures that the pupil receives additional practice, fluency building, at school and also has the opportunity to generalize learned skills to settings other than the classroom, particularly in home and community contexts.

Using the Portage service model

Parental involvement schemes have been one of the growth phenomena of the 1980s since unlike some previous attempts to encourage home-school liaison, parental involvement projects have viewed the home as an important learning environment in its own right and attempted systematically to involve parents in teaching basic skills. A number of schools have set up parental involvement projects by using the Portage model to supplement parent teaching skills by providing a home visiting service. Such projects not only encourage teachers to move out of the classrooms and into homes, but also represent a way of supplementing rather than supplanting what the parents are already doing at home.

The Portage model offers many advantages for schools and school staff. Teachers and parents can share in the selection, teaching, assessment and evaluation of curriculum objectives and avoid some of the worst problems of being isolated in one context. The formation of a Portage management team can offer important new managerial roles to the head teacher, deputy and senior school staff, and visiting support professionals like educational psychologists, advisers, and community medical officers can be given an indirect monitoring role which can utilize more fully their usually scarce professional services. The Portage model in school can also encourage positive organizational change in the re-assessment of staff attitudes, improved curriculum management, and agreed strategies for tackling whole school problems. In short, Portage has often brought about an organizational spring clean in schools!

New developments

Over the past decade the Portage model in the UK has proven itself to be remarkably robust. Components like criterion-referenced assessment using the Portage checklist, the use of activity charts, continuous monitoring record keeping survive almost unchanged from the early original project. These and other aspects of the model have been considerably fattened up by ongoing research by people who work within the Portage model. One result has been that the three-day workshop is a highly intensive one and has had to be recently supplemented by a practice manual (White and Cameron, 1987).

There has, however, been one other unusual aspect of the Portage service. The self-evaluation component has ensured that Portage has attempted not only to *maintain* but also to *improve* service delivery. As a result, people working within Portage have not only retained and added to the original model but have expanded the technology into new problem areas. These major areas of future development have been identified by Cameron (1986) as:

1. Children with extra special needs. In particular, children in families from different ethnic groups, children with sensory handicaps and children who are severely or profoundly handicapped;
2. The selection and teaching of language objectives for developmentally young children;
3. The encouragement of high quality learning especially the consideration of generalization and adaptation aspects in higher order learning;
4. Helping parents to manage non-educational problems including personal problems, and relationships with other members of the family or supporting professionals working with the family.

These four topics are relatively new and form the basis of the advanced Portage workshop referred to earlier. Advanced Portage workshops are restricted to experienced Portage home teachers, supervisors, parents and management team members.

Final comments

In 1985, a National Portage Association was set up. This association, which represents Portage schemes from all over England and Wales has provided guidelines for setting up and maintaining Portage schemes and has produced ethical guidelines for home teachers. The NPA also monitors the standard of training and service delivery. National Portage Conferences have been held annually since 1982 and the proceedings have been published.

It is clear, therefore, that the Portage Home Teaching Model represents a highly effective way of helping parents to deal with the everyday problems of bringing up a handicapped child. The Portage model recognizes that children gain most from education when their parents are closely involved in the teaching. Until now, many administrators and policy makers seeking to help handicapped children and their families have often looked for service improvements outside the home as with smaller classes, purpose-built centres, more specialized professional training, sophisticated teaching aids, and complex teaching methods. People working with the Portage model have explored an alternative to these 'hi-tech' solutions. As a result, Portage remains the outstanding example of a service which readily concedes that among the many experts working with preschool children, the most useful and effective are the ones which nature provided — the parents themselves!

References

BLACHER, J. (ed.) (1984) *Severely Handicapped Young Children and Their Families: Research in Review*, Orlando, Florida, Academic Press.

CAMERON, R. J. (1986) *Portage: Preschoolers, Parents and Professionals*, Windsor, NFER-Nelson.

COURT, S. D. M. (1976) *Fit for the Future*, Report of the Committee of Child Health Services, London, HMSO.

EDUCATION (HANDICAPPED CHILDREN) ACT (1970) London, HMSO.

EDUCATION ACT (1981) London, HMSO.

JESIEN, G. (1984) 'Home-based early intervention: a description of the Portage Project model' in Strutton, D. (ed.), *Management of the Motor Disorders of Children with Cerebral Palsy*, Oxford, Basil Blackwell.

NATIONAL PORTAGE ASSOCIATION (1985) *Code of Practice and Ethical Guidelines*, Available from Honorary Secretary, 4, Clifton Road, Winchester, Hants.

NATIONAL DEVELOPMENT GROUP FOR THE MENTALLY HANDICAPPED (1977) *Mentally Handicapped Children: A Plea for Action*, London, HMSO.

REVILL, S. and BLUNDEN, R. (1979) 'A home training service for pre-school developmentally handicapped children', *Behaviour Research and Therapy,* 17, pp. 207–14.

SHEARER, M. S. and SHEARER, D. E. (1972) 'The Portage Project: A model for early childhood education', *Exceptional Children*, 39, pp. 210–17.

SMITH, J., KUSHLICK, A. and GLOSSOP, C. (1977) *The Wessex Portage Project*, Wessex Health Care Evaluation Research Team, Research Report No. 125.

TIZARD, B. and HUGHES, M. (1984) *Young Children Learning: Talking and Thinking at Home and at School*, London, Fontana.

TOPPING, K. (1986) *Parents as Educators: Training Parents to Teach Their Children*, Beckenham, Croom Helm.

WARNOCK, M. (1978) *Report on Enquiry into the Education of Handicapped Children and Young People*, London, HMSO.

WHITE, M. and CAMERON, R. J. (1987) *The Portage Early Education Programme: A Practical Manual*, Windsor, NFER-Nelson.

7
Paired Reading: Issues and Development

Roger Morgan

Introduction

Much of the help children have had in learning to read, and to learn much else in their education as well, has always come from their parents. What has changed over the years is the professional educator's attitude towards this parental involvement, not the existence — or even, to a great extent, the nature — of that involvement.

It is not many years since schools actively discouraged parents from entering the building; the school near my home in the early 1970s sported the notice on its high metal fence NO PARENTS BEYOND THIS POINT. At the same time, and until quite recently, the strong professional stance was that parents should not try to help their children read in any systematic manner, in case they confused the child or pressured him inappropriately, and that the input on reading should be left strictly to the professionals at school. This message was given out all the more strongly if the child was very young or if he had any difficulty in reading.

Three factors have changed this attitude in recent years. Firstly, it has now become respectable again to acknowledge that most parents always did give their child help with reading at home. Also that their input can be more influential than the teacher's in terms of time and the attitudes towards reading given to the child. Secondly, the potency of parental involvement in reading has been given a respectable research basis by the work of Jenny Hewison (Hewison and Tizard, 1980; Tizard *et al.*, 1982). This research showed that children whose parents regularly listened to them read at home were definitely better at reading than children who did not have this help at home. This was followed up with the logical next step of asking parents to listen regularly to their children reading at home to assess the effects on the children's reading skills. The result was improved reading.

Finally, and perhaps to some extent allied to today's resource issues, parental involvement has become recognized as complementary to professional input, quite capable of being appropriately skilled and, as needs be, of responding to training in specialized approaches — even in the sensitive areas of very early teaching of reading or where the child has even a serious reading problem. The view of the parent as potentially problematic amateur has increasingly given way to that of the parent as potentially skilled and effective ally. It is of interest to note that the trend towards greater recognition and involvement of families in giving skilled help is to be found in many fields outside education; family members are much involved as primary helpers in medical and clinical psychological fields, and in social services work the role of the family member as main carer is being increasingly recognized and supported.

As parents are increasingly involved in their children's learning to read, and are also increasingly being given specialist support to do this and to take a key role where their children require particular help, it is essential that the parent/professional partnership *is* a complementary one, and not one of conflict and confusion. There are always risks that parents and teachers will differ in their view of the methods being employed and in their expectations and appraisals of progress. Sadly, there is still in some places a history of parent/teacher conflict over the teaching of reading — some of which has arisen from contrary views over issues such as the existence, diagnosis or nature of dyslexia. Both the development of the parents' role, and the need to reduce areas of misunderstanding, stress the importance of training for both parents and teachers in established and effective methods of parental involvement, with adequate communication and facilities for troubleshooting, both at the start of any home/school partnership reading scheme and continuously while it is under way.

The origins of paired reading

Paired reading was not originally developed for parental use, but has proved to be particularly suitable for the purpose. The technique originated when I was treating a child for a severe stammer, and as part of the treatment was using simultaneous reading from a simple book to increase speech fluency and give practice in speaking without a stammer. It is often the case that speech improves for someone with such a speech disorder when they are speaking alongside someone else's example, and when they are not under pressure to work out what to say; both conditions likely to be met by reading simultaneously out loud rather than in holding a normal conversation. The child also had a very low reading age, and I was encouraged to find that the practice at simultaneous reading appeared to be associated with improved reading skills as well as improved speech. As a behavioural therapist, I tried the same approach with children with reading problems, and added other behavioural components, principally that of positive reinforcement, which had also a good 'track record' in encouraging correct reading, to create the package of simple reading training techniques that forms paired reading.

It is important to stress that there is nothing inherently new in paired reading. The technique is a new recipe combining well established and common-sense ingredients. It uses basic elements whose pedigree goes back centuries — the judicious use of praise to reinforce learning, for example, and the practice of reading simultaneously, which many of us can remember from our own childhood in the form of the class reading aloud. Paired reading is, however, a *package* of these and other elements, which has been found to be effective as a whole. It is all too easy to react to a simple and commonsense technique by declaring that 'we do all that anyway', in one way or another. We don't — not in the same combination, with the same degree of consistency, and with the same degree of intensive focus on the specific elements involved.

The first study of paired reading (Morgan, 1976) did not involve its use by parents, but with children who came regularly to a tuition centre for evening paired reading sessions. By the second study (Morgan and Lyon, 1979), we had realized that the technique was simple enough and robust enough to be used just as effectively by parents at home as by professionals in school or reading centre. Equally, it was obvious that by adopting the strategy of 'little and often' for home sessions, parents were going to give their children far more reading practice with the technique than was possible in school or clinic. The use, and the effective use, of paired reading by non-professionals has recently undergone another quantum step in the rapidly increasing use of the technique by children tutoring other children, either younger than themselves, or of the same age but with lower reading skills.

The technique of paired reading is set out in the section at the end of this chapter, in a form suitable for use as a handout for parents or adult volunteers to use when tutoring children at home. This account of the technique includes a number of practical hints which I hope will be useful to those intending to teach paired reading to parents; the same principles are applicable to the context of peer tutoring of one child by another, or of adult literacy work, although of course the wording of any handout would need amendment. More detailed guidance on using and evaluating paired reading is given in the recently published paired reading handbook *Helping Children Read* (Morgan, 1986).

Paired reading comprises a number of components, of which the key ones are:

1. The child's free choice of reading material, including material appropriate to chronological age and interests but well above current reading age, giving an 'escape' from simplified texts, and the motivation of being able to use the technique to support one in reading material previously out of one's reach because it was out of one's ability range;

2. Simultaneous reading, giving 'participant modelling' in which the child learns to read even complex words by having the tutor's example to follow and against which to compare and adjust his own efforts while he is attempting each word;

3. Positive reinforcement, praise or 'feedback that you are right', of correct reading while reading alone, an extremely simple but well established and

powerful means of strengthening learning, and something often absent or only occasionally provided by many adults while listening to a child read;

4. Automatic adjustment of the amount of help given by the tutor, according to the child's needs, the child's wishes and level of confidence at the time, and the difficulty being encountered in the text. This by the two simple expedients of the child signalling when he wants the tutor to stop reading simultaneously, and the tutor resuming reading simultaneously whenever the child gets stuck and needs to have a word given or a mistake corrected;

5. Avoidance of pressure on the child, help being given four seconds after the child either gets stuck on a word or cannot self-correct an error. This represents a reversal of the pressures to 'try it again' that most children have experienced when they run into difficulty;

6. Capitalization upon any word decoding strategy that works for the child, rather than teaching him a new one. This both allows the technique to be flexible in encouraging even idiosyncratic methods of word-decoding and recognition, provided that they work for the particular child, and it renders paired reading safe for general consumption in that it will not damage, confuse or conflict with any more specialized techniques that may be in use alongside it. It is important that paired reading does not 'argue' with other methods, from the point of view of both the individual child, and of the parent and teacher involved where a number of methods may be in use at the same time;

7. Encouragement of mature reading strategies, which are usually inhibited by frequent stops to 'sound out' or 'try again', such as effective use of contextual cues because paired reading is predominantly continuous rather than halting, and of scanning ahead in the reading material encouraged by the child trying to spot words or passages to signal his wish to read alone.

The technique is specific, with specific instructions on what to do, in contrast to the parental listening approach which Hewison and her colleagues found helpful to children's reading. Hewison did not give instructions to parents on *how* they should help their children read at home, but simply asked them to listen to their children reading aloud, and when the child was stuck, to wait a short while before giving the correct word. Parents who wished to, could prompt the child in any way they wished.

Use of paired reading probably encourages correct reading as much by relieving the child of inhibiting influences as it does by teaching anything new. It reduces stress, while increasing the motivation to read by choice of preferred material and experience of coping, with support, with more complex material than the child could manage before. At the same time as reinforcing any successful word decoding strategies in the child's repertoire, it also has the effect of 'culling' out any unsuccessful strategies.

Evaluation of paired reading

Following the initial papers describing the paired reading technique, paired reading was subjected to a number of major controlled trials, of which the first was by Heath (1981). Heath reported twice the normal chronological rate of progress in reading accuracy and three and a half times the normal rate of progress in reading comprehension, with significant improvement over controls, amongst children of average age 7 years. Subsequent controlled trials were published by Robson *et al.* (1984), reporting positive results for paired reading in a rigorous study with a crossover design and 'blind' assessment, Winter (1984), reporting accuracy improvement of 4.9 times normal progress and comprehension improvement of 8.6 times normal progress after only four weeks of paired reading with junior age children, O'Hara (1985) reporting paired reading superior to control with physically handicapped children, and Carrick-Smith (1986) reporting three times normal progress for accuracy and six times normal rates of progress for comprehension. These studies recorded a number of important themes in paired reading evaluation reports.

An improvement in comprehension of what is read is consistently reported as being greater than the nevertheless significant improvement in the accuracy of reading; an important feature of paired reading, and one allaying the concern often expressed in its early stages that the technique might teach children to emulate the correct reading model of an adult tutor but without understanding the content of the material. Of a 'softer' type of evidence, but just as important and just as consistently reported in these and other studies of paired reading, is the positive report that paired reading is generally enjoyed, and that it tends to forge a positive parent-child relationship. It is also frequently reported that a child doing paired reading tends to generalize his interest to other reading material than that used in tuition sessions, becoming more positively interested in reading in general.

Paired reading has been most widely evaluated in a major government funded study in Kirklees, England. The third annual report of this study (Topping, 1987) reports evaluative results for 1,595 children, with average gains in reading accuracy of $3 \cdot 4$ times normal progress and $4 \cdot 7$ times normal progress in comprehension.

Paired reading is typically used in short courses of, perhaps, two to three months' duration, fifteen minutes per day. The questions arises, therefore, as to whether the technique is primarily a one-off booster to reading performance, or whether it can have a repeated or long term effect. Research evidence is less widely available on this topic than on the immediate outcome of short term projects, but what there is is encouraging. Lee (1986), studying the long term effects of paired reading with secondary age children, reported that the technique was associated with better reading than control children over a 12 month follow-up period, and that it led to improved fluency and rate of reading, and, importantly, improved skills in self-correction of errors and use of context.

There have been numerous studies of paired reading, of varying degrees of research rigour, and the reported results have been encouragingly consistent in supporting paired reading as a generally applicable and effective technique in improving children's reading. Where the research remains relatively weak however, is in the number of long-term studies available, and in the limited number of studies comparing paired reading in combination or in isolation with alternative approaches. The latter type of study is not so much important in identifying whether paired reading is a useful technique in the range of methods of helping children read that are currently available (controlled trials and increasing growth in its use demonstrate that it is) but would be useful in identifying further whether there are any factors that render paired reading more appropriate than, for example, unstructured listening to a child read, or whether paired reading and any other, more specifically 'diagnosed problem directed' technique would be useful in combination.

Wider uses of paired reading

From its beginnings as a remedial reading technique, paired reading was soon adopted as a method of assisting children with normal reading skills to progress with their reading. Evaluative studies such as those referred to above reported paired reading to be effective where the child has reading problems. Fawcett and Bruce (1985) reported that a group of eleven junior school children, with reading ages on average one year four months above average to start with, progressed at four times normal rate of progress with paired reading. Bruce (1985) separately reported that in an infant school, average and above average readers did just as well on paired reading as did those who needed help with reading. The same technique is applicable to average or above average readers as with those having difficulties, but there are some additional points to watch under these circumstances. Firstly, the child is likely to read at a greater rate using age-appropriate material, and it is sometimes therefore necessary to point out more minor errors, one aim being to increase accuracy, and thus ability to read fast without sacrificing accuracy, and secondly, it is more important that praise or 'feedback that you are right' is focused on self-corrections and achievement of difficult or recently mastered words or phrases. Choice of reading material of sufficient challenge to present the need for tutor support and so the opportunity to develop reading skill from the technique, beyond the benefit arising from straightforward reading practice, becomes more difficult with the more advanced reader. The problem of fiction that is technically challenging enough being too adult in content soon arises. One antidote to this is to move on to non-fiction material written for the lay adult rather than for children, on a subject of particular interest to the child or young person.

Paired reading has been increasingly used at both ends of the educational age range. Jungnitz (1983) has shown that the technique is effective with beginning readers in the infant school. Some writers have suggested that the whole technique is too much for very young children to cope with, particularly given that different components of paired reading have been found effective when used alone, as well as in combination. Thus Heath (1981) found the 'praise while reading alone' half of the technique capable of improving reading, but not to the same extent as the full technique, and Greening and Spenceley (1984) found just reading together with an adult to improve reading in very young children. Greening and Spenceley used the reading together component on its own with beginning readers to good effect, terming this abbreviated form of paired reading 'shared reading'. Gillham (1986) advocates leaving out the child's choice, by signalling, of when the parent should stop reading together with him. I have not found the full technique to be at all problematic for beginning readers to cope with.

At the other end of the age range, paired reading has recently begun to be deployed as a technique within adult literacy schemes. It has been slower to be tried in this context, probably because there is already a strong tradition of volunteer tutor choice of individual method, and the boost of the desire to use a suitable technique to boost home/school cooperation is absent. Scoble *et al.* (1987) have reported paired reading to be effective with adults learning to read, producing an improvement in accuracy of reading of $3 \cdot 75$ times normal rate of progress, and an improvement of $4 \cdot 7$ times normal for reading comprehension. The similarity of these results to the consistent findings with children is significant, and very encouraging.

Bush (1985) and Jungnitz (1985) have both reported paired reading to be suitable for use with children whose mother tongue is not English, and whose families may not be fluent English readers. In these circumstances, it may be practical for adult (or older child) volunteers to be identified to tutor the child.

What emerges from the research work on the wider applications of paired reading is that the technique is sufficiently flexible to cope with tutees of widely differing ages and reading abilities, different types of reading problem, and using reading material of widely differing types and levels; and that its effects are remarkably consistent in all contexts. These effects are a significant increase in reading accuracy, an even greater increase in reading comprehension, and reports of the tuition being both easy to do and, for most, more enjoyable than they anticipated reading tuition would be.

Peer tutoring

The use of paired reading by children or young people tutoring other children or young people has been referred to above. Again the research findings are remarkably consistent and perhaps surprisingly encouraging. A number of studies have reported peer tutoring with paired reading to be effective (Winter and Low, 1984; Gale and Kendall, 1985; Free *et al.*, 1985; Cawood and Lee, 1985; Carrick-Smith, 1985; Limbrick *et al.* 1985). A recent controlled study by Crombie and Low (1986) involved 46 children and reported the familiar improvements in both accuracy and comprehension, with the latter improving to the greater extent. The vital findings of the research on peer tutoring are, firstly, that children both accept and enjoy doing it responsibly, both as tutors and as tutees; and secondly, that the *children doing the tutoring improve their reading as much as, or slightly more than, those being tutored.* In his major report on the Kirklees paired reading project, Topping (1987) recorded that being tutored by a parent was only marginally superior to being tutored by another child, and that children doing the tutoring with other children progressed in their reading skills to a greater extent than their tutees.

The finding that child-*tutors* progress significantly, as well as their tutees, is consistently reported in the relevant studies. Paired reading as a peer tutoring technique has a major potential in schools, and within families where a sibling as well as a parent can carry out the tutoring. Just as important are the implications of the phenomenon of tutor-improvement. Using good readers to help poor or younger readers through paired reading is not to waste the time and energies of the better readers, but to boost their reading as well. Furthermore, since the better reader of the pair does not have to be a 'good reader' in absolute terms, but simply a better reader than his or her tutee, to the extent of about two years better in reading age, children and young people with reading difficulties themselves can experience the satisfactions and personal boost of helping someone else to read, while developing their own skills at the same time. Equally, paired reading can be used successfully by parents who themselves have reading problems, as long as they are sufficiently further along the road than their children. This is important as reading difficulty does tend to run in families.

Criticisms of paired reading

As with any technique, paired reading has been the subject of justifiable criticisms. A number of studies and reviews have underlined the need for caution, and wisely counselled against over-enthusiasm. Certainly, paired reading has become both widespread and fashionable in education today, and careful consideration of critiques of the technique are timely.

In general, it must be recognized that while paired reading is a very economical technique, being fairly readily taught to parents and readily supervised in use, it is not a *free* technique. It does consume significant resources. Even training parents and children in groups rather than in individual pairs takes both significant professional input and follow-up to resolve difficulties and misconceptions. Supervision during a course of paired reading requires regular contact at no more than fortnightly intervals. Equally, no technique is everyone's cup of tea, and there are both parents and children, even if relatively few, who simply do not like the technique, or who do not succeed with it. Some parents prefer to help their children in a less structured manner and it has been demonstrated that doing nothing more than regularly hearing a child read will have a beneficial influence on his reading skill.

Published critiques of paired reading by Swinson (1986) and Pumfrey (1986) warn that many of the early research studies on paired reading were limited in scope and research design, and should therefore be interpreted with caution. Pumfrey notes that the later studies reporting positive results were better-designed. Both critics stress that other forms of helping children read have been found effective, such as listening to children read, and that paired reading has its cons as well as its well-rehearsed pros, for example that it may not be suitable for all parent/child pairs, and that its blanket use in all settings would be unwise. Swinson comments that 'each approach has its strengths and weaknesses, and it is these characteristics that should be thoroughly evaluated by any school or teacher wishing to initiate a home-reading scheme'. He considers that the simpler straightforward listening approach may be suitable for prolonged use, while if schools 'are looking for a short intensive intervention which will not interfere with classroom activities then the paired reading approach may be for them'. Pumfrey calls for more and better designed evaluations, but considers that paired reading merits serious considerations by all teachers and parents interested in optimizing their children's reading development. In a later commentary, Pumfrey (1987) concludes that 'whether paired reading turns out to be a "breakthrough" of pedagogic importance, a " bandwaggon" of educational fashion that will rapidly be replaced, or something in between, remains to be seen'.

Referring to the relevant literature, Swinson (1986) quotes a number of projects which compared paired reading with other methods of helping children read. In one, the effects of paired reading and traditional regular parent listening were found to be comparable, but paired reading was suggested as the more effective in the beginning stages of learning to read. In another, emphasis on praise was found comparable in its effect to the full paired reading technique. In relation to this, it is important to note that both the simultaneous reading and reinforced individual reading elements of the technique have been reported as improving reading, and it is thus logical to combine them when the combination has been reported so consistently to have positive results. Combination of two active ingredients offers the possibility of effects greater than the individual elements themselves, and, perhaps more importantly, the likelihood that one or the other, even if not both, will help any particular child.

A very significant study of paired reading, in which it did not prove superior to other approaches, was conducted by Wareing (1985). Wareing found that paired reading did no better than listening to children read without any particular technique being used. She also, however, found that not having supervised parents' use of the technique, the parents had drifted away from the instructions they had been given. Paired reading was thus not being used by the end of the study, which had become a comparison of two groups of families both using a basic listening approach. Wareing's study does not, therefore, tell us about the comparative effectiveness of techniques, but demonstrates a weakness of any 'taught' technique that, without close attention to regular supervision, the technique will 'drift' away and eventually peter out.

Current issues in paired reading

Paired reading is clearly established as a generally useful technique in education, and as an established way in which families can help their children at home with a good expectation of success. A number of issues are of current concern in the field, and some of the major ones are summarized below:

Research and evaluation

Paired reading has been subjected to more and more rigorous outcome evaluation than most other aspects of education with children or adults, indeed, evaluation of paired reading has become a favourite subject for higher degree theses. It has always been sold on its research base, however, and it is both natural and right that there should be a call for further research. The basic technique is now well underwritten by well-designed research, but outstanding research questions concerning predictive factors, long term effects, and details of process remain deserving of further work.

Training

Use of paired reading requires parents and children to be trained in its use. This is done in various ways; principally by either group workshops, often including video presentation or by individual training sessions with parent/child, child/child, or tutor/student pairs. The resources implications of different training patterns are variable and significant, and further study of the efficacy of, and consumer satisfaction with, the alternatives is called for.

Variation

There are numerous variations on the basic technique, and different practitioners are inevitably using slightly different emphases, as are the same practitioners over time. It has been pointed out (Topping, 1987b) that my own technique has developed in minor ways over time, by introducing greater emphasis on pointing out errors and pacing the child's reading than I was doing ten years ago. Equally, I note minor differences in approach within the same technique when reading the published reports of research studies. The point to remember is that the possibility of changing the effects of the technique probably increases in proportion to the size of any changes that are made. Significant changes should not be made in any 'standard' technique like paired reading without separately evaluating the amended procedure. The positive research findings applicable to the basic technique cannot be assumed to apply to any significantly amended version.

That major changes in technique can produce major changes in effects was illustrated by a report by Spalding *et al.* (1984). In this study, the procedure was changed so that the parent started reading together with the child, but then faded out to leave the child reading alone. The same passage of the book was also read and then re-read, rather than progressing through the book as in the 'standard' technique. The results differed markedly from the consistent reports of paired reading itself; while comprehension improved significantly, the improvement in reading accuracy was lost. A major variant on the paired reading theme by Bryans *et al.* (1985), in which the same passage was read first to the child, then by the child and parent together, and finally by the child alone with praise and correction of mistakes from the parent, produced gains in reading accuracy, but this time not in comprehension.

One risk in the current popularity of paired reading is that instructions on how to do it have proliferated and differ. As an example, the instructions appearing in one currently published children's reading series acknowledge that they were derived from my own original instructions, but then make major variations likely to change the effects of the technique, replacing the child's signalling with the parent 'fading out', leaving praise out altogether, repeating the same passage rather than keeping going through the book, and advocating the use of special reading materials rather than offering the child a free choice of material.

Reading materials

The rising popularity of parents and children reading together has led to the publication of a number of special reading series designed for this purpose. While many of these offer excellent stories, and use the availability of parental help to avoid the stilted and limited easy vocabulary of many older 'readers', they are no better and no worse than any other book on the bookshop or library shelves for use in paired reading. Nor, for that matter, are they any better than any book the child wants to read at the car boot sale. Paired reading can be used with *any* reading material the child wants to read. It does not need any special materials.

Monitoring

Commonly available standardized reading tests were not designed for repeated use over relatively short periods of time, and while most studies reported have used reading tests to evaluate the technique, testing is not suitable for continuous monitoring of an individual child's progress during tuition. Monitoring by means of a 'progress book' in which percentage accuracy can be assessed regularly on different and previously unread passages of the same book, has been suggested as a suitable, if time consuming, method of monitoring. Simple three or five point rating scales also offer a limited monitoring option for home use. In future research projects it is important that more sophisticated evaluative techniques are employed to assess progress such as error analysis techniques.

Conclusion

The original form of paired reading, which is the most widely evaluated, now has sound research evidence to support its continued use, and has not been found in need of major amendment in order to be used with very young children, remedial or advanced readers, adults, or by children tutoring other children. It is certainly not a panacea but can usefully be regarded as a safe beneficial general reading tonic.

Appendix

Paired Reading

In Paired Reading, your child is helped to read better by all of the following:

1. Reading aloud with you, so that he is adjusting his efforts all the time to fit your example, and so learning how to read the difficult words from you.

2. You making sure that when he is reading on his own rather than with you, he always knows when he is getting words right.

3. Reading a book he really wants to read, rather than a 'baby' book or a reading scheme book — and getting through the book without having to keep stopping to sound words out. This makes reading enjoyable rather than an effort.

4. Automatically getting the sort of help he needs to keep on reading, whenever, he needs it, rather than getting stuck.

Most parents and children enjoy doing paired reading together.

How to do Paired Reading

1. Let your child choose a book he really wants to read (visit the library, bookshop or a car boot sale if needs be). The right book is one your child wants to read, and which is suitable in its content for children of his age who can read well. It does not matter if he finds it much too difficult to read on his own — he is going to be getting plenty of help with it. Some children are keen to try a book about a hobby or special interest, instead of a story book. You do *not* need a special book for paired reading; any book can be used.

2. Find somewhere quiet for you (Mum or Dad) and your child to sit next to each other at home — on the settee, on the edge of the bed, or at a table are fine; but not in a room with everyone else (or the TV!) disturbing you. Put the book where you can both see it easily.

3. Start off by reading out aloud together. At first you will find this hard, so practice for a couple of sessions, and only go on to add step 4 below when you both feel happy at reading together.

Some hints on reading out loud together are:

— read each word at exactly the same time as each other (not one after the other!).

— If you 'lose' each other, or if your child is missing bits of words out to keep up with you, *slow down*.

— one of you pointing to each word as you say it will help you to keep together.

— make sure you do start difficult words at the same time as each other; practise this because it is very tempting to wait for each other when you reach a difficult word, but that is not such a good way of your child learning the word.

— don't slow down or stop reading to see if your child is going to manage any of the words on his own, and don't ask him to 'sound out' any of the words.

— if your child hasn't managed to stay with you for a difficult word, simply point to the beginning of it with your finger and try it again together.

4. When you are happy with reading aloud together, tell your child that he may ask you to stop reading with him (to have a go on his own) by giving you a signal. The best signal is a knock on the table, bed or chair — simply asking you to stop is no good because it interrupts the reading. Tell him that he can signal you to stop even if it is only a word or two that he thinks he can manage on his own.

5. When your child signals, you stop reading with him and let him carry on reading on his own. While he is reading on his own, you need to do three things:

— keep letting him know all the time he is getting the words right — by keeping up a constant 'patter' of comments like 'good' 'that's right', 'well done', or 'yes'. It is especially important to make a positive comment like this when he manages a particularly difficult word, or manages to put right a mistake he has made. You will feel self-conscious doing this at first, but it is very important that he is never in any doubt that something he has just read is right. The 'feedback' that he is getting it right will 'seal in' to his memory the right way of reading any words he may not have been sure about

— watch out for mistakes he makes. Whenever he makes a mistake, use your finger to point it out, and ask him to have another try. If he hasn't got it right after about four seconds, tell him what it is, and start reading together again until he signals you to stop once more.

— if he gets stuck on a word, again wait for about four seconds, and then if he is still stuck, tell him what the word is and start reading together again. Do *not* ask him to 'sound it out'.

6. While he is reading on his own, remember that whenever he cannot manage a word (either when he is trying it for a second time after getting it wrong, or because he can't manage it at all), you *never* leave him struggling for more than about four seconds, and you *always* help him in the same way — by saying the word together with him (telling him what it is first if needs be) and then carrying on with reading together until he again signals you to stop for another try on his own.

To sum up

You always start reading together, when your child wants to try some reading on his own, he signals and you stop. While he is reading on his own, you praise him all the time he is getting things right, point out his mistakes, and always go back to reading together again if he is stuck for as long as four seconds. It is like driving a car with two gears — reading together gear and reading alone gear. Your child changes you both into reading alone gear by signalling when he wants to, and you change back into reading together gear whenever he is stuck for four seconds.

If your child wants to, you can change the book you are using. You will notice that if you are using an easier book, your child will signal often. With a more difficult book he will keep you both in 'reading together' gear more. This is the way that paired reading copes with both easy and difficult books.

Aim to do paired reading together for about a quarter of an hour each day, and enjoy talking together about the book as well as paired reading it together. Have frequent short breaks from reading to do this.

References

BRUCE, P. (1985) 'Paired Reading with mixed-ability middle infants'. *Paired Reading Bulletin*, 1, pp. 5–9.

BRYANS, T., *et al.* (1985) 'The King's Heath Project', in TOPPING, K. J. and WOLFENDALE, S. W. *Parental Involvement in Children's Reading* London, Croom Helm.

BUSH, A. M. (1983) 'Can pupils' reading be improved by involving their parents?' *Remedial Education*, **18**, 4, pp. 167–170.

CARRICK-SMITH, L. (1985) 'A research project in paired reading', in TOPPING, K. J. and WOLFENDALE, S. W. *Parental Involvement in Children's Reading*, London, Croom Helm.

CAWOOD, S. and LEE, A. (1985) 'Paired reading at Colne Valley High School'. *Paired Reading Bulletin*, 1, pp. 46–50.

CROMBIE, R. and LOW, A. (1986) 'Using a paired reading technique in cross-age peer tutoring'. *Paired Reading Bulletin*, 2, pp. 10–15.

FAWCETT, B. (1985) 'The Cowlersley Junior School P. R. Project'. *Paired Reading Bulletin*, 1, pp. 42–45.

FREE, L., *et al.* (1985) 'Parent, peer and cross-age tutors'. *Paired Reading Bulletin*, 1, pp. 38–41.

GALE, I. and KENDALL, D. (1985) '"Working Together": the Marsden Junior School peer tutor project'. *Paired Reading Bulletin*, 1, pp. 59–64.

GREENING, M. and SPENCELEY, J. (1984) 'Shared Reading: A review of the Cleveland Project'. *'In-Psych.' — Bulletin of Cleveland County Psychological Service*, 11, 2, pp. 10–14.

HEWISON, J. and TIZARD, J. (1980) 'Parental involvement and reading attainment'. *British Journal of Educational Psychology*, 50, pp. 209–215.

HEATH, A. (1981) 'A Paired Reading programme'. *'Edition 2' — ILEA School Psychological Service*, pp. 22–32.

JUNGNITZ, G., OLIVE, S. and TOPPING, K. J. (1983) 'The development and evaluation of a paired reading project'. *Journal of Community Education*, 2, 4, pp. 14–22.

LEE, A. (1986) 'A study of the longer term effects of paired reading'. *Paired Reading Bulletin*, 2, 36–43.

LIMBRICK, E., McNAUGHTON, S. and GLYNN, T. (1985) 'Reading gains for underachieving tutors and tutees in a cross-age tutoring programme'. *Journal of Child Psychology and Psychiatry*, 26, pp. 939–953.

MORGAN, R. T. T. (1976) '"Paired Reading" tuition: a preliminary report on a technique for cases of reading deficit'. *Child Care, Health and Development*, 2, pp. 13–28.

MORGAN, R. T. T. and LYON, E. (1979) '"Paired Reading" — a preliminary report on a technique for parental tuition of reading-retarded children'. *Journal of Child Psychology and Psychiatry*, 20, pp. 151–160.

MORGAN, R. T. T. (1984) *Behavioural Treatments with Children*, Heinemann, London.

MORGAN, R. T. T. (1986) *Helping Children Read — The Paired Reading Handbook*, Methuen, London.

O'HARA, M. (1985) 'Paired reading in a school for the physically handicapped'. *Paired Reading Bulletin*, 1, pp. 16–19.

PUMFREY, P. (1986) 'Paired reading: promise and pitfalls'. *Educational Research*, 28, pp. 89–94.

PUMFREY, P. (1987) 'A critique of paired reading'. *Paired Reading Bulletin*, 3, pp. 62–66.

ROBSON, D., MILLER, A. and BUSHELL, R. (1984) 'The development of paired reading in High Peak and West Derbyshire'. *Remedial Education*, 19, pp. 177–183.

SCOBLE, J., TOPPING, K. J. and WIGGLESWORTH, C. (1987) 'The Ryedale adult literacy paired reading project'. *Paired Reading Bulletin*, 3, pp. 67–73.

SPALDING, B., *et al.* (1984) '"If you want to improve your reading, ask your Mum"'. *Remedial Education*, 19, pp. 157–161.

SWINSON, J. M. (1986) 'Paired reading: a critique'. *Support for Learning*, 1, pp. 29–32.

TIZARD, J., SCHOFIELD, W. N. and HEWISON, J. (1982) 'Collaboration between teachers and parents in assisting children's reading'. *British Journal of Educational Psychology*, 52, pp. 1–15.

TOPPING, K. J. (1987a) 'Kirklees Psychological Service Paired Reading Project: third annual report'. *Paired Reading Bulletin*, 3, pp., 96–101.

TOPPING, K. J. (1987b) 'Peer tutored paired reading: outcome data from ten projects'. *Educational Psychology*, 7, 2.

WAREING, L. (1983) Comparison of the relative merits of three methods of parental involvement in reading. M.Sc. thesis, North East London Polytechnic.

WINTER, S. and LOW, A. (1984) 'The Rossmere Peer Tutor Project'. *Behavioural Approaches with Children*, 8, 2, pp. 62–65.

Part Three
Behaviour Difficulties in Schools

8
The Good Behaviour Guide:
HMI Observations on School Discipline

Jim Docking

Introduction

The last decade or so has seen a burgeoning interest in pupil behaviour as a subject for educational research. Apart from numerous small-scale investigations by professional researchers, and surveys conducted by the teacher unions, behaviour has featured in the major British studies on school effectiveness, both in the secondary sector (Galloway *et al.*, 1982; Gray *et al*; 1983; Reynolds 1976; Rutter *et al.*, 1979) and the primary (Mortimore *et al.*, 1986). It has also been the subject of reports commissioned by the British Psychological Society (1980), the Association of Educational Psychologists (1983) and the Scottish Council for Research in Education (Cumming *et al.*, 1981; Johnstone and Munn, 1987). Moreover, following the seminal work of Kounin (1970) in the United States, considerable attention in Britain has recently been given to classroom management styles in an attempt to identify those strategies which appear to be optimal in preventing disruption and facilitating an environment which is conducive to effective learning (Coulby and Harper, 1985; Lake, 1985; Lawrence *et al.*, 1984; Wragg, 1981). More controversially, the Centre of Child Study at the University of Birmingham has produced numerous publications advocating the use of behavioural techniques as a means of promoting classroom order (Merrett, 1985; Wheldall *et al.*, 1985).

One of the most recent contributions to our thinking about pupil behaviour has come from Her Majesty's Inspectors for Schools. A recent report (HMI, 1987) in the 'Education Observed' series called *Good Behaviour and Discipline in Schools* is based upon observations made by HMI during the course of inspections made over the previous four years.

To many teachers, the inspectors' reassuring picture of standards of pupil behaviour in schools today will come as a surprise:

> The overwhelming majority of schools are orderly communities in which there are good standards of behaviour and discipline; poor behaviour is unusual, and serious indiscipline a rare occurrence … [This] applies equally well to schools in all kinds of areas (para. 10).

Moreover, the above state of affairs is held to be 'consistent with the findings of research' and has also 'remained remarkably consistent over time'. Such conclusions are presumably based upon the inspectors' earlier observations (HMI, 1979) together with findings which have emerged in various studies of London schools (Denscombe, 1984; Mortimore *et al.*, 1986; Rutter *et al.*, 1979) as well as the survey of 465 comprehensive schools in forty-one local education authorities by Dierenfield (1982).

It has to be said, however, that the favourable view of behavioural standards painted by HMI is at variance with recent findings reported by some of the teacher unions. The report by the Assistant Masters and Mistresses Association (1984) on behaviour at infant and junior levels, maintains that three-quarters of the responding schools believed there had been a 'marked deterioration' in young children's conduct over the last five years. The National Association of Schoolmasters/Union of Women Teachers (1985) has claimed that comments received from almost 4,000 of its members justified the belief that serious disorder was a feature of many secondary schools, almost one in five teachers having experienced violence 'resulting in serious injury' on at least one occasion over a period of six months. The most recent survey comes from the Professional Association of Teachers. Warning of a 'disciplinary crisis which threatens to overwhelm the education system', the union, backed by a campaign in the Daily Express, has claimed that a third of respondents had been subjected to physical attack at school, while around 90 per cent believe that indiscipline is increasing (*Times Educational Supplement*, 4.12.87).

There are various reasons which can be suggested for this unmistakable mismatch between the perceptions of those on the shop floor and those of outside observers (for a discussion see Docking, 1987). These need not concern us now, but it is worth noting how the official HMI picture contrasts with the belief held by many teachers that serious misbehaviour is prevalent and worsening. In January this year the Secretary of State for Education was sufficiently alarmed by the teachers' evidence on school violence to promise an inquiry. The team, announced in March, includes representation from higher education, schools and industry — but no inspectors!

It is, however, the account of '*good practice*' that is the main subject of this report. For HMI, pupils are more likely to behave well if school policies:

> Establish clear and defensible principles and set boundaries of acceptable
>   behaviour;
> Depend on a carefully developed professional agreement;
> Provide guidelines for action;
> Are made explicit to pupils and parents;
> Are firmly and consistently applied.

The success of such policies is seen to depend upon the development of a positive school climate 'based on a quiet yet firm insistence on high standards of behaviour at all times'. In this respect, HMI regard the quality of relationships, not only between teachers and pupils but between teachers and between pupils, as crucial:

> Such relationships are characterized by mutual respect, by the valuing of pupils, by a willingness to listen and understand, and by a positive view of teachers as professionals and pupils as learners (para. 68).

HMI consider that standards of behaviour are a reflection of all the school's activities, so that both the overt curriculum and extra-curricular activities should allow opportunities for pupils to take initiatives and accept responsibility. The inspectors found behaviour better in schools where an emphasis is placed upon rewards, praise and privileges rather than sanctions, and where the latter are applied flexibly and with discrimination. A key factor in all this is the quality of leadership whereby the head and senior staff set clear and high expectations while exercising constant vigilance. Another hallmark of effective leadership is seen to lie in the quality of support given to teachers, and this importantly includes action to meet staff development needs through in-service training. Finally, HMI consider that standards of behaviour are affected by the quality of links with parents, the local community, and supporting agencies.

There is no doubt that the Report provides a detailed checklist which should provide invaluable material for agendas in meetings of heads and school staff and of governors. This writer has also found it very useful as a source for discussion among student teachers and those on in-service courses. For a major strength of the HMI analysis of the conditions conducive to good conduct is the conviction that pupil behaviour can be materially affected by policies and actions which are within the control of heads and teachers, regardless of pupils' home background.

Particularly useful in this respect is the attention given to those features which produce positive teacher-pupil relationships and effective school/class management. Here it is interesting to compare the conclusions drawn by the inspectors on the basis of their observations with those of professional researchers who frequently control for a range of background variables and whose findings are often based on more structured observations. Such a comparison will form the basis of the discussion which now follows. At the same time, however, it will be suggested that the weaknesses of the HMI viewpoint lie in its oversimplification of certain issues and in the absence of any explanation of how the terms contained in the document's title, 'good behaviour' and 'discipline', should be construed.

The significance of school factors

It is clear that HMI wish to emphasize that the responsibility for the quality of pupil behaviour lies essentially with the schools. In spite of brief statements regretting that some parents opt out of their responsibilities to ensure that their children develop high standards of behaviour, and that teachers do not always get the support they need from society, the clear thrust of the comments contained in the report is that it is the characteristics of the school which make all the difference to the behaviour within it. This perspective is entirely consistent with recent research studies in school effectiveness. Thus Reynolds (1976), reporting on a study of a group of secondary modern schools in South Wales, concludes as follows:

> Instead of continually merely treating the deviant and delinquent children, we should perhaps begin to look and see if the reason for their rebellion lies squarely in the nature, process and operation of some of the schools that we offer them. If the reason does lie there, then perhaps we ought to seek changes in some of our delinquents' schools (p. 229).

Three years later, Rutter and his colleagues (1979), in their survey of twelve inner-London comprehensive schools, also concluded that schools matter over and above background factors:

> Although schools differed in the proportion of behaviourally difficult or low achieving children they admitted, these differences did *not* wholly account for the variations between schools in their pupils' later behaviour and attainment (pp. 177–8).

Similar findings have emerged in the more recent London Junior School Project (Mortimore *et al.*, 1986) which measured pupil progress in terms of attainment, attitude and behaviour:

> It should be emphasized that a major finding of this study concerns the importance of the school in explaining variations in pupils' progress over the junior years. It has been shown that the school makes a far larger contribution to the explanation of progress than is made by pupils' background characteristics, sex and age (p. 16).

Comparable conclusions to those cited above have been reached in studies of school suspension rates. For instance, in his report of a recent investigation into suspensions in Leeds high schools, McManus (1987) writes:

> The main conclusion is that school-related factors are the principal influence on the number of pupils a school suspends. There was no support for the view that high suspension rates reflect deprived catchment areas.

Of course it would be idle to pretend that pupil behaviour is entirely a response to the school situation. Stress within the family and social disadvantage are undoubtedly important factors. But it is sensible to concentrate on school factors not only because these have been shown to be crucially important but also because they are, by and large, within the direct control of heads and teachers and therefore amenable to change. There is some evidence to suggest, however, that the success of schools in preventing and handling misbehaviour is affected by the extent to which the staff *believe* that they are able to control the situation (Maxwell, 1987). The evidence of HMI should help schools to feel confident that they can indeed affect the quality of pupil behaviour.

Leadership and policy

Turning now to some of the specific school factors which are identified in the report, HMI state that 'skilled and sensitive leadership ... is the most consistent feature of those schools where pupils behave well'. Such leadership, we are told, involves the head and senior staff cultivating commitment to the school by teachers, pupils and parents; ensuring effective communication; ensuring expected standards are agreed and consistently applied and that all teachers accept responsibility for pupil behaviour; making certain that management decisions do not adversely affect teacher and pupil morale; helping pupils and teachers over disciplinary problems; and 'establishing the principle that good relationships are a fundamental prerequisite of good behaviour'.

This belief in the significance of leadership style is certainly consistent with the findings from recent school effectiveness studies. Indeed the first of the twelve key factors of effectiveness identified in the London Junior School Project was 'purposeful leadership ... where the headteacher understood the needs of the school and was actively involved in the school's work, without exerting total control over the rest of the staff' (Mortimore *et al.*, 1986). Factors which were found to be particularly related to good pupil behaviour included the practice of seeing parents at regular fixed times and the involvement of staff in decision-making. A comparable finding in the earlier London study (Rutter *et al.*, 1979) was that behaviour was better in secondary schools in which senior staff provided a clear sense of direction and secured a consensus view about values and aims.

The emphasis given by HMI to *all* teachers feeling responsible for maintaining good behaviour can be related to findings of studies which have examined pastoral care practices in secondary schools. For instance, investigations by Galloway (1983), Denscombe (1984) and Lawrence *et al.* (1984) have demonstrated the unproductive consequences of relying upon arrangements which involve routine 'referral upwards', whereby house or year heads are used as troubleshooters. Senior staff can become resentful of colleagues whose referrals they perceive, however unfairly, as stemming from unimaginative teaching. A system which encourages routine referrals simply leaves less time for pastoral heads to perform their more positive roles, whilst also sometimes allowing minor incidents with a junior teacher to escalate into major confrontations with senior authority. Instead, the responsibility of senior staff to their junior colleagues should be to encourage an atmosphere of openness in which problems are exposed and discussed and not kept bottled up for fear of accusations of professional incompetence. Referrals can then be reserved for serious incidents. As HMI acknowledge, confrontations between teachers and pupils can often be attributed to inappropriate teaching style or curriculum provision. Alas, we are also told that schools rarely supply the kind of support which would enable teachers to adopt a more positive classroom profile. In this respect, an important role for senior staff is to identify relevant in-service needs and to take action accordingly.

It could be argued that a policy which discourages easy referrals will increase teacher stress and therefore compound the situation; but if, alongside this, there are strategies to provide for staff support and development, plus clear rules about the kinds of occasion when referrals *are* legitimate, the long-term effect should be to increase teachers' self-esteem and confidence as relationships with pupils improve.

The quality of teaching and learning experiences

When pupils are given an environment which arouses their curiosity and interest, when work is well matched to their abilities, and when they are involved in worthwhile activities and encouraged to take some responsibility for their own learning, they respond positively (para. 18).

This is a key sentence in the HMI document. Its implications need spelling out, however, if it is to be interpreted in the best educational interests of the pupils.

First, what is it to 'arouse curiosity and interest'? For there is an important difference between 'making lessons interesting', on the one hand, and 'helping children to see what there is of interest in the activity' on the other. The first alternative serves a *managerial* function, arresting apathy and to that extent facilitating classroom control; the appeal, however, is to factors which are extrinsic to the activity itself. By contrast, the second alternative goes beyond simple managerial concerns and serves an *educative* function, drawing attention to those features which are intrinsically interesting and which enable pupils to deepen their interest in that activity for its own sake (Wilson, 1971).

This failure to distinguish between ways of arousing curiosity and interest can be illustrated by reference to HMI's comments on the use of rewards. The inspectors observe (para. 37) that 'the best results are found where schools lay particular emphasis on rewards'. More specifically, it is asserted that 'pupils appear to achieve more, to be better motivated, and to behave better, when teachers commend and reward their successes and emphasize their potential rather than focussing on their failures and shortcomings'.

The emphasis here on positive rather than negative teacher behaviour is certainly to be welcomed as an important corrective to the view that discipline entails a rigid adherence to rules, breaches of which inexorably lead to punishment. Rewards may encourage some children to behave better when good conduct seems otherwise unattractive, and a system of rewards may help children to adopt better behavioural habits. Nonetheless, in relation to recent research findings, the statement on rewards is too sweeping. For one thing, no distinction is made between tangible and non-tangible rewards. Evidence from the school effectiveness studies suggests that the giving of prizes to secondary pupils is not significantly associated with either behaviour or work (Rutter *et al.*, 1979), while the head's use of stars and certificates for junior pupils is related to behaviour and attitude to school but not to cognitive outcomes (Mortimore *et al.*, 1986).

Moreover, from recent experimental evidence involving various age groups and curriculum areas it would appear that the offer of tangible rewards can actually undermine intrinsic interest, perhaps because the children shift their focus of attention from the features of the activity that make it interesting to prospects of receiving a reward (Lepper, 1983). In terms of attribution theory, it is also possible that knowledge of a reward adversely affects children's feelings of personal competence in that they attribute their success to external incentives rather than to their own effort or ability. It is clearly vital that pupils are not effectively encouraged to respond to the prospect of rewards by covering up their learning problems when they need help. A related factor here is that rewards may impair creative, insightful responses since children may 'play safe' in order to achieve a reward.

However, from other evidence it appears that rewards can be educationally productive if two conditions are ensured. First, rewards should be contingent on the achievement of certain standards and not on simple engagement in the activity (Boggiano and Ruble, 1979). Secondly, the teacher should give careful feedback which encourages the child to attribute the reward to his or her personal competence (Boggiano *et al.*, 1982). In this respect it is worth noting how a major finding of the London junior school project was that behaviour and achievement are better when teachers provide a 'work-centred environment', giving regular feedback on children's work. In short, whether rewards can be a useful *educative* as well as *managerial* tool depends very much on what the teacher is also doing to help children develop both an intrinsic interest in the activity and a sense of personal achievement. Undoubtedly school should be a *rewarding experience* for children.

HMI are on firmer ground in their remarks on the significance of praise, arguing persuasively that teachers are more likely to be aware of the potent effect which praise can have on pupils' motivation if they work in an atmosphere where colleagues commend each other for their successes. Recent reviews on the use of classroom praise in American schools (Brophy, 1981) and British (Schwieso and Hastings, 1987) show that teachers are sparing with their praise for social conduct compared with academic achievement, and especially with respect to low achievers and troublesome pupils.

HMI also rightly draw attention to another important matter in the effective use of praise when they cite a policy guideline from an urban comprehensive school:

> The test question to be used in all praise should be: does it identify and instance the nature of the satisfactory behaviour ... The idea of what is satisfactory in school behaviour and achievement is not automatically learned or maintained but needs to be taught and supported (para 38).

In short, praise needs to be specific if the pupil is to profit from its message.

One might qualify this, however, in two ways. The first is by suggesting that with older pupils, who are often more concerned about positive feedback from peers than from adults, praise should be administered quietly and privately. According to a recent investigation, this seems to be what older pupils want (Sharpe *et al.*, 1987) presumably because it minimizes the risk of causing personal embarrassment. Secondly, praise comments should convey to pupils that they have the inherent ability to succeed. As Schunk (1987) has suggested, if a pupil thinks a task is easy the communication 'That's good. You've been working hard!' signals that the teacher believes the pupil to have low ability.

A qualifying comment needs also to be made about HMI's assertion, in the passage quoted at the start of this section, that behaviour is better 'when work is well matched to the children's ability'. It is important that the concept of matching is taken to mean identifying what the pupils can do as a basis for providing rather more demanding experiences, not for providing more experiences at the same level of difficulty. Activities which are too hard will be demotivating and may therefore animate frustration, while activities which literally match the children's present attainment are unlikely to meet the criterion of challenge which HMI importantly emphasize elsewhere. Following the work of Deci (1975), we can say that optimal conditions for arousing intrinsic interest are provided when children are set goals which, although within their reach, are also beyond their present levels of achievement. It is this particular construction of 'match', whereby children are offered *moderate* challenge, which is a motivational prerequisite for an effective learning experience. Recent evidence suggests, however, that primary school teachers find difficulty in correctly diagnosing children's abilities and planning appropriately matching tasks (Bennett *et al.*, 1984).

The final assertion which HMI make in the passage quoted at the start of this section suggests that behaviour will be better if children are encouraged to take responsibility for their own learning. If this is related to attribution theory, the hypothesis is two-fold: that children are more likely to learn effectively not only if they feel success but also if they attribute that success primarily to their own efforts and ability rather than to help received from others, the easiness of the task, or just luck. Children who tend to be disruptive are particularly prone to see the causes of their successes in terms of external and unstable factors, chance or the teacher's mood, and such beliefs are likely to contribute to feelings of anxiety and personal helplessness (Fry and Grover, 1984). That 'nothing succeeds like success' imperfectly states that position; a more accurate formulation would be 'nothing succeeds like the success *which you can contribute to your own agency*'.

There is little doubt that pupils' beliefs about their competencies are susceptible to influence by teachers. Certainly the literature is rich in examples on how children conform to negative expectations when they sense they are being labelled as problems. Fortunately, it is also the case that teachers can help children to think more positively about their own capabilities. In a recent review of research on self-efficacy, Schunk (1987) has suggested the following factors, each of which has important practical implications for teachers:

1. Pupils must believe that their success is not temporary but that they are making continual progress — and not too slowly; the teacher's feedback should therefore convey this information;
2. Pupils with self-doubts and anxiety about their competencies are more

likely to believe in the power of their own efforts if they are exposed to peer models who have similar attributes to themselves but have managed to achieve success in the relevant task. The best practice here is for teachers to choose models from low-achievers who have overcome a learning problem, rather than from pupils who learn with ease;

3. Pupils need to take complex tasks in small steps; hence the teacher should break down difficult material into smaller units with plenty of practice opportunities;

4. Pupils need to feel that their efforts will be worthwhile. Telling them that their successes with complex tasks were due to trying will therefore encourage persistence in the belief that further effort is likely to produce success. After a time, however, it is important for the teacher to switch from effort-feedback to ability-feedback since otherwise pupils may begin to wonder why they have to work so hard to succeed;

5. Goal-setting is important, but pupils are more likely to achieve those goals which they set for themselves for they will be committed to them. Self-initiated goals will also help pupils to learn to judge their abilities accurately and hence provide better opportunities for experiencing success.

Galloway and Goodwin (1987) sum up the problem of self-efficacy nicely when they say this:

> Many children with learning and adjustment difficulties interpret failure as a message about *themselves* ... The teacher's task is to show pupils that failure carries a message about the *task* and not about them.

Sanctions

The section on sanctions in the HMI report deserves special attention given that corporal punishment has now been abolished in maintained schools. It is important to realize that the use of the term corporal punishment in the 1986 Education Act, as clarified in DES Circular 7/86, includes any intentional application of force such as slapping and cuffing, throwing chalk and rough handling.

Whilst recognizing that even in the most orderly schools the need for punishment will arise, HMI persuasively point out that the more teachers are positive and sensitive in their regular dealing with children, the more powerful is the sanction of disapproval. Although the report lists possible punishments, HMI wisely do not give their seal of approval to any of these but instead identify the principles which should govern the use of sanctions. The first is that sanctions should be varied so that a clear distinction is made between minor and serious offences. Most teachers, no doubt, can recall instances when punishment in school must have offered children a confused picture of adult morality, as when infringements of arbitrary, local conventions such as the regulation colour of socks have been treated in much the same way as violations of moral rules such as truth-telling and treating others as persons.

On first reading, the next two principles might seem self-contradictory: a school should 'indicate which sanctions are likely to be appropriate to particular offences' yet also 'insist on flexibility in the application of sanctions to suit individual circumstances'. Presumably the first of these helps to make the boundaries of unacceptable behaviour explicit while the latter is necessary in the interests of justice. Certainly it is both unproductive managerially and undesirable educationally to apply a particular, or any, punishment inexorably for a given offence since this takes no account of circumstance or motive. Hence it would be wrong to treat two culprits in the same way for identical offences if one was the consequence of calculated maliciousness and the other unintentional, the result of a misunderstanding, or a direct consequence of parental negligence. Nor will it attend to the child's emotional needs if a teacher relentlessly punishes for an offence whose commission is effectively a cry for help. One is reminded here of Reynold's (1976) hypothesis, based on observations in a group of secondary modern schools in South Wales, that better behaviour is found in schools were there is a tolerance for a limited amount of 'acting out' and where instances of deviance evoke therapeutic rather than punitive responses. In short, the oft-heard pleas for consistency should relate to the thoughtful application of principles of practice, not to a rigid application of a code of practice.

Fourthly, HMI maintain that good sanction policy should discourage punishment of a whole group. As Piaget (1932) showed, many children beyond the infant stage are sensitive to the injustice of punishing innocent members of a group when the offenders are not known or will not own up.

The fifth and sixth principles perhaps should have come first. The inspectors suggest 'that sanctions should be applied without infringement of the school's aim and principles' and should not 'damage relationships and pupils' self-esteem'. An illustration which might be useful here is the practice of immoderately shouting at pupils. Like corporal punishment, this can have a dramatic shock effect which can be rewarding for the teacher, who can then easily slide into the habit of intimidating and denigrating pupils as a means of control. But, again like corporal punishment, its long-term effect will be to set up a model of violence and to destroy pupils' sense of pride and self-respect. In any case, on purely instrumental grounds, there is experimental evidence that soft reprimands are more efficacious than loud ones (O'Leary *et al.*, 1970).

Next, HMI advise that schools should 'indicate the balance to be kept between sanctions and rewards' and 'provide guidelines also on positive ways of achieving good behaviour'. Rutter *et al.* (1979) found that third-year secondary pupils reported twice as many reprimands as instances of praise and three times as many punishments as rewards. Certainly it is important that the use of reprimand or punishment does not undo the school's efforts to promote a positive atmosphere.

This is not to say, however, that punishment is just a necessary nuisance which has no part to play in promoting a positive school atmosphere. Used discriminatively and sensitively, it can serve to remind children, as they grow older, that they are moral agents, who deserve to be treated as responsible for their actions. As HMI assert in their last proposition, 'Above all ... pupils should be brought to understand why what they have done is unacceptable, and how they can put it right.' Writing from his experience as a Junior school head Winkley (1987) has recently emphasized that punishments are 'best thought of as reminders and inhibitors, intended in an almost theatrical sense to mark a pause in the game. At best they are active encouragers of thinking'. In short, the *focus* of punishment should be on the inherent reasonableness of the rule which has been infringed and not the power of the punisher, while the *manner* of punishment should convey to the culprit that it is the behaviour that is unacceptable and not the child as a person.

The concepts of good behaviour and discipline

The HMI report opens with a crucial sentence:

> Good behaviour is a *necessary condition* for effective teaching and learning to take place, and an *outcome* of *education* which society rightly expects (para. 1, emphasis added).

At first sight this statement appears to be logically contradictory, for how can something be both a necessary condition and an outcome? Unfortunately, HMI say nothing in their report to help us out of this dilemma, since nowhere do they discuss what, for them, counts as good behaviour. Of course, HMI do not intend reports in this series to count as fully-fledged curriculum documents, and there are limits to the range of issues which can be discussed in a short publication which is itself based on a series of short visits to schools. Nonetheless, the inspectors could be expected to explain to us the criteria on which their evaluations were based, especially as the report enjoins teachers to provide 'defensible principles with a strong positive rationale' (para 12) and to follow through the implications of the conceptual distinction which they themselves seem to raise at the very start of their report.

It is possible that HMI see good behaviour simply in terms of conformity to certain conventions. In this case the only intelligible interpretation of the opening sentence is that learning cannot take place unless pupils are already, to some extent, abiding by such a behavioural code, and that, as a product of their education, pupils will come to abide by this code ever more diligently. Yet whilst code-abiding is self-evidently a condition for any social organization, good behaviour must surely be more than this if it is to be an outcome of education.

Of course children must learn to conform to a disciplinary code which not only makes them possible to teach and pleasant to live with but also provides individuals with a sense of physical and psychological security. They must therefore learn to obey simple requests from those in authority, to show common courtesies, to refrain from violent or threatening behaviour and using foul language, and so forth. But if their behaviour is to be qualitatively affected as 'an important outcome of education', children must also be encouraged to cultivate a sensitivity to the needs and claims of others, to foresee the consequences of their actions on others, to feel committed to certain behavioural principles, and generally to see themselves and others as persons. No doubt HMI would accept this — but, unlike the Board of Education fifty years ago, they have not said so. In the later editions of the *Handbook of Suggestions for the Consideration of Teachers* (1937), the criteria by which a school's discipline should be evaluated were discussed in some detail. The crucial test for discipline was held to be

> whether it represents a real sense, on the part of the children, of the rightness of the behaviour that is expected of them (Board of Education, 1937, p. 24).

The distinction, then, which HMI might have made between 'good behaviour' as a 'condition for effective teaching and learning to take place' and as 'an important outcome of education' is that the former relates to a limited range of desirable, conventional behaviours: for example, children must be made to be attentive and courteous, to concentrate, not to prevent others learning, and so forth, whilst the latter stems from a state of mind involving understanding, insight, sensibility and commitment.

Now all this may seem to be academic quibbling. After all, can we not all recognize 'good behaviour' when we encounter it, and do we not know what it feels like to be in a school where the 'discipline' is 'good'? But the distinction which is being suggested is important for very practical purposes. This is because the manipulative kinds of classroom strategies and school policies which may be perfectly effective in providing minimal conditions for effective learning may do nothing to bring about good behaviour in the second, educative, sense. The question to ask about a school's disciplinary practice, therefore, is this: Are the features of teaching styles, classroom management practices and school ethos, together with the range of curriculum and extra-curricular opportunities, those which are likely not only to provide a climate for effective teaching and learning but also to help pupils develop a sensitive perception of others' needs and a sense of moral obligation?

Consider, for instance, the recent proposal leaked from DES in the late summer of 1987 and made public at the beginning of the New Year (*Times Educational Supplement*, 8.1.88), that schools should be given behavioural ratings to help them and the public assess their achievements and value for money. Do HMI believe that good behaviour, as an outcome of education, is appropriately defined in terms of a limited range of performance indicators such as truancy, lateness, and demeanour, which DES are suggesting? An example of the last indicator according to a DES official is 'that shoes are polished and socks are pulled up' — and we are told that staff demeanour is to be assessed too!

Thankfully, there is indirect evidence in their report that HMI see good behaviour in terms which go beyond the DES performance indicators. For instance we are told that 'good relationships are a fundamental prerequisite of good behaviour' (para. 14) and that where teachers 'treat one another and the pupils with courtesy and consideration, they demonstrate a commitment to which pupils can and do respond with respect and often with liking' (para. 15). More specifically, amongst the factors which are 'more subtly ... prevalent in lessons where good behaviour is well established' are 'the nurturing of genuine involvement based on an understanding of concepts', 'the encouragement of pupils to contribute ideas' and 'an encouragement to define their ideas in discussion' (para. 19). Later we are also told that in schools with high standards of behaviour 'there is an emphasis on sensitivity towards pupils, so that teachers become aware of the need to listen to them and to be seen to be listening' (para. 41). And although HMI leave out the role of pupils when they urge that the policies for behaviour are 'worked out cooperatively and command the assent of all teachers' (para. 13), they approve of pupils being involved in discussion concerning sanctions (para. 42). In other words, it looks as if HMI do have a notion of an educative discipline in mind since otherwise they would have devoted more space to extolling the virtues of an efficient system of manipulatory devices such as rewards and sanctions. Yet without an explicit discussion about the kind of good behaviour which schools, as educational institutions, should be cultivating, the Report is about the means to undefined ends. It is vital that in a society of shifting and uncertain values, the ends of a school's *educational* behaviour policy are not taken for granted but are seen as part of general curricular aims.

Conclusions

HMIs have provided a report which is humane and constructive. They might have dwelt on all they found which was wrong. Instead, they have wisely provided a well-stocked inventory of ideas to help schools make behaviour better. It may be, as has been suggested in this chapter, that some statements are too general and that insufficient attention has been given to conceptual clarification. It may be, too, that the picture painted of behavioural standards in schools today is too rosy. But at least the inspectors have confirmed that behaviour is best in schools where children are engaged in enriching experiences and feel they are significant. This is important at a time when schools are being evaluated in terms of benchmarks and performance indicators and value for money.

Note

Since this chapter was written, further surveys on pupil behaviour have been published. For a review of all recent work, see Docking, J. (1989) 'Elton's four questions: Some general considerations', in Jones, N. (Ed.) *School Management and Pupil Behaviour*, Lewes, Falmer Press.

References

ASSISTANT MASTERS AND MISTRESSES ASSOCIATION (1984) *The Reception Class Today*, London, AMMA.

ASSOCIATION OF EDUCATIONAL PSYCHOLOGISTS (1983) *Alternatives to Corporal Punishment*, Durham, AEP.

BENNETT, S. N., DESFORGES, C., COCKBURN, A. and WILKINSON, B. (1984) *The Quality of Pupil Learning Experiences*, Hillsdale, N.J., Erlbaum.

BOARD OF EDUCATION (1937) *Handbook of Suggestions for the Consideration of Teachers*, London, HMSO.

BOGGIANO, A. K. and RUBLE, D. N. (1979) 'Competence and the overjustification effect: a developmental study', *Journal of Personality and Social Psychology*, 37, pp. 1462–8.

BOGGIANO, A. K., RUBLE, D. N. and PITTMAN, D. S. (1982) 'The mastery hypothesis and the overjustification effect', *Social Cognition* 1, pp. 38–49.

BRITISH PSYCHOLOGICAL SOCIETY (1980) *Report of a Working Party on Corporal Punishment in Schools*, Leicester: British Psychological Society.

BROPHY, J. E. (1981) 'Teacher praise: a functional analysis', *Review of Educational Research*, 51, pp. 5–32.

COULBY, D. and HARPER, T. (1985) *Preventing Classroom Disruption*, Beckenham, Croom Helm.

CUMMING, C. E., LOWE, T., TULIPS, J. and WAKELING, C. (1981) *Making the Changing: A Study of the Process of the Abolition of Corporal Punishment*, London, Hodder and Stoughton/Scottish Council for Research in Education.

DECI, E. L. (1975) *Intrinsic Motivation*, New York, Plenum.

DENSCOMBE, M. (1984) 'Control, controversy and the comprehensive school', in Ball, S. (ed.) *Comprehensive Schooling*, Lewes, Falmer Press.

DIERENFIELD, R. (1982) 'All you need to know about disruption', *Times Educational Supplement*, 29 January.

DOCKING, J. W. (1987) *Control and Discipline in Schools: Perspectives and Approaches*, 2nd ed., London, Harper and Row.

DWECK, C., DAVIDSON, W., NELSON, S. and ENNA, B. (1978) 'Sex differences in learned helplessness', II and III, *Developmental Psychology*, 14, pp. 268–76.

FRY, P. S. and GROVER, S. C. (1984) 'Problem and non-problem children's causal explanations of success and failure in primary school settings', *British Journal of Social Psychology*, 23, pp. 51–60.

GALLOWAY, D., BALL, T., BLOMFIELD, D. and SEYD, R. (1982) *Schools and Disruptive Pupils*, London, Longman.

GALLOWAY, D., BALL, T., BLOOMFIELD, D. and SEYED, R. (1982) *Schools and Disruptive Pupils*, London, Longman.

GALLOWAY, D. and GOODWIN, C. (1987) *The Education of Disturbing Children*, London, Longman.

GRAY, J., MCPHERSON, A. F. and RAFFE, D. (1983) *Reconstructions of Secondary Education*, London, Routledge and Kegan Paul.

HER MAJESTY'S INSPECTORATE (1979) *Aspects of Secondary Education in England*, London, HMSO.

HER MAJESTY'S INSPECTORATE (1987) *Good Behaviour and Discipline in Schools*, Education Observed 5, London, DES.

JOHNSTONE, M. and MUNN, P., (1987) *Discipline in Schools: A Review of 'Causes' and 'Cures'*, Edinburgh, SCRE.

KOUNIN, J. (1970) *Discipline and Group Management in Classrooms*, New York, Holt, Rinehart and Winston.

LAKE, C. (1985) 'Preventive approaches to disruption', *Maladjustment and Therapeutic Education*, 3, pp. 47–52.

LAWRENCE, J., STEED, D. and YOUNG, P. (1984) *Disruptive Children — Disruptive Schools*, Beckenham, Croom Helm.

LEPPER, M. (1983) 'Extrinsic reward and intrinsic motivation: implications for classroom practice', in: Levine, J. M. and Wang, M. C. (eds.) *Teacher and Student Perspectives: Implications for Learning*, Hillsdale, N.J., Erlbaum.

MAXWELL, W. S. (1987) 'Teachers' attitudes towards disruptive behaviour in secondary schools', *Educational Review*, pp. 203–216.

MCMANUS, M. (1987) 'Suspension and exclusion from high schools: the association with catchment and school variables', *School Organisation*, 7, pp. 261–271.

MERRETT, F. E. (1985) *Encouragement Works Better than Punishment*, Birmingham, Positive Products.

MORTIMORE, P., SAMMONS, P., STOLL, L., LEWIS, D. and ECOB, R. (1986) *The Junior School Project*, London, ILEA Research and Statistics Branch.

NATIONAL ASSOCIATION OF SCHOOLMASTERS/UNION OF WOMEN TEACHERS (1985) *Pupil Violence and Disorder in Schools*, Birmingham, NAS/UWT.

O'LEARY, K. D., KAUFMAN, K. F., KASS, K. F. and DRABMAN, R. S. (1970) 'The effects of loud and soft reprimands on the behaviour of disruptive students', *Exceptional Children*, 37, pp. 144–5.

PIAGET, J. (1932) *The Moral Judgement of the Child*, London, Routledge and Kegan Paul.

REYNOLDS, D. (1976) 'The delinquent school', in HAMMERSLEY, M. and WOODS, P. (eds.) *The Process of Schooling*, London, Routledge and Kegan Paul/Open University Press.

RUTTER, M., MAUGHAN, B., MORTIMORE, P., and OUSTEN, J. (1979) *Fifteen Thousand Hours: Secondary Schools and their Effects on Children*, London, Open Books.

SCHUNK, D. H. (1987) 'Self efficacy and motivated learning', in. HASTINGS, N. and SCHWIESO, J. (eds.) *New Directions in Educational Psychology: 2 Behaviour and Motivation in the Classroom*, Lewes, Falmer Press.

SCHWIESO, J. and HASTINGS, N. (1987) 'Teachers' use of approval', in, Hastings, N. and Schwieso, J. (eds.) *New Directions in Educational Psychology: 2 Behaviour and Motivation in the Classroom*, Lewes, Falmer Press.

SHARPE, P., WHELDALL, K. and MERRETT, F. (1987) 'The attitudes of British secondary school pupils to praise and reward', *Educational Studies*, 13, pp. 293–302.

WHELDALL, K., MERRETT, F. and BORG, M. (1985) 'The Behavioural Approach to Teaching (BATPACK): An Experimental Evaluation'. *British Journal of Educational Psychology*, 55, pp. 65–75.

WILSON, P. S. (1971) *Interest and Discipline in Education*, London, Routledge and Kegan Paul.

WINKLEY, D. (1987) 'The paradox of discipline'. *Education 3–13*, October.

WRAGG, E. C. (1981) *Classroom Management and Control*, London, Macmillan.

WRAGG, E. C. (ed.) (1984) *Classroom Teaching Skills*, Beckenham, Croom Helm.

9
Violent, Aggressive and Disruptive Behaviour

Delwyn P. Tattum

Disruptive behaviour

Deviant behaviour is a part of organizational life, and as complex organizations, schools are no exceptions. This is particularly true of secondary schools where young people with varying degrees of reluctance attend, and are 'boxed' for set times and redistributed about the building at regular intervals. Within these experiences they can express their deviance in different ways with some opting out of the work cycle, others staying away, with a third group striking out.

When considering the emergence of disruptive behaviour as a problem we need to examine the matter of incidence, that is, how extensive and extreme is the behaviour, and whether the situation teachers face in the 1980s is worse than in earlier decades. The degree of incidence will be discussed in a later section, but when we address the issue of providing an historical dimension to indiscipline we find that there has been little systematic investigation of the topic. Ariés (1960) does provide startling accounts of rebellions and riots in public schools during the eighteenth and nineteenth centuries: Eton's famous rebellion in 1768 was followed by five serious rebellions in Winchester between 1770 and 1818. Schools like Harrow, Charterhouse, Merchant Taylors' and Shrewsbury were not exempt and from the 1780s Rugby experienced a number of serious upheavals: even under Matthew Arnold there was a near rebellion in 1833 (Lawson and Silver, 1973).

In an attempt to provide a more recent historical perspective on indiscipline in state schools Furlong (1985) examined the mid-nineteenth century, the early twentieth century, and the 1950s, but because of the lack of systematic research information was obliged to turn to less conventional sources, such as, oral histories, diaries, biographies and semi-fictional accounts of schooling. 'Whether such evidence gives a true picture of disruption and truancy in earlier periods is impossible to say. All that can be said with any certainty is that challenging behaviour at schools is nothing new ... it has a history as long as mass education itself'. Interestingly, a conclusion from this historical survey is that the most distinctive feature of the last two decades has been the continuing expression of public concern. The moral panic of the middle classes found regular expression in the mass media, provoked questions in parliament, preoccupied teacher union conferences, and spawned a vast body of educational literature on the subject.

The Pack Report (1977) reviewed and focused on school-based factors which may have contributed to the emergence of disruptive behaviour and identified the following reasons:

1. Earlier maturation of young people than in the past;
2. Raising of the school-leaving age;
3. Unsettlement arising from a period of rapid educational change;
4. Disenchantment of many young pupils with the type of secondary education provided;
5. Teacher shortage and/or a high rate of staff turnover;
6. Teachers who cannot cope with the situation.

In an attempt to widen the context of the debate Coulby and Harper (1985) drew attention to what they called the 'urban crisis' and the 'youth crisis'. Consideration of the conditions in many inner cities provides a backcloth against which to examine violent and aggressive behaviour. In the summer of 1981 we witnessed rioting in many cities and reports (HMI, 1978b) confirmed that disruptive behaviour was most severely experienced in inner-city schools. Many of these schools reflect the run-down and neglected neighbourhoods they serve, the low morale of teachers and pupils, low academic achievement, job prospects for school-leavers being depressed, and youngsters and their parents regarding the nature of the schooling offered to be an irrelevance. Coupled with this manifestation of social malaise is the challenging emergence of youth culture. This is a post-war phenomenon as the spending power of adolescents is independently catered for in music, magazines, dress, and hairstyles, and characterized in its extreme forms by groups such as Teds, Mods, Rockers, Skinheads, and Punks. In addition to experimenting with music and dress many experiment with alcohol, drugs, and in their relations with the opposite sex. The secondary school provides a social meeting place for the consumers of youth culture.

> In this respect the school provides a forum for teenage ideas, and yet, in the pursuit of traditional values, formal authority relationships, outmoded rituals, debilitating routines, and a liturgy of rules, it is the very antithesis of the 'other' world of many young people (Tattum, 1982).

The language of disruption

Disruptive behaviour is easier to describe than define. In the language of teachers it is behaviour that is uncooperative and rude; insolent and disobedient; provocative and aggressive; hostile and abusive; impertinent and argumentative; surly and arrogant; threatening and intimidatory. But this kind of language has been used by teachers since the beginning of formal education because it contains within it the responses of pupils to the compulsory nature and authority structure of popular schooling. The significant difference that has occurred in the last two decades is the application of a new label — disrupter, as if we have now identified a new category of pupil. For once a label has been created it makes it easier for the person to be identified, typified and stigmatized. The danger with person labels is that they come to encompass the total identity in the minds of others, so that a galaxy of status traits may be ascribed, many of which have nothing to do with the prescribed behaviour. In the short history of the term disrupter, the act of selection and segregation have been significant mechanisms in the process of confirming the category in the consciousness of teachers and pupils alike.

> Categories are not pre-existent but are socially constructed so that people may classify others, and before anyone can be seen as a deviant there must be a category to which he or she can be assigned — the official establishment of units facilitates the public labelling process of disrupters (Tattum, 1982).

In earlier decades pupils who were disobedient, aggressive or abusive were contained within the school but the education system has recently taken a major step such that it can now select and isolate from mainstream schooling a new category of pupil within the definition of children with special needs. One of the many dangers of isolating pupils is that they come to be looked upon as abnormal. The process can also contribute to the adoption of an innate pathological model within the profession, thus enabling schools to absolve themselves of any blame as the pupil's 'condition' will be seen as a mental aberration rather than a chosen solution to a social problem.

Continuing the theme of the lexicology of the disruptive pupil the semantic distinction between 'problem children' and 'children with problems' (Lawrence *et al.*, 1984) and, the personally preferred, 'disturbed' or 'disturbing' child, further engages the nature of the issues involved. For decades the field of special education has been the domain of psychiatrists and psychologists, and in the past the ideology they have favoured has been the *medical model*. This is a way of looking at social deviance and abnormality as a form of illness and the focus of approach is the individual in whom the signs or symptoms are manifest, such that an appropriate form of treatment is prescribed to bring about a recovery. More recently sociologists have shown an interest in special education (Tomlinson, 1982) and they are more interested in organizations, social contexts, and social interaction, and so by definition they approach social problems from a different direction and ask different questions. In fact, Frude (1984) identifies a meeting-point between the two perspectives, although the way in which disruptive pupils have been dealt with over the last fifteen years does query his view-point.

> The individualisation of the problem is seen in a comparison between such descriptive terms as 'disturbed' and 'disturbing', or 'maladjusted' and 'maladapted'. Disturbed (or maladjusted) locates the problems within the individual pupil, but fails to explore the context in which the

behaviour manifests itself. The solution is therefore to extract problem pupils and transfer them to a special place where they will receive medical or pseudo-medical treatment. But concentration on the social pathology of the individual permits us to ignore deficiencies in the system. To look beyond the pupil takes us into the school and classroom, and requires us to consider whether the nature of the organisation places constraints and controls on the pupil which are themselves problematic. What is more, the attitudes and expectations of teachers can create confrontational situations for pupils who lack the social skills to 'please teacher'. If this is the case, then the handicap is social and not medical, and though recognising that children behave badly the approach also concentrates our attention on the context and relationships in which they display their inappropriate behaviour (Tattum, 1985).

The above quotation further indicates the problems associated with the language of the disturbing child when it links it with the maladjusted. Provision for maladjusted pupils pre-dates that for disrupters by decades, so that from the late 1960s we witnessed a massive increase in the number of pupils who, by their category of handicap, were described as presenting ordinary schools with behavioural problems. In 1950 there were 587 pupils in schools for the malad-justed, but by 1979 the figure had risen to 22,402 in England and Wales. In Tattum (1985) it is argued that special education has operated as a means of social control through the exclusion of the defective and troublesome, and that the identification and exclusion of disruptive pupils is an extension of this policy with a comparable increase in provision through the 1970s and 1980s. (The issue of incidence and provision is dealt with in the following sections.) On this issue Galloway (1985) writes of a 'spurious distinction, rapidly becoming enshrined in DES folklore, between maladjusted and disruptive'. The Warnock Report (1978) does not distinguish between the two categories, but one of the groups identified as continuing to require placement in special schools includes 'those with severe emotional or behaviour disorders who have very great difficulty in forming relationships with others or whose behaviour is so extreme or unpredictable that it causes severe disruption in an ordinary school or inhibits the educational progress of other children (paragraph 6.10)'.

Subsequent government legislation does not appear to have clarified the distinction between maladjusted and disruptive, as the 1981 Act requires that pupils transferred to special schools must be 'statemented' following formal assessment, but a later circular (DES, 1983) advises that formal procedures

are not required when ordinary schools provide special educational provision from their own resources in the form of additional tuition and remedial provision or, in normal circumstances, where the child attends a reading centre or unit for disruptive pupils (para. 15).

Given that the concept of maladjustment is equally as vague as that of the disrupter (Laslett, 1977; Wilson and Evans, 1980) the above distinction becomes problematic. What is more, the available screening devices have many limitations (Tizard, 1968; Mortimore *et al.*, 1983), so that any clarity of distinction between the two groups emanates more from legal and administrative considerations than from professionally assessed special educational, psychological or medical needs. Consequently, whether a child is sent to a school for the maladjusted or a special unit for disrupters may depend on arbitrary factors, none more apparent than the availability of facilities.

To conclude this section on the vocabulary of disruptive behaviour a selection of definitions is offered as further illustration of the confused state of our understanding of the problem. Saunders (1979) defines problem behaviour as:

> that behaviour of pupils which prevents the teacher from achieving his legitimate and appropriate objectives.

To allow for the fact that misbehaviour is context-bound Mortimore *et al.* (1983) provide a definition which focuses on *the behaviour* rather than on *the child* in defining it as:

> any act which interferes with the learning, development or happiness of a pupil or his or her peers, or with the teacher's attempts to foster those processes or feelings.

Finally, in an attempt to focus on the interactional nature of disruptive behaviour Tattum (1982) includes relationships, social context and rules in his definition:

> Rule-breaking in the form of conscious action or inaction, which brings about an interruption or curtailment of a classroom or school activity, and damages interpersonal relationships.

The incidence of disruptive behaviour

Not only is it difficult to ascertain whether there has been an *actual*, as opposed to a perceived, increase in disruptive incidents, but the methodology associated with the exercise is notoriously difficult, as will be evident from the studies to be discussed. The data gathering difficulties arise, firstly, from a lack of agreement about what constitutes disruptive behaviour, as indicated in the previous section, and secondly, from the associated factor that some teachers are more tolerant than others. Similarly, there is evidence of a reluctance on the part of local authorities, schools, and individual teachers, to openly admit that they are experiencing problems of indiscipline. In the exercise of quantifying acts of disruption, Furlong (1985) notes that four approaches have been attempted, namely, teachers' estimates; recording incidents; rates of suspensions and exclusions; teachers' rating scales; each of which, with their associated problems, will be noted in the following review of research extending over the last two decades.

Teacher Unions

It is not surprising that teacher unions have been particularly active in surveys and reports on indiscipline, and the most prolific has been the NAS/UWT. They commissioned Lowenstein to conduct two early surveys into violence in schools in England and Wales. In the 1972 survey, *Violence in Schools and its Treatment*, questionnaires were sent to NAS representatives in 13,500 schools, and from a low return rate of 10 per cent of primary schools and 25 per cent of secondary schools, approximately 60 per cent (622) reported violence of some kind but only twenty-four schools indicated violence to be a very frequent occurrence. In his follow-up survey, *Violent and Disruptive Behaviour in Schools* (1975), Lowenstein requested that schools record all incidents of violent and disruptive behaviour over a three month period, October to December, 1974. Completed questionnaires were returned from 5 per cent of primary, 15 per cent of middle, and 18 per cent of secondary schools. Considering primary, middle and secondary schools in that order, 1.49, 1.72, 5.32 *incidents of violence* were reported per school, and 4.52, 6.16, 37.34 *incidents of disruptive behaviour* were reported for each type of school. As with the first survey, one is obliged to counsel caution about generalizing from such low return rates, and also, in the second survey, about the lack of objectivity in the teachers' perceptions and lack of account taken of the intensity of incidents. From his data Lowenstein concluded that incidents of violent and disruptive behaviour are more frequent in secondary schools, that boys are more involved than girls, and that the final year of schooling was the peak period. He found no evidence to associate these behaviour patterns with big schools, and legitimately notes that the figures may have been depressed because many teachers were reluctant to report problems in case it reflected on their competence.

A third NAS/UWT survey was conducted by Comber and Whitfield (1979), *Action on Indiscipline*, in which a questionnaire was sent to a representative sample of approximately 1,600 union members from whom 642 (40 per cent) completed returns were received. The purpose of the survey was to gather 'first hand accounts of recent incidents in schools, perceived as being stressful to the teacher which would serve as a basis for discussion on the nature and treatment of indiscipline'. Once again, from the low response rates, of which nearly half were nil returns, 'often backed by specific statements claiming that their school work never caused them considerable stress', it is difficult to agree with the authors' conclusions that, 'It is apparent that indiscipline in many schools is a serious problem impairing the efficiency of the school and imposing considerable stress on teachers' (Comber and Whitfield, 1979).

The Union also produced reports in 1976 and 1985. In the latter, its journal, *The Schoolmaster and Career Teacher*, invited members to report on *'Pupil Violence and Serious Disorder in Schools'* (1985), between September 1984 and February 1985. From just 3,910 replies out of a membership of over 10,000 they conclude that the survey 'has revealed a disturbing picture of the problems facing teachers in today's schools. Pupil violence towards teachers is no longer a headline grabbing exception, while occurrences such as pupil vandalism of teachers' personal property and verbal abuse toward teachers appears to be becoming commonplace' (NAS/UWT, 1985).

Most other teacher unions have eschewed major national surveys and confined themselves to expressing concern through documentary statements on indiscipline, for example, NUT (1976) and PAT (1985). Interestingly, the AMMA (1984) conducted a survey of assistant teachers on behaviour problems at infant and junior levels. Approximately three-quarters of the responding schools indicated a belief that there had been a 'marked deterioration' in young children's conduct and social training over the previous five years. But once again the response rate was low (31.2 per cent), and therefore the representativeness of the views expressed is questionable, as is the reliability of teachers' subjective assessment of behavioural trends over a five year period.

The criticisms made of these surveys is of their methodological weaknesses and as Laslett (1977) comments, 'The chief criticism is of the assumption that such surveys could produce reliable evidence'. Other evidence may support the unions' views, for they do represent the perceptions of very many members of the professions and so must be taken seriously, but it would be premature on the evidence to-date to claim that many of our schools are 'blackboard jungles'.

Government and local authorities

In 1973 a collaborative research project involving the DES and the Association of Education Committees circulated a questionnaire on violence and indiscipline in schools and received returns from sixty of the 100 local education authorities contacted — thus accounting for approximately 56 per cent of all primary pupils and about 57 per cent of secondary pupils in England and Wales. The main findings of the survey were:

1. The number of pupils in schools involved in incidents was proportionately very low, although noticeably greater in secondary than in primary schools.
2. About 60 per cent of the responding authorities thought that there had been no significant increase in misdemeanours.
3. Over three-quarters of responding authorities thought that boys were more involved in misbehaviour than girls.
4. There were proportionately three or four times as many incidents reported in the more densely populated areas.
5. The average size of primary and secondary schools involved in incidents was greater than the national average for these schools.
6. Much of the vandalism affecting schools had occurred out of normal hours.
7. Social problems related to home and community influences, in particular

marital break-up or domestic tension, were the factors mainly blamed for misbehaviour.

8. Better cooperation and communication, both within school and between schools and their local communities, were the remedies most often mentioned. Following these in order of frequency of mention came sound pastoral care arrangements, leadership and concern on the part of the headteacher and senior staff, and good supporting social agencies.

These general findings were supported by the Pack Report (SED, 1977) and the DES report on *Aspects of Secondary Education in England* (1979). The Pack Committee found no evidence to indicate that indiscipline was anywhere out of control in Scotland although there was thought to be an increase in some areas. More significantly, it gained the impression that it had 'to some extent changed in character in recent years, making it harder to combat and contain'. Two years later the DES survey of a 10 per cent sample of maintained secondary schools in England asked the headteachers of the 384 schools visited by inspectors to assess the extent of pupil behaviour problems in their own school. The overwhelming majority of schools indicated nothing worse than some minor problems of indiscipline, in fact, 64 per cent reported that they had no disruptive pupils and only 13 per cent estimated that they had ten or more. This general picture is supported by the HMI report on *'Good behaviour and discipline in schools'* (1987). The report is based on evidence gained from inspections since January 1983 and supplemented from special attention given to behaviour and discipline during visits to schools in the summer term of 1986.

> The general picture of behaviour within schools which emerges from these publications is that the overwhelming majority of schools are orderly communities in which there are good standards of behaviour and discipline; poor behaviour is unusual, and serious indiscipline a rare occurrence (DES, 1987).

These government surveys suffer from some of the problems associated with subjective assessments that were mentioned earlier. The probability exists that many headteachers would be reluctant to give HMI an adverse picture of their schools, and at the time of inspections it is most probable that everyone would be on their 'best' behaviour.

A number of local education authorities have produced reports on the incidence of disruptive behaviour, amongst them are Berkshire, Essex, Lancashire, Cumbria, Avon and Mid Glamorgan, but the more extensive reviews have been conducted by the ILEA. In 1978–79 the ILEA embarked on a massive extension of its provision of support centres such that a total of 2,280 places were created. More recently, the SERP (1984) survey into off-site units in England and Wales showed a steady growth of provision to 7,000 pupils. The point to note about these figures is that they only apply to extreme cases of violence and disruption, and therefore do not reflect the minor, daily infractions with which teachers have to cope. A similar observation applies to rates of suspensions and exclusions. As is the case with pupils placed in special units so the government does not gather national figures on suspensions and exclusions, and so, within the national profile of special needs the above pupils represent lost statistics. There are a number of reasons why the DES is reluctant to gather these data, and Galloway (1982) deals with them in detail. His most apposite observation is that:

> Disruptive pupils have become a politically sensitive issue. Collecting, let alone publishing, details about them could give the topic greater attention from educationalists than it deserves. Few administrators welcome public discussion, let alone public accountability. Yet if the issues are not discussed, there is a serious risk of decisions being based on administrative expediency rather than educational need.

Considering data on exclusions and suspensions, York *et al.* (1972) reported that thirty-one pupils were suspended from Edinburgh schools in a two year period (1967–69) from a total school population of 67,500. Similar figures were reported by Grunsell (1979) and Galloway (1976); for out of the seventy-four comprehensives in his fictitiously named Baxbridge LEA, Grunsell demonstrated how the figures may be distorted as the top three suspending schools contributed 45 per cent of the total and the top five, 60 per cent, over a period of three years. His figures of permanent suspensions were forty-two (1975), forty (1976), and sixty-three (1977). He thus concluded that the figures probably reflect a school's willingness to exclude rather than the degree of disruptive behaviour, and therefore 'there is no objective consistency in what the figures measure'.

Individual and local surveys

In this section space permits no more than a brief review of a number of small-scale surveys and the tenor of teachers' responses and perceptions of the problem. The advantage of small-scale surveys is that the research can be more thoroughly executed, yet, on the other hand, one has to be cautious about generalizing from the findings. McNamara (1975) requested the headteachers of 233 primary and forty-seven secondary schools to list their problem pupils. The average number of disrupters in secondary schools ranged from 1.5 per cent in selective grammar schools to 4.2 per cent in schools where there was the greatest concentration of social problems. In a study of sixty-one secondary schools Mills (1976) confirmed McNamara's relatively small numbers, and indicated a hard core of 3 per cent seriously disruptive in any one school, supported by another 10 per cent who occasionally got involved. The most frequent kinds of disruptive behaviour were found to be rejection of school uniform, persistent truancy, cutting lessons, refusal to work and cooperate in lessons, and individual misbehaviour which interrupted lessons. Physical assaults on teachers were most uncommon. A similar picture is provided by Rutter *et al.*'s (1979) research into twelve inner London secondary schools. During a twelve-week period of observation only one incident brought a lesson to a complete stop, and relatively little behaviour fell into their 'severe' category.

An American's analysis of disruption in English comprehensive schools is provided by Dierenfield (1982). His survey covered 125 schools in forty-one LEAs, and questionnaires were directed to headteachers or their deputies and six classroom teachers. He received 465 replies (53.1 per cent), of which 70 per cent were returned by classteachers; once again the response rate does not permit us to make inferences about the general secondary population. His findings on teacher estimates are contained in the following tables:

Question: 'How would you assess the extent of classroom disruption in comprehensive schools?'

Extent of Disruption	*Percentage*
Not really a problem	7·7
Only a mild difficulty	19·3
A problem but one which it is possible to cope with	67·8
A severe situation	3·6
Totally out of control	0·0

Question: 'In what direction do you believe disruption has been moving during your experience in comprehensive schools?'

Becoming *less* severe	8·7
Remaining about the same	49·3
Becoming *more* severe	40·4

It is possible for the above figures to be interpreted in either direction, but the general findings from the survey would indicate that whilst most teachers are concerned about classroom disruption it is not conceived of as a critical problem. There was substantial agreement about the factors which could control indiscipline, and the five regarded as the most effective in rank order were positive teacher personality, effective teaching methods, establishing and maintaining classroom standards early on, support from senior colleagues, and consistent application of behaviour standards to all pupils. By comparison, measures such as streaming, special units, expulsions, or corporal punishment, were not deemed to be worthwhile solutions to the problem behaviour.

Finally, a number of projects have been conducted by a team at Goldsmiths' College, and in Lawrence, Steed and Young (1984) they present a detailed analysis of two systematic 'whole-school' studies in a boys' senior high school and an all-through 11–18 coeducational school. In both instances the research lasted one week and involved issuing all staff with a standard form to record incidents in detail, interviews and observation. In the first study data on 101 incidents was collected and on 144 incidents in the second case-study. The types of behaviour stressed by teachers were refusal to be taught, general disruption, doing no work, tardiness in settling, refusal to obey, and insolence.

In 1986 Lawrence *et al.* extended their interest in disruptive behaviour to include primary schools. Eight-five schools from forty local education authorities cooperated, and the schools were designated by the LEAs as having potentially 'difficult', 'average', or 'easy' intakes, and in most cases the headteacher's categorization was in agreement. Most pertinently 62 per cent of headteachers expressed the view that over the last ten years the onset of disruptive behaviour was getting earlier. A rank order of types of behaviour listed as occurring earlier was not listening, poor concentration, aggression towards other pupils, disobedience, and bad or abusive language. Teachers in the schools were also asked to complete an 'incident sheet' similar to the one used in the secondary schools; and on a randomly chosen day 587 staff reported a total of 312 incidents mentioning disobedience, aggression and defiance in one third of the cases. In a useful review of research into the prevalence and persistence of aggressive behaviour in children aged 3–7 Laing and Chazan (1986) suggest that 'most nursery staff and infant school teachers will have at least one moderately or severely aggressive child in their class'. The most disconcerting aspect of these findings, once allowance has been made for any methodological weaknesses, is that the problem of disruptive behaviour is not mainly to be found in secondary schools but that it also needs to be monitored and tackled in primary schools.

From this review it will be evident that research into the incidence of disruptive pupil behaviour is beset with problems. The emergence of the problem itself is not recent but the available hard data are limited, and also suspect, because of methodological and statistical difficulties. What is more, the research projects are very different in form and style which prevents data comparisons with any great confidence.

The aetiology of disruptive behaviour

Tracing the causes of disruptive behaviour is plagued with difficulties as the previous two sections will have conveyed. One problem is the recency of interest in this form of deviant behaviour when compared with the work done on truancy, delinquency and maladjustment. And although there may be a measure of association between disruption and the other behaviours they are not one and the same, and there are as many differences between them as there are similarities. For this reason transposition of research findings needs to be selectively and cautiously applied. It is also the case that behaviour is not influenced by a single cause but by a complexity of factors including innate, familial, societal and educational influences. 'The child is at the centre of a matrix of interrelated forces, each of which acts as a potential stimulus to the child's own capacity to respond' (Fontana, 1985). But before examining causal association we should sound a cautionary note about taking a too deterministic position. It was evident from the interviews conducted by Tattum (1982) that the extremely disruptive pupils involved in the study were fully aware of the extremity of their actions and actually chose when and whose class they would disrupt. They were not driven by inner forces but consciously directed the nature, direction and intensity of their behaviour. This alternative position does not deny that previous experiences may have predisposed them to act and react in an aggressive way; furthermore, social interactions, as between teacher and pupil, do not exist in a vacuum but have social histories and are staged within a social setting and audience. It is with this interactionist perspective foremost that studies of the aetiology of disruptive behaviour will be discussed within two broad categories; firstly, the child, the family and society; and secondly, the school and the education system.

The child, family and society

Approaches which concentrate exclusively, or even predominantly, on locating the cause of deviant behaviour in the individual have been heavily criticized, mainly because the 'child-deficit' model individualizes the problem and so fails to give due regard to environmental factors. However, the majority of those who would emphasize the role of personality on deviant behaviour would also acknowledge the importance of home and other influences, and so it would be mistaken of us if we ignored the fact that innate factors may play some part in determining personality and social behaviour, for 'among the many millions of children in our schools there will certainly be a number who are disadvantaged by neurological impairment, and in some cases this will find expression in disruptive behaviour' (Frude, 1984).

Herbert (1978) classifies the behaviour of the disrupter in the 'conduct disorder' dimension as opposed to a 'personality problem' dimension, although he does emphasize that the labels must not be rigidly interpreted as 'both problems are personality expressions and both affect conduct'. Rutter (1975) also argues for a 'mixed' category of conduct and personality disorders, and in a consideration of conduct disorders he expresses the opinion that 'the problem lies in the interaction between the child and his environment, and not just within the child himself'. Supportive interpretations of the above come from research into troublesome children with physical impairment of a congenital origin; for example, West (1982) in his study of delinquents; Wolff (1967) when comparing children with adverse obstetric histories; and Stott (1966), who, in his intensive study of thirty-three troublesome children, found that in twenty-six cases with symptoms of somatic-neural impairment, it was more likely that their difficult behaviour arose from the fact that physical problems made the children more susceptible to stress in certain situations than a direct causal link between condition and behaviour.

As the main agency of socialization the family is regarded as having prime responsibility for inappropriate or inadequate social learning. In a further consideration of conduct disorders Rutter (1975) distinguishes between 'socialized delinquency' and 'unsocialized aggressive behaviour', and summarizes the temperament of conduct disordered children as impulsive, unpredictable and unmalleable; also aggressive and assertive in their relationships, showing little feeling for others. Most significantly he presents a depressing picture of family life from which discordant relationships extend into other interpersonal relations. Child-rearing practices display inconsistent and ineffective displays of affection. Supportive findings are in the work of Hoffman (1970), West (1982), and Lefkowitz *et al.* (1977), whose longitudinal study of over 800 ten-year-olds found that the most violent boys came from homes where parental control was either permissive or harshly punitive. From these and other findings it is evident that interventionist strategies would need to be directed towards the family, and, more specifically, parent-training schemes. Having first noted how ill-developed this area of intervention really is, Topping (1986), in his review of various programmes, observes that 'many successes have been achieved, and indeed some workers report better effectiveness via direct work with parents than via direct work with children or both combined'.

Extending our review into the neighbourhood and peer group influences, the subcultural model of deviance demonstrates how delinquency is bound up with the prevailing way of life and social traditions transmitted from one generation to another (Mays, 1972). And Miller (1958) argues that lower working-class culture is characterized by six 'focal concerns': trouble, toughness, smartness, excitement, fate and autonomy. It is evident that such 'concerns' are contrary to the authority structure of schools and if displayed would present teachers with severe discipline problems.

Family, community and school do not exist apart from the wider influences of society. The conflictual nature of the relationship between family and school, and the influence of current trends and movements in wider society is fully expressed in the Pack Report (SED, 1977):

> According to the Evidence, society affects the schools mainly through the attitudes of parents, values derived from the media and the changed approach to moral questions generally associated with the 'permissive society'. The Committee sees the latter as conflicting with the school because a wider section of society now accepts or at least tolerates standards of behaviour that were previously considered unacceptable and which schools by and large strive to resist. Children have always been confronted, sooner or later, with different standards from which to choose, but today the gap is wider and more widely spread through the community. The same problem of double standards arises in relation to violence and crime, which is increasing and to which children are more and more exposed through what they see and experience. This, too, poses a dilemma for children — to imitate or not.

Adverse societal influences frequently cited are violence on TV, pornographic literature, video-nasties, and also, teenage sex, drinking, glue-sniffing and drugs. Those who maintain that television is a contributory factor in the causal chain of behaviour problems may do so from different standpoints. Social learning theorists would claim that children may display aggressive behaviour as a consequence of modelling actions seen on the screen. Alternatively, others may hold to the view that exposure to violence may be emotionally and physically arousing; whilst a third position may argue that repeated exposure may dull sensibilities or inhibitions. Research by Belson (1978), and Eysenck and Nias (1978), would appear to confirm the causal relationship between the mass media and violent behaviour, but Gunter (1984) counsels caution against too simplistic an interpretation. He argues that not only can it divert our attention away from other social problems but also that wholesome television programmes may actually counteract the antisocial content and facilitate good behaviour in children.

On 'video nasties' Hartshorn (1983) found that a high percentage of children viewed them, and Reid (1983) suggests that their influence may be much greater than has hitherto been appreciated. Finally, some findings have indicated that the levels of lead in the atmosphere may adversely affect intellectual ability and behaviour (Yule *et al.*, 1984), and it is also suggested that food additives and diet deficiencies could cause hyperactivity with the resultant symptoms of destructiveness, excitability and unpredictable behaviour (Weiss, 1982).

The school and the education system

Over the last twenty years there have been cumulative research findings to support the contention that aspects of school organization, policy and practice can affect the learning and behaviour of children in attendance. Earlier research worked mainly on the premise that schools were sufficiently similar in basic organization, curriculum and teaching methods so that any variation in outcome was due mainly to the nature and quality of the intake (Douglas, 1964; Plowden, 1967; Davie *et al.*, 1972; Jenks, 1972). In an influential paper Bernstein (1970) argued that 'education cannot compensate for society'. The more recent 'school effectiveness' literature (Rutter, 1983; Reynolds, 1985) also recognizes that children arrive at school with different attitudes, expectations and behaviour patterns but that some schools 'rather than support pupils with personal problems and difficulties actually contribute to their difficulties and exacerbate the pupil's problems. Conversely, there are schools which provide a supportive atmosphere for their pupils which is conducive to good behaviour and academic success' (Tattum, 1984). In other words, 'schools do make a difference'.

An early, influential study into the effects of schooling on anti-social behaviour, irrespective of the nature of the intake and catchment area, was by Power *et al.* (1967; 1972), who examined the differential delinquency rates in twenty secondary schools in Tower Hamlets. Broadly similar findings were produced by Gath and colleagues (1977), although they were concerned to investigate probation rates and rates of referral to child psychiatrists both from primary and secondary schools in Croydon. In a study of schools in Sheffield Galloway (1980) found no linear relationship between the numbers of exclusions and suspensions from schools and their catchment areas — thus supporting an earlier study into persistent absenteeism (Galloway, 1976). A within-school factor which showed some connection with high rates was whether a school during its reorganization included a selective school in its composite institution — a factor more related to teacher attitudes towards pupils' work and behaviour than physical resources. Further research into in-school influences has been carried out by Reynolds (1976) and Reynolds and Sullivan (1979), who found that the more successful schools in their South Wales sample included a high proportion of senior pupils in authority positions, lower levels of institutional control and use of corporal punishment, smaller school size, and more favourable teacher-pupil ratios. A significant finding concerning teacher-pupil relationships was what Reynolds called 'a truce', whereby teachers judiciously enforced rules governing such sensitive matters as dress, smoking, and gum-chewing. Finally, the Rutter team (1979), from their sample of twelve inner London comprehensive schools, chose to measure attendance rates, delinquency rates, in-school behaviour, and public examination results. They found considerable variation between schools on all four measures even when pupil intake had been allowed for; and invariably those schools which were successful on one outcome tended to do well on the others and vice versa. The study found no measurable association between the indicators of school outcome and institutional features such as school size and buildings, teacher-pupil ratios and size of class, or school resources. What did emerge was that the more successful schools had an identifiable 'ethos' which Mortimore (1980), one of the co-authors, summarized under five main general headings:

1. A common staff policy on behaviour to encourage consistency.
2. Positive staff attitudes towards pupils' academic progress were reflected in improved behaviour.
3. Teachers presented themselves as good models in the way they prepared and conducted their lessons.
4. The use of effective praise and rewards was strongly related to good behaviour.
5. There was less misbehaviour where conditions were pleasant and pupils were encouraged to take on responsibilities and participate in school activities.

Each of these studies has been criticized; for example, the Rutter study has been criticized because of the selection of intake variables, choice of schools, and statistical analysis (Goldstein, 1980; Hargreaves, 1980). And yet, despite these criticisms the studies do focus our attention on the context in which the unwanted behaviour occurs, and if only part of the problem lies within the school itself then it is an area over which teachers have some control.

An alternative approach to understanding why children behave in an extreme way is to ask the pupils. Applying Mills' (1940) concept 'vocabularies of motive' Tattum (1982) provides the subjective accounts of twenty-nine disruptive pupils who were interviewed and observed during their placement in a special unit. As a group they made no attempt to deny that they had behaved very badly — though in each case they were able to explain or justify their behaviour. There was nothing exceptional in their justifications, but as Mills explains, motives are learned from others through socialization into approved or disapproved ways of behaving. The accounts therefore draw upon the culture and language of the school and in that respect support some of the findings described in the previous section.

1. It was the teacher's fault.
2. Being treated with disrespect.
3. Inconsistency of rule application.
4. We were only messing — having a laugh.
5. It's the fault of the school system.

In their vocabularies they range from blaming teacher to blaming the system — which is not surprising, 'but it is not the general attribution of blame that is important but the specific things that they point to that is of value. For whilst these pupils are the extreme exponents of disruptive behaviour they do not stand in isolation from *all* other pupils ... Other pupils misbehave and many are critical of aspects of school life, and it is this knowledge that should make us take their words seriously as they are, by their actions and outbursts, drawing attention to features which their less demonstrative peers also find frustrating, distressing, and unjust' (Tattum, 1982). In fact, most of the recent work on disruptive behaviour indicate schools to be generators of anti-authority identities and attitudes in young people (Bird *et al.*, 1980; Galloway *et al.*, 1982; Schostak, 1983; Lawrence *et al.*, 1984).

Many pupils are disaffected, harbouring negative feelings towards schooling, and the pupils in Tattum (1982) criticized teachers who did not respect them as 'persons', because they showed no respect for their feelings or concern for their welfare, or as 'pupils', because they showed little interest in their progress and attainment. Branch *et al.* (1977) demonstrated a significant relationship between low self-concept as a learner and disruptive behaviour. McGuiness and Craggs (1986) refer to the pathogenic effect of schools, and Hargreaves (1982) is critical of the unintended, but no less damaging, effects of the hidden curriculum on the dignity and sense of worth of many pupils. As one adolescent girl caustically remarked, 'School is for learning, but all it learnt me is that I'm no good for anything' (Tattum, 1982), and so rejection of school and all it represents may be a self-defensive mechanism against further assaults on self-esteem. But, once again, we must be cautious about drawing simplistic cause and effect linkages, for, as Fontana (1985) observes, some children experience personal and family problems which may cause them to feel vulnerable and insecure. 'Their need for attention and sympathy may lead them into attention-seeking behaviours ... unreasonable demands on teacher's time and energies. Or they may start deliberately performing badly in class ...' (Fontana, 1985). Continuing with the theme of teacher-pupil relations, Wilson and Herbert (1978), when writing about families who live in circumstances of poverty, comment that, 'Children adapt to family and neighbourhood, but in doing so they become maladapted to school'. A further application of the inappropriate socialization thesis encourages us to see behaviour problems as a lack of the social skills necessary to meet teachers' expectations or adequately cope with adult authority relations, that is, they fail to 'please teacher'.

Finally, in this section on the school, it is important that reference be made to teaching skills and classroom management, and the nature of the curriculum and its relationships to external examinations. Treatment can but be very brief as these are massive issues, each in its own right. Teaching is a highly skilled activity which can be learned and improved through study, experiment and practice, and this applies to teachers at every phase of their professional career. In recent years the growth in the research and literature on effective classroom techniques has been extensive, including Robertson (1981); Wragg (1984); Kyriacou (1986); Bull and Solity (1987). For just as effective teaching can prevent unwanted behaviour so ineffective teaching can precipitate and escalate problem behaviour. Hargreaves *et al.* (1975) distinguish between the 'deviance-proactive' and 'deviance-insulative' teacher. In summary, the former thinks that it is impossible to provide conditions under which difficult pupils will work, and in 'disciplinary matters he sees his interaction with these pupils as a contest or battle ... He is unable to "de-fuse" difficult situations'. In contrast the latter believes that these pupils want to work and if they do not work the conditions are assumed to be at fault. 'He believes that these conditions can be changed and that it is his responsibility to initiate that change.' In disciplinary matters he is firm and believes that is what they prefer — he avoids confrontations. Whilst it is unlikely that any teacher fits exactly into either type the model does provide a continuum along which teachers range in their attitudes and relationships with pupils.

The school curriculum serves individual, societal and vocational functions, but to be accepted by children it must be seen to be interesting and relevant to their lives and needs. One problem is that the secondary school curriculum in particular is too academically orientated and serves a narrow purpose and clientele, despite recent innovations to modify this situation. Unfortunately, where the 'hot-house' climate exists it rewards the successful and accentuates the feelings of failure in many other youngsters.

Coping with disruptive behaviour

A *crisis-management response*

A major response to disruptive behaviour has been the establishment of a new type of educational provision, namely, the special unit. They have proliferated throughout the United Kingdom and are known by various labels, such as school support unit, adjustment unit, pupil placement unit or exclusive unit — more emotive names are 'sin-bins' or 'mini-borstals'. In some cases they are attached to a school and pupils may be placed there for all or some of their lessons. Off-site units usually serve a number of schools, they may be physically and administratively independent; and pupils may attend them on a part-time or full-time basis. In most instances the pupils remain on the roll of their school. Many questions about the benefits and disadvantages of units have not been adequately addressed; the most detailed evaluative study was by the ILEA (Mortimore *et al.*, 1983), whilst other reviews may be found in Lloyd-Smith (1984), Topping (1983).

The peak year for the setting up of special units was 1974, and in a DES survey it was found that in 1977 as many as sixty-nine of the ninety-six English LEAs had one or more units, giving a total of 239 units providing 3962 pupil places (HMI, 1978b). Evidence of further expansion in the 1970s was provided by ACE (1980) in a survey which indicated the existence of units in Scotland, Wales, the Isle of Man and the Channel Islands. The total number was markedly increased in 1979 when ILEA approved 240 support centres to accommodate 2,280 pupils; and the latest national survey by the Social Education Research Project (Ling and Davies, 1984), found that there had been a further increase of 140 per cent in off-site units compared with the DES figures (HMI, 1978b). In a survey of European countries Lawrence *et al.* (1986) found that few countries had adopted segregation as a solution to school behaviour problems. Most had initiated schemes to tackle the problem where it occurs, in the school and classroom.

In an analysis of the characteristics of pupils in ILEA centres West *et al.* (1986) found that the majority were in the 14–16 age group (60 per cent); boys outnumbered girls by a 2 : 1 ratio; children classified as Caribbean were disproportionately represented, as were pupils whose parents were in semi-skilled or unskilled occupations. The research team also expressed concern about the quality of the curriculum and the difficulties associated with reintegrating pupils into mainstream schools. Following a review of its off-site provision, ILEA (5042 and 5141) recommended that there should be a reduction in their numbers and that they should be larger so that they could offer a broader curriculum and reduce the feeling of professional isolation experienced by many staff. Even more constructively, it was recommended that there was a need to change the concept of where units actually fit into a local authority's provision for children with special needs, so that larger units could become centres of alternative education which would offer pupils something worthwhile in educational terms.

In Tattum (1985) three critical questions are asked about the social control function of special units.

1. *Who benefits from the transfer?*

   In most cases the interests of other pupils and teachers are probably given priority concern, which runs contrary to the entire philosophy of children with special needs where the interests of the child are paramount.

2. *Who decides and on the basis of what information?*

   Local authorities have widely varying admissions procedures, from a multi-disciplinary team to a single person (Tattum, 1982). Behavioural criteria are problematic because of their subjectivity, and the measurement schedules available only describe behaviour, concentrate on negative aspects, and focus on the individual pupils without taking teacher-pupil interaction into account.

3. *What are the functions of units?*

Their functions have been variously described as *diagnostic* and *therapeutic*, but negative elements of *containment* and *punishment* are implicit in their place in the system. Units must have an *educative* function, but the quality of physical provision and education is unacceptable in many cases (HMI, 1978b; Dawson, 1980; Topping, 1983).

Units conform to a crisis-management approach to disruptive behaviour in that they can only cope in a negative and reactive way with a small number of extreme cases. For this reason they will continue, and as a result of the abolition of corporal punishment in 1987 the pressure will increase for their proliferation. Finally, there are many sound educational reasons for the support of on-site units in preference to off-site (Tattum, 1982).

Interventionist approaches

Whilst units will continue to cater for a minority of disruptive pupils, alternative approaches which focus less on the individual pupil and more on the context and interaction need to be developed. Intervention in a school or classroom may be carried out by individuals. Topping (1986) considers the strengths and handicaps of consultancy by educational psychologists, local authority advisors, peripatetic support teachers, and higher education teachers, and advocates the 'problem-solving model' of problem specification, data collection, objective setting, intervention, and evaluation. The objective is to work with schools to initiate person and/or organizational change.

The individual change agent approach has been extended into a peripatetic team approach by a number of local authorities. Griffiths (1981) described how a 'Special Education Team' operates on an itinerant casework basis with disruptive pupils in twenty-three comprehensive schools in a northern LEA. The team consists of six teachers who are invited to work within schools, sometimes on a one-to-one basis with a particular pupil, or to negotiate a strategy with a teacher or group of teachers. Because each problem is different the emphasis is on flexibility in the process of problem analysis and negotiated intervention. Similar teams exist in a number of other authorities, but the best documented operations are the two 'Schools Support Teams' in ILEA. Coulby and Harper (1985) describe in detail the development of one team's objectives and procedures from its 1979 date of operation. When at full strength it consisted of a teacher-in-charge, twelve scale three teachers, an educational psychologist, a clerical officer, and a senior educational welfare officer. One teacher was responsible for running a small class of secondary pupils at the Centre. In all, the team catered for the eighty primary schools and fifteen secondary schools in the Borough. The area is divided into 'patches', so that two or three team members are responsible for working in all the primary and secondary schools in that patch. This means that during a given week a support teacher would work in a range of settings — schools, classrooms, pupils' homes, other agencies; work with a number of different teachers, other adults, and pupils; and face a multiplicity of presenting problems. The role is a challenging and stressful one, and 'team teachers need not only training and supervision, but support and advice. These are provided through the processes of induction, consultation, and in-service training' (Coulby and Harper, 1985). The team also has a five-stage model — referral, assessment, formulation, intervention, and evaluation, which can be applied at different levels — pupil, classroom, school, and LEA, and, as such, can take account of how change at one level may affect others.

Describing similar operations in the other support team Lane (1986) subscribes strongly to an interactionist approach to behaviour problems. 'Deviance in schools is not a product of specific deficits in the child or the school; it is an interactive, dynamic process'. It is that interaction which is the main focus of attention and therefore the success of the team's interventionist programmes depend upon 'the combined efforts of the schools, the children, the families, other agencies, and the centre in pooling resources and skills to meet complex problems and the use of validated techniques of analysis and intervention. The importance of that partnership has been established at the experimental, theoretical, and practical level' (Lane, 1986). Regardless of the level or nature of the intervention specific principles should be followed and Lane (1986) provides an excellent framework for application:

1. No intervention can be predetermined in advance of the situation and the construction of a formulation which explains why the behaviour occurs in a given context. An intervention has to be based on the formulation.
2. As far as possible, interventions should take place in the context in which difficulties were reported.
3. The principle is maintained that any action taken should be aimed at the minimum level of intervention necessary to achieve agreed objectives in the setting.
4. The range of response offered should be flexible, to ensure rapid movement between levels of intervention, as necessary.

Preventative approaches

The two previous sections on coping strategies are reactive, in that they are a response to a problem; how much better for a school to create policies which are proactive, that is, they initiate practices which are anticipatory and so reduce the incidence of indiscipline throughout the pupil body. Therefore, the recommendation in this section is the adoption of a 'whole-school approach' to discipline (Watkins and Wagner, 1987; Tattum, 1988). In working towards a whole-school approach the aim is to create an ethos of good order supported by a system of monitoring pupil behaviour and progress. Ethos has both content and process (Purkey and Smith, 1982). Content refers to policy, structure and curriculum, and process refers to the school culture, quality of social relationships, and channels of communication. To achieve and maintain a whole-school policy there is need for coherence and consistency within the content and process of effective management (Tattum, 1986). *Coherence* refers to the ways by which policies, plans and procedures are formulated and articulated. *Consistency* refers to the actions taken by everyone to put the policies and practices into operation. In this way discipline and social control are regarded as an integral part of the entire teaching function, involving curriculum, pastoral care, class management, teacher-pupil and teacher-parent relations, rules and regulations, rewards and punishments, amongst others.

Tattum (1988) discusses four steps a school must follow in developing a whole-school, preventative approach to discipline.

1. Teachers, ancillary staff and pupils, need to be involved in the creation and review of the policy and practice for better understanding and commitment. How individual schools set about devising a policy will vary, but one model is to set up a working group so that the proposals are democratically arrived at. The school may then set aside an INSET day to discuss the programme and decide priorities for a staff development programme. Material available to assist schools in in-service training include *Preventative Approaches to Disruption* (Chisholm *et al.*, 1986); *Finding Answers to Disruption* (Grunsell, 1985).

2. If the rationale and application of the policy are to be understood it must be articulated to all adult members of the school, pupils, parents, and governors.

3. If a positive ethos is to be established then staff need to present and conduct themselves as good models as they display their commitment to the agreed policy. Disruptive pupils were highly critical of teachers who were inconsistent in the way they applied school rules, and also of those teachers who failed to apply similar disciplinary expectations to their own behaviour as they did to the pupils (Tattum, 1982).

4. Schools need to keep accurate, up-to-date records of pupil attainment and behaviour. Various methods of record-keeping may be adopted, but any scheme is only as good as the diligence shown by teachers in recording events, and the specific and explicit nature of their comments on the incident and misbehaviour.

A whole-school approach to discipline is therefore predicated on the belief that good order and a positive learning environment are created when *all* members of staff accept responsibility for the behaviour of *all* pupils, not only in their own classrooms, but as they move about the school. In working towards a developmental, preventative approach a school needs to address a number of internal sub-systems, some of which will be listed below with supportive references. An effective pastoral system is central to a whole-school approach (Watkins and Wagner, 1987; Tattum, 1988), with a constructive function given to the pastoral tutor to improve pupil self-confidence and self-esteem. Integrated with the pastoral tutor's role is the development of teaching and class management skills across the school, and Jones (1986) reviews trends and critical issues in this field from the United States. (Some recent UK literature is listed on page 20.) Lawrence *et al.* (1984) provide a list of coping strategies when dealing with indiscipline, and Bowers (1986) deals with an area of growing interest and importance, namely, conflict management. Schools are rule-governed organizations and therefore it is essential that schools regularly review their rules and regulations (Tattum, 1982), whilst in America 'school discipline plans' (Duke, 1986) are to be found in many school districts, which, in essence provide a detailed code of expected behaviour and a graduated list of consequences according to severity and frequency of rule infringement. Finally, in their thinking about good order and discipline schools have been too preoccupied with the negative aspects of punishment to the neglect of a constructive approach through praise and encouragement, rewards and incentives (Tattum, 1988). In the HMI review of 'good behaviour and discipline in schools' (DES, 1987) it was found that, 'The *balance* between rewards and sanctions, in both policy and practice, is a useful touchstone of a school's approach to maintaining good standards of behaviour'.

In summary, one can but conclude that the majority of schools are not facing crises of indiscipline, and although the media may focus on the excessive acts of pupil violence and aggression, the problems faced daily by the vast majority of teachers are low-key, but nonetheless frustrating, irritating and stressful. The trend in our understanding and coping with disruptive behaviour is also in keeping with this analysis, that is, to progress from individualizing blame, to focusing on the school as an organization, which, by its policies and practices can, either, create a climate of dissension and disaffection, or a positive ethos of whole-school concern for mutual respect, high expectations, and an orderly community.

References

ADVISORY CENTRE FOR EDUCATION (1980) 'Disruptive Units', *Where*, 158, pp. 6–7.
ARIÉS, P. (1960) *Centuries of Childhood*, Harmondsworth, Penguin Books.
ASSISTANT MASTERS and MISTRESSES ASSOCIATION (AMMA) (1984) *The Reception Class Today*, Report, 7 (1), pp. 6–9.
BELSON, W. A. (1978) *Television, Violence and the Adolescent Boy*, London, Saxon House.
BERNSTEIN, B. (1970) 'Education cannot compensate for society', *New Society*', 26 February, pp. 344–7.
BIRD, C., CHESSUM, R., FURLONG, J. and JOHNSON, D. (1980) *Disaffected Pupils*, Brunel University, Education Studies Unit.
BOOTH, T., and COULBY, D. (eds.) (1987) *Producing and Reducing Disaffection*, Milton Keynes, Open University Press.
BOWERS, A. (1986) 'Interpersonal Skills and Conflict Management', in TATTUM, D. P. *Management of Disruptive Pupil Behaviour in Schools*, London, Fulton.
BRANCH, C., DAMICO, S. and PURKEY, W. (1977) 'A comparison between the self-concepts as learners of disruptive and non-disruptive middle school students', *Middle School Journal*, 7, pp. 15–16.

BULL, S. L. and SOLITY, J. E. (1987) *Classroom Management: Principles to Practice,* Beckenham, Croom Helm.

CHISHOLM, B., KEARNEY, D., KNIGHT, G., LITTLE, H., MORRIS, S. and TWEDDLE, D. (1986) *Preventive Approaches to Disruption: Developing Teaching Skills,* London, MacMillan.

COHEN, L. and COHEN, A. (eds.) (1987) *Disruptive Behaviour: A Sourcebook for Teachers,* London, Harper and Row.

COMBER, L. C. and WHITFIELD, R. C. (1979) 'Action on indiscipline: A practical guide for teachers', NAS/UWT in association with the Department of Educational Enquiry, University of Aston.

CORRIGAN, P. (1979) *Schooling the Smash Street Kids,* London, MacMillan.

COULBY, D. and HARPER, T. (1985) *Preventing Classroom Disruption,* Beckenham, Croom Helm.

DAVIE, R., BUTLER, N. and GOLDSTEIN, H. (1972) *From Birth to Seven,* London, Longman in association with National Children's Bureau.

DAWSON, R. L. (1980) *Special Provision for Disturbed Pupils: A Survey,* London, Macmillan.

DENSCOMBE, M. (1985) *Classroom Control: A Sociological Perspective,* London, Allen and Unwin.

DEPARTMENT OF EDUCATION AND SCIENCE (1983) 'Assessments and Statements of Special Educational Needs', Circular 1/83, London, HMSO.

DIERENFIELD, R. B. (1982) 'Classroom Disruption in English Comprehensive Schools', Minnesota, Macalester College, St Paul.

DOCKING, J. W. (1987) *Control and Discipline in Schools,* 2nd ed., London, Harper and Row.

DOUGLAS, J. W. B. (1964) *The Home and the School,* London, MacGibbon and Kee.

DUKE, D. L. (1986) 'School discipline plans and the quest for order in American schools', in TATTUM, D. P. *Management of Disruptive Pupil Behaviour in Schools,* London, Fulton.

EYSENCK, H. J. and NIAS, D. K. B. (1978) *Sex, Violence and the Media,* London, Temple Smith.

FEINGOLD, B. F. (1985) *Why Your Child Is Hyperactive,* New York, Random House.

FONTANA, D. (1985) *Classroom Control,* London, British Psychological Society and Methuen.

FORD, J., MONGON, D. and WHELAN, M. (1982) *Special Education and Social Control: Invisible Disasters,* London, Routledge and Kegan Paul.

FRUDE, N. and GAULT, H. (eds.) (1984) *Disruptive Behaviour in Schools,* Chichester, Wiley.

FURLONG, V. J. (1985) *The Deviant Pupil,* Milton Keynes, Open University Press.

GALLOWAY, D. M. (1976) 'Size of school, socioeconomic hardship, suspension rates and persistent unjustified absence from school', *British Journal of Educational Psychology,* 4, pp. 40–47.

GALLOWAY, D. M. (1980) 'Exclusion and suspension from school', *Trends in Education,* 2, pp. 33–38.

GALLOWAY, D. M. (1985) *Schools, Pupils and Special Educational Needs,* London, Croom Helm.

GALLOWAY, D. M., BALL, T., BLOMFIELD, D. and SEYD, R. (1982) *Schools and Disruptive Pupils,* London, Longman.

GATH, D., COOPER, B., GATTONI, F. and ROCKETT, D. (1977) *Child Guidance and Delinquency in a London Borough*, Oxford, Oxford University Press.

GILLHAM, B. (ed.) (1981) *Problem Behaviour in the Secondary School*, Beckenham, Croom Helm.

GOLDSTEIN, H. (1980) 'Fifteen thousand hours: A review of the statistical procedures', *Journal of Child Psychology and Psychiatry*, 21, pp. 363–69.

GRIFFITHS, D. (1981) 'A team approach to disruption', *Forward Trends*, 1. pp. 8–10.

GRUNSELL, R. (1980) *Beyond Control? Schools and Suspension*, London, Writers and Readers.

GRUNSELL, R. (1985) *Finding Answers to Disruption: Discussion Exercises for Secondary Teachers*, London, Longman.

GUNTER, B. (1984) 'Television as a facilitator of good behaviour amongst children', *Journal of Moral Education*, 13, pp. 152–59.

HARGREAVES, A. (1980) 'Review of Fifteen Thousand Hours', *British Journal of Sociology of Education*, 1, pp. 211–16.

HARGREAVES, D. H. (1982) *The Challenge For The Comprehensive School*, London, Routledge and Kegan Paul.

HARGREAVES, D. H., HESTER, S. K. and MELLOR, F. J. (1975) *Deviance in Classrooms*, London, Routledge and Kegan Paul.

HARTSHORN, D. J. (1983) 'Children and video films at home', *Educational Studies*, 9, pp. 145–50.

HERBERT, M. (1978) *Conduct Disorders of Childhood and Adolescence*, Chichester, Wiley.

HER MAJESTY'S INSPECTORATE (1978a) *Truancy and Behavioural Problems in some Urban Schools*, London, HMSO.

HER MAJESTY'S INSPECTORATE (1978b) *Behavioural Units: A Survey of Special Units for Pupils with Behavioural Problems*, London, HMSO.

HER MAJESTY'S INSPECTORATE (1979) *Aspects of Secondary Education in England*, London, HMSO.

HER MAJESTY'S INSPECTORATE (1987) *Education Observed 5: Good Behaviour and Discipline in Schools*, London, HMSO.

HOFFMAN, M. L. (1970) 'Conscience, personality and socialisation techniques', *Human Development*, 13, pp. 90–126.

JENKS, C. (1972) *Inequality: A Reassessment of the Effect of Family and Schooling in America*, New York: Basic Books.

JONES, V. F. (1986) 'Classroom management in the United States: Trends and critical issues', in TATTUM, D. P. *Management of Disruptive Pupil Behaviour in Schools*, London, Fulton.

LAING, A. F., and CHAZAN, M. (1986) 'The management of aggressive behaviour in young children', in TATTUM, D. P. *Management of Disruptive Pupil Behaviour in Schools*, London, Fulton.

LAING, A. F., and CHAZAN, M. (1987) *Teachers' Strategies in Coping with Behaviour Difficulties in First Year Junior School Children*, Maidstone, Association of Workers for Maladjusted Children.

LANE, D. A. (1986) 'Promoting positive behaviour in the classroom', in TATTUM, D. P. *Management of Disruptive Pupil Behaviour in Schools*, London, Fulton.

LASLETT, R. (1977) 'Disruptive and violent pupils: the facts and fallacies', *Education Review*, 29, pp. 152–62.

LAWRENCE, J., STEED, D. and YOUNG, P. (1984) *Disruptive Children — Disruptive Schools?* London, Croom Helm.

LAWRENCE, J., STEED, D. and YOUNG, P. (1986) 'The Management of Disruptive Behaviour in Western Europe', in TATTUM, D. P. *Management of Disruptive Pupil Behaviour in Schools*, London, Fulton.

LAWSON, J. and SILVER, H. (1973) *A Social History of Education in England*, London, Methuen.

LLOYD-SMITH, M. (1984) *Disrupted Schooling*, London, Murray.

LOWENSTEIN, L. F. (1972) *Violence in Schools and its Treatment*, Hemel Hempstead, National Association of Schoolmasters.

LOWENSTEIN, L. F. (1975) *Violent and Disruptive Behaviour in Schools*, Hemel Hempstead, National Association of Schoolmasters.

MAYS, J. D. (ed.) (1972) *Juvenile Delinquency, the Family and the Social Group*, London, Longman.

McGUINESS, J. and CRAGGS, D. (1986) 'Disruption as a school-generated problem', in TATTUM, D. F. *Management and Pupil Behaviour in Schools*, London, Fulton.

McNAMARA, D. (1975) 'Distribution and incidence of problem children in an English county', Paper presented to the British Association (Paper L251).

MARSH, P., ROSSER, E. and HARRÉ, R. (1978) *The Rules of Disorder*, London, Routledge and Kegan Paul.

MILLER, W. B. (1958) 'Lower class life as a generating milieu of gang delinquency', *Journal of Social Issues*, XIV, pp. 5–19.

MILLS, C. W. (1940) 'Situated actions and vocabularies of motives', *American Sociological Review*, 5, pp. 904–13.

MILLS, W. P. C. (1976) 'The seriously disruptive behaviour of pupils in secondary schools in one local education authority', Unpublished M.Ed. Thesis, Birmingham University.

MORTIMORE, P. (1980) 'Misbehaviour in schools', in UPTON, G. and GOBELL, A. (eds.) *Behaviour Problems in the Comprehensive School*, Cardiff, Faculty of Education, University College.

MORTIMORE, P., DAVIES, J., VARLAAM, A. and WEST, A. (1983) *Behaviour Problems in Schools*, London, Croom Helm.

NATIONAL ASSOCIATION OF SCHOOLMASTERS/UNION OF WOMEN TEACHERS (1985) *Pupil Violence and Serious Disorder in Schools*, Hemel Hempstead, NAS/UWT.

NATIONAL UNION OF TEACHERS (1976) *Discipline in Schools*, London, National Union of Teachers.

PACK REPORT (1977) *Truancy and Indiscipline in Scotland*, London, HMSO/SED.

PLOWDEN REPORT (1967) *Children and their Primary Schools*, Vol. 1, London, HMSO.

POWER, M. J., ALDERSON, M. R., PHILLIPSON, C. M., SCHOENBERG, E. and MORRIS, J. N. (1967) 'Delinquent Schools?', *New Society*, 10, pp. 542–43.

POWER, M. J., BENN, R. T. and MORRIS, J. N. (1972) 'Neighbourhood, school and juveniles before the Courts', *British Journal of Criminology*, 12, pp. 111–32.

PROFESSIONAL ASSOCIATION OF TEACHERS (1985) *Corporal Punishment and Alternative Sanctions*, Derby, Professional Association of Teachers.

PURKEY, C. S. and SMITH, M. S. (1982) 'Too soon to cheer? Synthesis of research of effective schools', *Educational Leadership*, December, pp. 64–69.

REID, K. (1986) *Disaffection From School*, London, Methuen.

REID, K. (ed.) (1988) *Helping Troubled Pupils in Secondary Schools*, Volumes 1 and 2. Oxford, Basil Blackwell.

REID, P. and REID, K. (1983) 'Porn in a wider game', *Times Educational Supplement*, April.

REYNOLDS, D. (1976) 'The delinquent school', in HAMMERSLEY, M. and WOODS, P., (eds.)

The Process of Schooling, London, Routledge and Kegan Paul in association with the Open University Press.

REYNOLDS, D. (ed.) (1985) *Studying School Effectiveness*, Lewes, Falmer Press.

REYNOLDS, D. and SULLIVAN, M. (1979) 'Bringing schools back in'. in BARTON, L. and MEIGHAN, R. (eds.) *Schools, Pupils and Deviance*, Driffield, Nafferton Books.

ROBERTSON, J. (1981) *Effective Classroom Control*, London, Hodder and Stoughton.

RUTTER, M. (1975) *Helping Troubled Children*, Harmondsworth, Penguin Books.

RUTTER, M. (1983) 'School effects on pupil progress: Research findings and policy implications', *Child Development*, 54, pp. 1–29.

RUTTER, M., MAUGHAN, B., MORTIMORE, P. and OUSTEN, J. (1979) *Fifteen Thousand Hours*, London, Open Books.

SAUNDERS, M. (1979) *Class Control and Behaviour Problems*, Maidenhead, McGraw-Hill.

SCHOSTAK, J. F. (1983) *Maladjusted Schooling*, Lewes, Falmer Press.

SCHOSTAK, J. F., and LOGAN, T. (eds.) (1984) *Pupil Experience*, Beckenham, Croom Helm.

SKINNER, A. (1983) *Disaffection from School: Issues and Interagency Responses*, Leicester, National Youth Bureau.

SOCIAL EDUCATION RESEARCH PROJECT (1984) *A Survey of Off-Site Special Units in England and Wales (Excluding ILEA)*, City of Birmingham Polytechnic.

STOTT, D. H. (1966) *Studies of Troublesome Children*, London, Tavistock.

TATTUM, D. P. (1982) *Disruptive Pupils in Schools and Units*, Chichester, Wiley.

TATTUM, D. P. (1984a) 'Pastoral care and disruptive pupils: a rhetoric of caring', *Pastoral care in Education*, 2, pp. 4–15.

TATTUM, D. P. (1984b) 'Disruptive pupils: system rejects', in SCHOSTAK, J. F. and LOGAN, T. (eds.) *Pupil Experience*, Beckenham, Croom Helm.

TATTUM, D. P. (1985a) 'Control and welfare: Towards a theory of constructive discipline in schools', in RIBBINS, P. (ed.) *Schooling and Welfare*, Lewes, Falmer Press.

TATTUM, D. P. (1985b) 'Disruptive pupil behaviour: A sociological perspective', *Maladjustment and Therapeutic Education*, 3, pp. 12–18.

TATTUM, D. P. (ed.) (1986) *Management of Disruptive Pupil Behaviour in Schools*, London, Fulton.

TATTUM, D. P. (1988) 'Disruptive behaviour — A whole-school approach', in REID, K. (ed.) *Helping Troubled Pupils in Secondary Schools*, Vol. 2. Oxford, Blackwell.

TIZARD, J. (1968) 'Questionnaire measures of maladjustment', *British Journal of Educational Psychology*, 30, pp. 9–13.

TOMLINSON, S. (1982) *A Sociology of Special Education*, London, Routledge and Kegan Paul.

TOPPING, K. (1983) *Educational Systems for Disruptive Adolescents*, Beckenham, Croom Helm.

TOPPING, K. (1986) 'Consultative enhancement of school-based action', in TATTUM, D. P. *Management and Pupil Behaviour in Schools*, London, Fulton.

UPTON, G. and GOBELL, A. (eds.) (1980) *Behaviour Problems in the Comprehensive School*, Cardiff, Faculty of Education, University College.

WARNOCK REPORT (1978) *Special Educational Needs: Report of the Committee of Enquiry into the Education of Handicapped Children and Young People*, London, HMSO.

WATKINS, C., and WAGNER, P. (1987) *School Discipline: A Whole-school Approach*, Oxford, Blackwell.

WEISS, B. (1982) 'Food additives and environmental chemicals as sources of childhood behaviour disorders', *Journal of the American Academy of Child Psychiatry*, 21, pp. 144–52.

WEST, D. J. (1982) *Delinquency: Its Roots, Careers and Prospects*, London, Heinemann.

WEST, A., DAVIES, J., and VARLAAM, A. (1986) 'The management of behaviour problems: A Local Authority response', in TATTUM, D. P. *Management and Pupil Behaviour in Schools*, London, Fulton.

WILSON, D. M. and EVANS, M. (1980) *Education of Disturbed Pupils*, Schools Council Working Paper 65, London, Methuen.

WILSON, D. M. and HERBERT, G. W. (1978) *Parents and Children in the Inner City*, London, Routledge and Kegan Paul.

WOLFF, S. (1967) 'The contribution of obstetric complications to the aetiology of behaviour disorders in childhood', *Journal of Child Psychology and Psychiatry*, 8, pp. 57–66.

WRAGG, E. C. (ed.) (1984) *Classroom Teaching Skills*, Beckenham, Croom Helm.

YORK, R., HERON, J. M. and WOLFF, S. (1972) 'Exclusion from schools', *Journal of Child Psychology and Psychiatry*, 13, pp. 259–66.

YULE, W., URBANOWICZ, J., LANSDOWN, R. and MILLAR, I. B. (1984) 'Teachers' ratings of children's behaviour in relation to blood lead levels', *British Journal of Developmental Psychology*, 2, pp. 295–305.

Part Four
Teachers and In-service Training

10
Research into In-service Training and Special Educational Needs

Colin Robson and Judy Sebba

Introduction

This chapter describes the work and findings of a recently completed DES funded research project on in-service training and special educational needs. The implications of the project, and its outcomes, for carrying out and developing in-service training for special educational needs in the radically changed context provided by GRIST (Grant Related In-Service Training) are explored.

Project impact

Project Impact ran for three years from October 1983. It was funded by DES as part of a programme of research into special educational needs which also included concurrent projects based at the University of London Institute of Education (on the working of the 1981 Act) and the National Foundation for Educational Research (on the integration of pupils with special educational needs). Project Impact was conducted jointly between the Hester Adrian Research Centre and the Education Department, University of Manchester and the Behavioural Sciences Department, Huddersfield Polytechnic. The term 'Impact' is not an acronym but was meant to signify our concern for in-service training which makes an impact in the sense of assisting teachers to change and develop their teaching.

The project had three inter-related themes. First, the development and evaluation of a pilot version of a regional modular diploma for teachers and others working in the special needs field. Second, the development and evaluation of a range of short school-focused courses which might form constituent elements within the pilot regional diploma, but which could also be used and made available more widely. Third, the more detailed evaluation of an existing widely disseminated skills-based training course — the Education of the Developmentally Young (EDY) package (Foxen and McBrien, 1981; McBrien and Foxen, 1981) — which is also a constituent element within the pilot regional diploma.

The modular diploma

The original idea for what became the modular diploma arose from the observation that a substantial number of teachers and others involved with children and young people with special educational needs were assiduous attenders at short courses put on by institutions of higher education, teachers' centres and advisory services. However, while such courses appeared to fulfil a perceived need they were not part of any coherent pattern of provision, nor was there any form of quality control on what was provided. They did not lead to any form of qualification or award. In a situation where the overwhelming majority of teachers with responsibilities for pupils with special needs do not have a specialist qualification for this type of work, and where the number of secondments to attend full-time diploma and other courses has been so small as to constitute a drop in this particular ocean, an obvious question can be asked. Is there a way in which completing a number of short courses can be justified, both academically and professionally, as leading to a recognized qualification?

To seek an answer to this question, a successful grant application was made to the Nuffield Foundation in January 1981 by Professor Peter Mittler. The first author of this chapter was seconded on a half time basis from 1982–84 under this grant, to act as a coordinator. The efforts were overseen by a steering committee from the north-west branch of ASET (Association of Special Education Tutors) which included representatives from local authority advisory services and HMI. Full details of the resulting scheme are given in Robson (1984) and Robson *et al.* (1988; especially Chapter 6). Following extensive discussion with interested parties (including potential students) it was agreed to seek to develop a diploma whose main features are listed in Table 10.1. It was also agreed that, although the

Table 10.1

Main Features of the Diploma
  1. Provides a specialist qualification in the special needs area.
  2. Common modular framework involving different institutions.
  3. Cooperation between public sector institutions and universities.
  4. Involvement of advisory services and others having an in-service role.
  5. Concentration on professional relevance.
  6. Compulsory 'contextual studies' and 'school-focused studies'.
  7. Wide choice of 'professional studies units' (PSUs).
  8. 'Open' PSUs from a wide variety of sources.
  9. Flexibility in rate and timing of teachers' involvement with the course (min. 2 yrs — max. 6 yrs).
 10. Mixed mode — part-time evening; half-day and day release; one week and one term full-time.
 11. Open to professionals other than teachers working in the special eductional needs area.

---

ultimate aim was to develop a regional scheme for the north-west, a pilot version should first be mounted in the Manchester area involving Manchester Polytechnic, Manchester University and local authorities in Greater Manchester in the first instance.

There are three types of unit within the diploma:

1. *Contextual Studies* (weighted as three units; i.e. one quarter of the diploma). This gives a framework for understanding special educational needs and the ways that they have been, or might be, met. Any students who have successfully completed the Open University course E241 Special Needs in Education may claim exemption from this part of the diploma.

2. *Professional Studies Units* (six units in total which may be made up of single, double or triple weighted courses). These are the short courses from a wide variety of sources. They are 'open' in the sense that students registered for the diploma typically study alongside others who may be simply taking that unit by itself, or possibly for another award. School-based units are available, including the EDY course mentioned previously.

3. *School-Focused Study* (weighted as three units; i.e. one quarter of the diploma). A study, usually of the teacher's own classroom, school or authority, directly related to the teacher's own professional concerns or interests.

Approval to run the diploma, in time for a start in January 1984, was received from Manchester University and CNAA (the Council for National Academic Awards — the body responsible for validating degree awards in polytechnics and other public-sector institutions). Full and equal cooperation between a university and polytechnic is a notable feature of the scheme, undoubtedly fostered by the close working relationships which already existed between staff involved in special needs teaching in the two institutions.

Project Impact played a role in the further development of the diploma by providing continued funding for a coordinator until the end of 1986 (Geoff Davies, formerly a member of the Polytechnic staff and before that an LEA adviser) and an independent evaluator (Len Wharfe, Registrar for Teacher Education at CNAA). The continuation of the coordinator's role over the early formative years of the running of the diploma has been crucial. It has been necessary to devise procedures for coping in administrative and financial terms with what was for both institutions a new and different type of course. Now that routines have been established these functions can, and have been, devolved within the institutions. Evaluations carried out by the course team and by the independent evaluator (Wharfe, 1987) indicate that the course is now well established and is well received by the course members. Certainly the main function of the pilot has been achieved; the feasibility of this type of very open and flexible modular scheme has been demonstrated. The stringent validation and approval procedures, and subsequent evaluations, give strong reassurance about the quality of what is on offer.

Currently well over 100 teachers and others (including for example, nursery nurses and lecturers in further education) are registered for the diploma, with the first ones having already completed.

Development and evaluation of short courses

A major part of the effort of the project has fallen under this heading. With one exception, the role that the researchers have adopted is that of facilitator in connection with the short courses produced by other agencies. Table 10.2 gives details of these courses. The exception is the 'INSET Workshop' which was developed directly by the research team as a culmination of its work, and as a tangible outcome assisting in the dissemination of the project's findings. In the other cases the strategy adopted was to seek involvement with an individual or team known to have run courses which appeared to fall within the remit of the project. The 'deal' was that we would provide resources (e.g. in the development of course materials including the making of video-tapes); they would agree to our evaluating the course. Our intention was to cover a wide range of special needs and of types of course (e.g. behavioural, experiential). Constraints were that the course had to be school-focused, in the sense of relating directly to the professional concerns of course members, and, more specifically, that they had to be eligible for inclusion as a single professional studies unit within the modular diploma (e.g. in length thirty 'committed' hours — say a one week full-time course, or a one afternoon or evening session per week for a term).

We were involved with a variety of persons putting on courses, including a local authority advisor, an advisory teacher, a team of educational psychologists, and a team consisting of a researcher, a higher education lecturer and a special school teacher. The typical procedure was for us to be involved with an initial run of the course, and then to feed back information from our evaluation to the course team for them to consider possible modifications to the course aims, content, process or whatever else appeared to be indicated (e.g. target group for the course, type of pre-course information). We would also be involved with a second run of the course, where the focus would be more on a summative evaluation of the effects and effectiveness of the course, although the opportunity would also be taken to suggest further modification if that seemed appropriate.

Arrangements had previously been made for the course materials which survived this process, in the sense of appearing from the evaluation to be well received by the client group and effective in achieving worthwhile objectives, to be published within an 'Impact INSET' series. The first four courses listed in table 2 are being made generally available in this way (Mallon, 1987; Garrett and Dyke, 1988; Kiernan, Reid and Goldbart, 1987; Sebba, 1988). The course which appears under the pseudonym of 'Course A' was found on evaluation to have serious problems which the course team were not able to address within the time-scale of the project. It is, however, of interest to note that an exercise forming part of the INSET workshop (see Robson *et al.*, 1988; Part 2) which is based on a suitably

Table 10.2 *Description of short courses selected for development and evaluation*

Course	Focus		Provider	Mode	Location
	Population	*Content*			
An Introduction to Counselling Skills, for teachers with responsibility for special educational needs	Teachers in special or ordinary schools with counselling responsibilities	Introduction to counselling techniques: *not* a training course for school counsellors	LEA or university INSET department: single tutor	Workshop: validated NW Diploma	Centre
Microelectronics and Pupils with Special Educational Needs	Teachers of pupils with special educational needs and with responsibility for INSET on micros	Reviewing software, preparing support material and developing INSET	Council for Educational Technology/SEMERC; multi-tutored	Workshop: non-award-bearing	Centre
Foundations of Communication and Language	Teachers, speech therapists and others working with pupils with severe learning difficulties	Communication at preverbal level	LEA, university INSET department or British Institute of Mental Handicap: multi-tutored	Workshop based on manuals: validated NW Diploma	Centre or school
Education of People with Profound and Multiple Handicap	Staff in schools, hospitals and community services working with people with profound handicap	Curriculum and methods for profound handicap: multi-disciplinary approaches	British Institute of Mental Handicap: multi-tutored	Workshop: validated NW Diploma	Centre
'Course A'	Teachers of pupils with moderate or specific learning difficulties	Direct instruction and precision teaching	LEA (school psychological service): single tutor per two trainees	Workshop based on manuals	School
Organization, Management and Special Educational Needs	Heads and deputy heads of special schools and heads of SENs departments in ordinary schools	Managerial and organizational skills	LEA or university INSET department: single tutor	Workshop: validated NW Diploma	Centre

anonymized version of the evaluation of Course A has been regarded as a particularly instructive experience by participants. The course on organization and management was positively evaluated but time pressure did not permit a second run of the course within the project.

Details of the evaluation procedures are provided in Sebba and Robson (1987) and a more general discussion of the issues involved in evaluating this type of course is given in Robson *et al.* (1988).

A strong theme which emerged was the importance and value of incorporating different types and sources of information in the evaluation. It is not uncommon for course evaluations to rely solely on participants filling in rating scales on the course, or of sessions within the course (e.g. 'indicate on a 5 point scale your views as to the value of this session; 5 = very valuable, 1 = not at all valuable'). Such information is quick and easy to obtain, and can have value. We have, for example, normally asked for separate ratings on 'interest' and 'usefulness'. Typically, for what appear to be good well-run courses, these ratings are either essentially identical, or 'usefulness' is rated lower than 'interest'. The latter case may indicate a possible cause for concern on a school-focused course, and is usually associated with problems participants envisage in implementing approaches or techniques covered in the course.

Caution in relying solely on ratings is indicated by the fact that ratings for 'Course A' described above were relatively high, and it was only by discussions with and interviews of the staff involved that the serious concerns they had about the course began to surface. Other evaluations provided a good example of a course which was both highly rated and also referred to in very positive terms by all concerned, but which failed in the sense that follow-up reports, observation and interview in the schools three months after the course showed that the course's central objective had not been achieved by any of the participants.

Other general findings were the importance of careful preparation before the course. This included ensuring that details of the course and its objectives were circulated so that potential participants could be selected (or select themselves) and informed. It was also found to be helpful for these participations to have a voice in the detailed focus and approach of the course so that it could relate to their concerns. During the course the opportunity for participants to discuss with each other and to share experiences and problems, was in all cases cited as a valued aspect of the course. Follow-up after the courses highlighted many barriers to implementation of ideas and techniques covered in the course. These barriers could be reduced in a variety of ways including establishing pre-course with the head and others that the staff member was being sent on the course to help the school carry out some task or to deal with an issue or problem concerning the school. Explicit attention during the course to likely barriers to implementation also appeared to be of value. The practice of having two members from a school or unit on the course helps them to provide mutual support in relation to subsequent innovations. Guidelines and suggestions arising from our experience are provided in Robson *et al.* (1988).

Evaluation of the EDY course

The Education of the Developmentally Young (EDY) course is a widely disseminated in-service training course for staff working with persons with severe learning difficulties in the use of behavioural techniques. To date over 3,000 teachers, hospital staff and others have successfully completed the skills training part of the course. Our evaluation of the views of persons who have received a certificate for successful completion of the EDY course was complemented with a survey of the views of EDY instructors. This indicated that the course was highly valued by the overwhelming majority of those concerned, who considered that it is successful in developing the skills concerned and leads to beneficial effects in their schools and units. This impression was supported by a series of case studies involving observation of EDY in use in schools.

Notwithstanding this, it appears that in its present form EDY suffers from a number of deficiencies, including for example an excessive use of jargon, which were analyzed. Given attention to these matters in a revised version of the materials, and a flexible use of such materials, our conclusion was that there is a strong case for the use of this package in the next decade (Robson, 1988).

Project impact and GRIST

It will be clear, even from this short account, that this was not a 'pure' research project. The conception is that of research and development, where we have taken a facilitating rather than a direct role, and of evaluative studies, where we hope to have made some contribution particularly in providing examples of studies combining qualitative and quantitative approaches.

In dissemination terms, four sets of training materials have arisen from the project together with a companion volume which deals with the project findings and general issues to do with running short school-focused in-service training courses. This volume also incorporates materials for a workshop on INSET which, true to the model adopted in the project has itself been run and evaluated twice. We have been increasingly persuaded as to the utility of the 'flexible package' within the new GRIST framework, and have endeavoured to present all the materials in this light. With local authorities acquiring more direct control of their in-service, and particularly where local advisory services and schools are running their own staff development programmes, there is a great danger that many local groups will be separately and laboriously reinventing their own version of the wheel. Our hope is that the resource packs arising from the project will lead to savings and increased efficiencies in this process, both directly and by example and suggestion. Another major worry in this devolved system is that of quality control, and of potentially severe restrictions in the opportunities for teachers and others to acquire specialist in-service qualifications.

The pilot modular diploma provides one answer to both of these problems. It is encouraging to note that the pilot diploma is currently expanding to involve additional higher education institutions and local authorities. It is also noteworthy that several similar modular schemes are now starting in other parts of the country.

References

FOXEN, T. and MCBRIEN, J. (1981) *The EDY Course: Trainee Workbook*, Manchester, Manchester University Press.

GARRETT, J. and DYKE, B. (1988) *Microelectronics and Pupils with Special Educational Needs*, Manchester, Manchester University Press.

KIERNAN, C. C., REID, B. and GOLDBART, J. (1987) *Foundations of Communication and Language*, Manchester, Manchester University Press.

MALLON, V. (1987) *An Introduction to Counselling Skills for Special Educational Needs*, Manchester, Manchester University Press.

MCBRIEN, J. and FOXEN, T. (1981) *The EDY Course: Instructor's Handbook*, Manchester, Manchester University Press.

ROBSON, C. (1984) 'A modular In-Service advanced qualification for teachers of children with special needs', *British Journal of In-service Education*, 11, pp. 32–36.

ROBSON, C., SEBBA, J., MITTLER, P. and DAVIES, G. (1988) *In-Service Training and Special Educational Needs*, Manchester, Manchester University Press.

ROBSON, C. (1988) 'Evaluating the education of the developmentally young (EDY) course for training staff in behavioural methods', *European Journal of Special Needs Education* (in press).

SEBBA, J. (1988) *The Education of People with Profound and Multiple Handicaps*, Manchester, Manchester University Press.

SEBBA, J. and ROBSON, C. (1987) 'The development of short school-focused INSET courses in special educational needs', *Research Papers in Education*, 2, pp. 3–30.

WHARFE, L. (1987) *Evaluation of Diploma in Special Educational Needs — North West Regional Scheme*, Manchester, Project Impact.

11
Teacher Training and the Integration of Handicapped Pupils: a UNESCO Study

Irene Bowman

Introduction

During the past 20 years we have experienced an increasing international concern not only to ensure that all children have access to education, but to ensure that the rights to education of handicapped pupils are also safeguarded. Debates have ensued concerning the issue of integration and implications for education. (Warnock, 1978; Hegarty and Pocklington, 1981). Consequently, the term integration has come to be used to refer to a child with handicaps being provided with education in the same setting as 'ordinary' children. In this sense it refers to methods of educational organization which are a means to achieving social integration.

A second feature of recent debate is the change in conceptualization of handicap, arising from examining the effect of environmental resources and deficiencies upon the intellectual and social development of all children. Handicap is no longer considered to be determined by 'within child' factors, but the outcome of an interaction between resources and deficiencies of both the child and the environment. In this sense, special educational needs of children are conceptualized as part of a continuum of educational needs for which ordinary schools can constitute a resource or constraint. This conceptualization throws into sharp focus relations between school organization, school curricula and teacher competence (Stanziale and Chiagaveto 1981). It raises questions about teacher training and support in the extension of teachers' functions in ordinary schools (ACSET, 1984).

In this context, the University of London, Institute of Education was commissioned by UNESCO to participate in a Project designed to further integration; Professor K. Wedell and the present author collaborated with

Note: This chapter was published originally in the *European Journal of Special Needs Education*, Vol. 1, 1986. We are grateful to the Editor of that journal and to publishers John Wiley for permission to reproduce the article.

UNESCO in carrying out the work. The participation initially took the form of carrying out a study of teacher training and integration in the five UNESCO World Regions. This paper briefly describes the study and extracts some aspects of the findings as an introduction to more detailed accounts.

The study carried out for UNESCO

The aims of the study

These were: to review teacher training in the context of a variety of country systems, to consider teacher attitudes to integration, and to produce a report (Bowman *et al.* 1985) which could form the basis of meetings about teacher training and integration, in each of the five UNESCO world regions.

The countries

These were selected by UNESCO, which also identified in each country a respondent who was to collect data. Fourteen countries participated: Egypt, Jordan; Colombia, Mexico, Venezuela; Botswana, Senegal, Zambia; Australia, Thailand; Czechoslovakia, Italy, Norway, Portugal. This grouping of countries presented variations with regard to whether the population was stable or rising; whether the educational system was developing or established; whether special education was developing or established; whether integration was informally in process or a statutory requirement.

The methodology

At UNESCO's request the enquiry was carried out by means of two questionnaires, and a case study provided by each country showing current practice. UNESCO dealt with translation and despatch of all material, and appointed a respondent in each country who administered the enquiry.

The main questionnaire (MQ) was designed to obtain a picture of national policy and practice regarding education and integration, and of teacher provision and training. The MQ also contained questions designed to indicate those cultural, economic and topological features which appeared to affect access to education for all pupils.

The teacher questionnaire (TQ) was designed to discover the conditions in which teachers work, their experience of teaching handicapped pupils in ordinary classes, their training and their views on integration. A sample of 100 teachers from each country was intended to be equally distributed between urban/rural areas and primary/secondary ordinary schools. Whilst this sample size and distribution was not achieved in some countries, the sample nevertheless provides nearly 1000 teachers' experiences of having handicapped pupils in their classes, and their views about support and further training.

A case study of current practice was requested from each country, to show integration in varying conditions.

Terminology was especially problematical as terms are used in differing ways complicated by translation. Assumptions had to be made about understanding and misunderstanding. For the purposes of this paper, labels have been chosen to identify types of school and age phases of education. Both labels and age phases vary across countries, but those chosen here are broadly representative.

Findings

Fourteen countries returned MQs. Twelve countries returned TQs. Two areas have been extracted for brief discussion here. These areas are: I, Types of teacher training and II, Teacher attitudes to integration.

Types of teacher training

The wider context

MQ reports showed that the provision and form of teacher training closely related to the education provision available and the age range for which school attendance was compulsory. Countries varied in educational goals and methods of achieving these. Some countries reported centralized curricula and inflexible methods of assessment, in which teaching goals and styles related to the whole class. MQ reports indicated that between 4 and 45 per cent of pupils repeated one or more grades, revealing a 'hidden' population of pupils whom teachers probably found hard to teach.

Teacher training for ordinary education

In this introductory account, we want to focus upon dimensions of teacher competence — academic, professional and special needs — and the relative emphasis upon these across countries. Elements of these dimensions of teacher competence can be found in (i) training routes, through which teachers are produced to service differing age-phases of education and in (ii) teacher training curricula.

(i) *Teacher training routes* identified from MQs are presented in Tables 11.1a and 11.1b. Table 11.1a shows the main routes and Table 11.1b shows combinations of these routes which are more rarely available. Considerable variations in access to academic and professional competence is indicated in these tables. In Table 11.1a the extremes of the range of variations are represented by routes A and D (b). Route A shows that in four countries pre-service training takes place within the prospective teachers' secondary education. In two of these countries this is completed by the age of 14 years, which raises the question of the level of intellectual development and experience thought necessary for such teachers.

Table 11.1a   Pre-service teacher training for ordinary schools

Route	No. of countries N = 14	Location and mode of training	Qualification	Schools for which teachers are produced
A	4	Secondary school training during teacher's own secondary education (F/T)	Certificate	Nursery primary secondary (vocational)
B	2	College of further or vocational education (F/T)	Higher certificate	Nursery or middle
C	14	College of teacher training (F/T)	Diploma or degree in education	Nursery primary middle secondary
D	University			
	11	(a) Education degree of diploma courses (F/T)	Degree in education	All
	1	(b) Subject degree courses only (F/T)	First degree in academic subject	Middle secondary
	7	(c) Subject degree (F/T) + professional training (F/T or P/T)	Degree in academic subject + Post-graduate diploma	Middle secondary
	1	(d) Subject degree + practice (F/T)	Degree in academic subject + professional recognition	Middle secondary
E	1	Distance training (P/T)	Certificate	Primary

Table 11.1b   Combinations of routes for pre-service teacher training

Route	No. of countries	Location (mode not known)	Qualification	Schools for which teachers are produced
A + C	3	Secondary school + college of teacher training	Diploma	Nursery primary
B + C	2	College of further education + college of teacher training	Diploma	Middle secondary
C + D	2	College of teacher training + university	Diploma or degree	Primary middle secondary
D + C	1	University + college of teacher training	Subject degree + professional training	Secondary

Route D (b) shows that in one country a highly academic education including a subject degree qualifies to teach in middle or secondary schools. This is completed by the age of 22 years, but does not provide a professional training. This is a surprising finding in view of the fact that integration in the ordinary class is required by law in that country.

(ii) *Teacher training curricula* were reported in the MQs with varying degrees of precision. It is difficult to know how representative of the total sample were those countries for which given percentages of time were devoted to curricular elements. The percentage of course time given to professional elements varied from 0 to 30 per cent, the training of secondary school teachers showing the lowest. In some MQs teaching practice was not reported, in others neither educational method nor teaching practice was reported. Class management and curriculum studies were referred to in about half of the MQ reports but were more often absent from the training of teachers of young children. Very low percentages of course time were reported for the few countries mentioning psychology or child development.

The overall indicator was of higher proportions of time being devoted to academic studies.

Countries varied in the amount of information or practical work designed to give competence in meeting the basic educational needs of handicapped children in ordinary classrooms. Access to such competence ranged from none at all or one seminar on special education, to options in professional studies which offered more specific training. In one country 17 per cent of the training curriculum for secondary teachers was devoted to methods of teaching handicapped pupils.

In summary, MQ responses indicated that the training of ordinary school teachers varied considerably in dissemination of professional skills and knowledge required for teaching both 'ordinary' and handicapped pupils in their ordinary classes.

Teacher training for special education

Training routes are presented in Table 11.2 following the same pattern as those given in Table 11.1a.

Pre-service training in special education was available in nine countries. This training ranged from specialist options added to ordinary teacher training courses, to degree or to postgraduate diploma course in special education.

In-service training took place after qualification as a teacher, and was reported by twelve countries. Five of these countries offered full-time training, two of these sending teachers abroad for training to teach pupils with specific impairments (Table 11.2, route G). By implication, these countries did not have their own resources to train in these areas of competence. Ten countries offered part-time training, ranging from short, non-award-bearing courses in specific techniques or specific impairment, to diploma level courses which focused upon

Table 11.2   Special education teacher training Pre- and In-service routes available

Route	Pre-service		In-service	
	No. of countries $N = 14$	Location, mode and qualification	No. of countries $N = 14$	Location, mode and qualification
A	1	Secondary school within student's own secondary education (Certificate) (F/T)	0	(Secondary school not applicable here)
B	0	College of further or vocational education	0	College of further or vocational education
C	8	College of education: either option within ordinary training or special course added (F/T P/T)	3	College of education courses Diploma/certificate (F/T P/T)
D	(a) 6	(a) University degree in special education (F/T)	2	University courses (P/T) Qualification not known
	(b) 2	(b) Postgraduate diploma in special education (Mode not known)		
E	1	Distance training (F/T)	3	Distance training certificate (F/T P/T)
F	0	Short courses	6	Short courses run by various agencies
G	0	Training abroad only	2	Diploma/degree training abroad only (F/T)

functions of specialist teachers. Two of these countries used diploma level courses to train specialist resource teachers to work in ordinary schools.

Access to in-service training in remote areas was often through distance teaching (Table 11.2, route E) by radio, correspondence, TV, video and film. Satellite transmission of radio, TV and computer assisted learning is a current development.

Curricula for training in special education

There were few details given in most MQ responses. However, there was some indication that a high proportion of time was devoted to professional knowledge and skills. For example, one college for teachers of the handicapped was reported to time-table 72 40 min periods of observation and 240 periods of teaching practice, for those training to teach blind, deaf, physically handicapped and mentally handicapped pupils. Also time-tabled were between 99 and 149 periods devoted to teaching method, including the use of teaching aids. An average of 24 periods was devoted to theoretical or academic curricula in this college course.

The presence of training courses in special education indicates that a pool of qualified and experienced specialist class teachers and more recently trained specialist support teachers exists in some countries. This is an important indication for implementing integration. Differences in weighting of academic and professional curricula in ordinary and special teacher training, emerge as a source of further discussion for teacher trainers.

Teacher attitudes to integration

Between 67 and 90 per cent of the teacher sample reported having pupils with handicaps in their ordinary school classrooms. Several items in the TQ were intended to give a view of certain MQ issues from the perspective of these teachers. We have extracted two aspects of this data: 1. teachers' views on integration and 2. teachers' views about the forms of help they consider important with handicapped pupils in their classes.

1. Teachers' views on integration of pupils into ordinary classes are given in Table 11.3. The data in Table 11.3 refers to the median percentages of teachers favouring the integration of pupils with different kinds of handicaps into ordinary classes in different countries. The distribution of these median percentages indicates the following points:

— Medical and physical conditions (delicate and physical handicaps) were seen as easiest to manage in the classroom.
— About half the teachers felt that children with specific learning difficulties and speech defects could be taught within an ordinary class.
— Around a third of the teachers felt that children with moderate learning difficulties or severe behaviour and emotional problems could be helped in ordinary classes.
— Around a quarter of the teachers felt that children with sensory defect could be taught in ordinary classrooms.
— Under 10 per cent of teachers felt that children with severe mental handicap and with multiple handicap could be managed in the ordinary classroom.

Table 11.3   Percentage of teachers favouring integration into ordinary classes

Pupils	Percentages		
	Median	Range among countries	Size of range
Delicate	75.5	39–97	58
Physical handicap	63.0	28–93	65
Specific learning difficulty	54.0	27–92	65
Speech defect	50.0	26–88	62
Severe emotional and behavioural difficulties	38.0	17–63	46
Moderate mental handicap	31.0	17–50	33
Blind	23.5	0–67	67
Deaf	22.5	0–68	68
Multiple handicaps	7.5	1–54	53
Severe mental handicap	2.5	1–47	46

The above indications based on the median percentages have to be considered in relation to the range of percentages found. It is clear that there is a wide difference of opinion between the countries. The greatest difference of opinion relates to sensory handicaps (hearing and visual impairment). This range of variation is twice as great as the difference of opinion about the integration of children with moderate learning difficulties. A major factor underlying this difference of opinion is likely to be the level of support services available to teachers in each country, and their preparation through training. However, by consulting the range of responses *within* each country which are not tabled here, we notice another factor. The country where teachers return high percentages favouring education of all handicapped pupils in ordinary classes (ranging from 47 to 93 per cent) has a law *requiring* this in practice. Further, the teacher sample from the country which offers the most sophisticated segregated educational provision returns very low percentages (ranging from 0 to 28 per cent) favouring integration in ordinary classes, except for delicate children (67 per cent). It is just possible that these samples of teachers show an awareness of the official policy of each country, but more likely that they are reflecting their own experience which stems from such policies put into practice.

Teachers may perceive integration more favourably where they actually experience handicapped pupils in a context which offers support but demands a professional response to sustain the pupils in their classes.

2. *Teachers' views about forms of help with handicapped children in ordinary classrooms* are indicated in Table 11.4. We asked the teachers to indicate which of a list of twelve measures they thought most important in helping with handicapped children in ordinary classes. Table 11.4 presents the median percentages of teachers who indicated each form of help to be important. The table shows that these median percentages are all very high. Teachers generally do

Table 11.4   Forms of help rated important by teachers

	Percentages of teachers		
	Median	Range among countries	Size of range
Training in individual teaching methods	93	88–100	12
Smaller classes	93	59–100	41
Help and advice for parents	90	72–96	24
Special equipment	89	83–98	15
Support from education advisers	88	72–93	21
Freedom to change curriculum and methods	83	73–93	20
Support from medical staff	81	75–98	23
Training in classroom organization	80	57–94	37
Training in use of special equipment	79	64–95	31
Parental help with school work at home	78	66–87	21
Additional help in the classroom	74	49–96	47
Support from social services	70	41–79	38

want the forms of help listed. However, the range of percentages found indicates considerable differences of opinion between teacher samples for individual measures.

Three forms of further training were inserted into the list given to teachers. Of these 'training in individual teaching methods' outranks all other measures of help in terms of agreement between teacher samples. This is an interesting finding in view of the data on pre-service teacher training briefly indicated above, which suggested that training in professional skills was scarce. That teacher samples in many countries ranked 'smaller classes' equally highly, supports the idea that these teachers want to change their pedagogy.

A number of findings carry implications for teacher training. The high regard for support from education advisers is corroborated by findings from another part of the TQ, where the school psychologist, special teacher and educational welfare officer were considered to be important sources of help. Yet teacher training data, briefly discussed above, does not indicate any training in collaborative or organizational skills to facilitate the planned use of such help. The TQ responses indicate that teachers can identify at least some training needs, are willing to take further training and are prepared to innovate.

Discussion

Countries differ in the conditions which affect change in education. For example expanding populations may generate government priorities to increase current educational provision whereas stable populations may help to generate flexibility and extensions to the functions of ordinary schools. Consequently countries differ in demands made of teachers who may be directed to deliver centralized curricula at specified rates, to specified standards annually, or be asked to be creative and flexible in adapting and producing curricula and new methods of delivery and evaluation. Teachers may be required to work only at the level of whole classes in some countries and at various levels of individuals, group(s) and classes in others.

Similarly, for good historical reasons, conceptualizations of handicap differ across countries. In some the assumption is that handicap is intrinsic to the child and a complex segregated system of care or of sophisticated segregated education is necessary. Recently some have begun to draw upon a conceptualization of the educational needs of all pupils among which are special educational needs. In this view ordinary schools may constitute a resource and teacher training can help to produce and to sustain that resource.

Both MQ and TQ data suggests that a major problem is how to maintain continuity between the demands made of teachers in ordinary schools and their pre-service training. MQ data showing that 'ordinary' pupils repeat grades, some continually, can be partly understood in terms of gaps in teachers' professional skills and knowledge. The experience of integration throws into sharp relief such professional training needs, and TQ data suggest strongly that teachers can identify these. So consultations with teachers may help to produce both locally relevant in-service support and professionally relevant pre-service training. Several countries are giving priority to the latter, and are faced with the associated problem of training or retraining teacher trainers. Where countries are able to give priority to in-service training, they often report using multiplier systems, whereby those trained as support teachers themselves provide local in-service training.

The TQ data contains a number of potentially interesting features. Of particular interest is the variation across and within countries in teacher perceptions of integration. Variations appear to be related to training, experience of pupils with potentially handicapping conditions, and support available in the ordinary school. These variables will be examined more closely in a further paper.

References

ADVISORY COMMITTEE FOR THE SUPPLY AND EDUCATION OF TEACHERS (1984) *Teacher Training and Special Educational Needs*, UK, HMSO

BOWMAN, I., WEDELL, N. and WEDELL, K. (1985) 'Helping handicapped pupils in ordinary schools: strategies for teacher training', Report on a survey of 14 countries undertaken for the Special Education Unit, UNESCO, Paris.

DEPARTMENT OF EDUCATION AND SCIENCE (1978) *Special Educational Needs*, Warnock Report, London, HMSO

HEGARTY, S. and POCKLINGTON, K. (1981) *Educating Pupils with Special Needs in the Ordinary School*, Windsor: NFER, Nelson.

STANZIALE, D and CHIAGAVETO, G. (1981) *L'Unita Pedagogica*, Rome, Gruppo Editoriale Fabbri.

12
Stress in Teaching

Jack Dunham

Introduction

Research into stress into teaching has expanded rapidly in the last decade. These studies have been concerned with six interests: definition of stress; studies of the incidence of occupational stress in teaching; sources of stress; studies of coping strategies; studies of stress reactions; and recommendations for the reduction of stress in teaching.

Definition of stress

In the educational literature three major approaches to understanding stress can be identified. The first of these approaches looks at the pressure exerted on teachers. This engineering model equates stress with external pressures. The second approach is concerned with teachers' reactions to these pressures which consist of emotional, behavioural, mental and physical manifestations such as headache, muscular tension and stomach ailments. From this perspective stress is defined as 'an unpleasant emotional state, tension, frustration, anxiety, emotional exhaustion' (Kyriacou, 1981). The third approach to explaining stress is concerned with both pressures and reactions and also the coping resources which teachers use as they attempt to cope with their difficulties. Stress from this perspective means a significant excess of pressure over coping resources. Dunham (1986) supports this third approach when he writes:

> I use the interactionist model as the basis of my in-service training in stress reduction skills. My definition of stress is: a process of behavioural, emotional, mental and physical reactions caused by prolonged, increasing or new pressures which are significantly greater than coping resources.

Studies of the incidence of occupational stress in teaching

Subjective methods of assessment which ask teachers to report on their work pressures and stress reactions have been used in several investigations. Kyriacou and Sutcliffe (1978) in a series of studies of over 700 comprehensive school teachers in England asked the single question 'In general how stressful do you find being a teacher?' The answers were coded on a five point response scale from 0 (not at all stressful) to 4 (extremely stressful) and the research workers found that 25 per cent of the teachers in the study reported their job to be *very stressful* or *extremely stressful*. Knutton and Mycroft (1986) reported data from a study of 154 deputy heads of secondary schools who were asked the same question. The percentage of this sample who considered their work very or extremely stressful was also 25 per cent.

Dunham (1986) reported on the stress reactions of staff in three comprehensive schools. The teachers were asked to indicate on a check list which reactions they had experienced in the present school year and to give an assessment of their frequency by indicating which they had experienced *very often, often, sometimes* or *rarely*. The most frequent reactions were: feelings of exhaustion (41 per cent), marked reduction of contacts with people outside school (31 per cent), frustration because there is little sense of achievement (26 per cent), irritability (25 per cent), wanting to leave teaching (20 per cent) and apathy (19 per cent).

Sources of stress in teaching

Kyriacou and Sutcliffe (1978) in a study of 257 teachers in comprehensive schools in the north of England asked them to rate 51 possible sources of stress on a five point scale from no stress to extreme stress. Four major causes were identified:

1. Pupil misbehaviour (noisy pupils, difficult classes, difficult behaviour problems);
2. Poor working conditions (poor career structure, poor promotion opportunities, inadequate salary, shortage of equipment);
3. Time pressures (not enough time to do the work, too much work to do, administrative work);
4. Poor school ethos (inadequate disciplinary policy of school, lack of consensus on minimum standards, attitudes and behaviour of the headmaster).

Some of the items in this detailed analysis have received further research interest. A survey of disruptive behaviour has been conducted in two London secondary schools (Lawrence *et al.*, 1983). When these teachers called their students' behaviour disruptive they meant rowdiness, abuse, bad language, talking and refusing to accept the teacher's authority. Dunham (1986) found that staff who have to cope with student behaviour and language which are difficult to manage experience further stress when they are powerless to change the conditions in which the children live.

Other investigators have found that a major source of stress for staff was their heads' styles of management. Armes (1985) in his study of staff stress in eight

Bradford upper schools found that over 60 per cent of the respondents identified their headteacher in this way. Dunham (1986) has argued that the leadership behaviour of the head may increase stress 'and may make the school a place of frustration, anxiety, anger, threat and fear'. He concluded that the leadership styles which cause stress include autocratic management which ignores consultation, indecisive behaviour which does not provide clear guidelines and inconsistent behaviour which generates staff uncertainty and insecurity.

Dunham also reported that some kinds of staff behaviour put a lot of pressure on heads. He found four kinds of *problem* staff behaviour, for example, teachers who are incompetent, unadaptable, who disturb their colleagues, and attitudes of non cooperation with senior management. Dunham also identified additional pressures on heads. These include parents' behaviour, pressures from the local education authority, media publicity of an adverse kind, union activities and cuts in expenditure which are becoming increasingly significant.

Dunham (1987) has also investigated the pressures on middle management responsible for the pastoral care of pupils in secondary schools, for example, heads of year and houses. They have to cope with role conflict and heavy time pressures. These were identified by the teacher who wrote:

> There is the constant pressure on time. I am so often torn between pastoral and other teaching/administrative demands. Do I do any job properly?

The third major pressure for these middle managers was a very wide range of duties. These included:

— formal duties, which were intensified by teachers who opt out of lunchtime duties;
— liaison with primary schools;
— parental contacts covering a wide range of problems;
— contacts with welfare/social services relating to specific pupils;
— responsibility for fixtures/fittings and for keeping formal financial accounts,
— oversight of behaviour and discipline of all pupils in year or house;
— teaching commitments and staff leadership:
— development of a pastoral care team.

This last item on year and house heads' responsibilities to develop pastoral care teams was a source of considerable difficulty as the following comments indicate:

— clearing up other teachers' discipline problems — especially when the kids are in the right;
— staff expectations that you are the solver of all problems immediately;
— wanting to respond to criticism honestly, (from parents), but having to protect inadequate colleagues.

Dunham (1983) has also been concerned with the problems of teachers who work with children with special educational needs in day special schools, children's homes, residential schools for maladjusted children and secondary schools. This research indicated that staff are experiencing several different kinds of heavy demands at work. Such demands seem to have grown steadily in recent years, reflecting changes in social and economic conditions and government policies in the United Kingdom as a whole. These demands are caused by the unpredictable, depressing, disruptive and violent behaviour of some of the children, poor working conditions, communication difficulties with colleagues, external agencies and incompetent management.

There are also new problems arising from major changes in policy and resources. The worsening financial situation in schools has become increasingly significant. Reduced expenditure on equipment, books and help for the 18 per cent of pupils with special educational needs in primary and secondary schools cause major pressures. So, too, do the redeployment of teachers, poor promotion prospects, fears of school closures and redundancies and the new demands imposed by the 1981 Education Act.

This is a daunting survey of demands on teachers so it is important to find out what coping strategies they use to meet these pressures.

Studies of coping strategies

Little research has been aimed at investigating the coping actions used by teachers when they encounter heavy work pressures. Kyriacou (1980) reported his study of forty-two teachers in two comprehensive schools who rated the frequency with which they used each of thirty-three actions. The three most commonly used coping strategies were to *try to keep things in perspective*, to *try to avoid confrontation* and *try to relax after work*.

Dunham (1986) found that teachers were using a broad range of skills, techniques, knowledge, experience, relationships, thoughts and activities which he classified as personal, interpersonal, organizational and community resources. Personal resources were work strategies, positive attitudes and out-of-school activities including gardening, painting, walking, cooking, baking, cycling, driving their cars fast and praying. Their interpersonal resources were social support activities such as talking over stressful incidents with husband/wife/friend/family and meeting people who were not teachers. Organizational resources came from colleagues in school with whom they were able to discuss problems, worries and feelings. Community activities reported by teachers to take their mind off their work and to reduce their tension included bell ringing, squash, weight-lifting, drama and choral singing.

Further information about work strategies was provided by seventy headteachers, advisers and officers, who participated in a stress management workshop

Dunham had been invited to lead. They reported their in-school coping strategies as:

— sharing difficulties by talking to colleagues;
— avoiding clutter;
— denoting priority of jobs;
— delegating;
— more efficient use of time;
— writing stinging memos to superiors to get things off my chest — always ending with a positive proposal;
— accepting that industrial action is not personal;
— timetabling blocks of time for office work;
— using my switch off (sod it) button;
— trying to get the rules of the game from the LEA about how priorities are decided.

Positive attitudes are also important personal coping resources. Some of those used by teachers have been reported to be:

1. Recognizing the dangers of allowing stress factors to combine in my mind so that I reach hyper self-critical conclusions, for example, I'm under stress — I can't cope — I can't teach — I'm an inadequate person;
2. By seeing my problems in the context of the *great scheme of things*;
3. Planning several events, including new and interesting activities for future weeks or weekends;
4. Attempting to encourage within myself a more confident attitude towards the job;
5. Thinking positively, for example, the large majority of pupils are perfectly teachable and the minority which give rise to stressful situations must be viewed in perspective;
6. Trying not to worry about other people's jobs — doing your own well and leaving others to answer for their own decisions (Dunham, 1986).

Kyriacou (1980) has also asked teachers which resources they used to tackle their work pressures. The twenty most frequently used strategies were:

Try to keep things in perspective.
Try to avoid confrontations.
Try to relax after work.
Try to take some immediate action on the basis of your present understanding of the situation.
Think objectively about the situation and keep your feelings under control.
Stand back and rationalize the situation.
Try and nip potential sources of stress in the bud.
Try to reassure yourself everything is going to work out all right.
Do not let the problem go until you have solved it or reconciled it satisfactorily.
Make sure people are aware you are doing your best.

Try to forget work when day is finished.

Try to see the humour of the situation.

Consider a range of plans for handling the sources of stress-set priorities.

Make a concerted effort to enjoy yourself with some pleasurable activity after work.

Try not to worry or think about it.

Express your feelings and frustrations to others so that you can think rationally about the problem.

Throw yourself into work and work harder and longer.

Think of good things in the future.

Talk about the situation with someone at work.

Express your irritation to colleagues at work just to be able to let off steam.

Studies of stress reactions

Kyriacou and Sutcliffe (1978) in their review of teacher stress indicated that the symptoms are *physical*, for example, peptic ulcers, cardiovascular diseases, increased heart rate; *psychological* such as depression and anxiety, and *behavioural* in the deterioration in work performance and in interpersonal relationships. In their study of 257 teachers they asked them how frequently they experienced these reactions on a seventeen item check list. The most common symptoms were feeling exhausted, frustrated, very angry, very tense, anxious and depressed.

A later study by Kyriacou and a different research partner (Kyriacou and Pratt, 1985) investigated the stress reactions of 131 teachers in first, middle and comprehensive schools in the north of England. The teachers reported a whole range of symptoms. The most frequently mentioned were being unable to relax or switch off after work, feeling drained at the end of the school day and sleeplessness.

Dunham (1986) has grouped stress reactions into four main categories: behavioural, mental, emotional and physical. In his model these four categories form a framework of successive stages which teachers pass through as their pressures become increasingly severe. In the first stage old or newly acquired coping actions are used when a teacher becomes aware of increased demands. If these coping actions are unsuccessful mental and emotional symptoms are experienced. These include frustration, anger, anxiety, poor concentration and memory impairment. More severe reactions are psychosomatic. Prolonged exposure to heavy pressures in teaching without increases in coping resources brings the risks of emotional exhaustion and burnout.

The process of stress is indicated by Figure 12.1. which explores the interaction between the performance of the teacher's role, stress reactions and the pressures which are experienced by teachers.

In this model, says Hebb (1972), work with only a few demands leads to boredom. Increasing pressures are regarded as stimulating and energizing, but if they are beyond a teacher's coping resources they lead to high levels of anxiety,

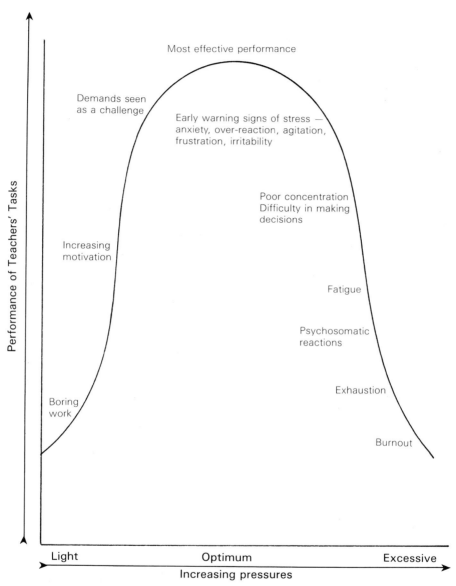

Figure 12.1   The Relationship between Work Pressures and Work Performance

poor concentration and reduced effectiveness in the performance of professional and family responsibilities. Continued pressures, without an increase in coping strategies results in fatigue, exhaustion and burnout.

Dunham (1988) has provided further insight into these different stress reactions in his recently completed study of teachers of home economics in the Republic of Ireland. They reported by questionnaire that their stress reactions were: headaches, fatigue and exhaustion, feelings of frustration leading to confrontation situations, for example, shouting, tightness in chest, find myself racing around the room, irritable with students and husband, always tired, fit for nothing at the end of week, feelings of panic, mind all clogged up, unable to cope with work, unable to cope with family demands, pains in eyes, confidence eroded at times, anger, extra day's sickness, lack of interest in the job and no imput into teaching.

In this list there are behavioural, physical, emotional and mental reactions. Similar signs of stress were also identified by the teachers referred to earlier who were under heavy pressure because of their pastoral care responsibilities. One teacher reported a number of physical reactions:

> I have constant headaches and constriction around the windpipe due to tension. There is inability to sleep properly because of an over-reactive mind at 3 a.m. When things get bad at the end of term I get indigestion and palpitations.

One teacher identified his behavioural reactions as: 'heavy smoking, driving too fast and an inability to sit still and relax'.

A report of mental reactions noted:

> Constant self-control is essential for me to establish my priorities and to stick to them. My judgment suffers by virtue of having too much *on the plate* and so little time to give full consideration to a problem.

A report of emotional symptoms identified:

> A general feeling that the workload is so heavy that it is impossible to cope. Much of the pastoral work makes me feel that I am wasting my time. Thinking about it causes headaches and depression.

Armes (1985) in his study of teachers in upper schools in Bradford noted the effects of some of these reactions, particularly frustration and irritability, on interpersonal relationships:

> The saddest thing is to find that about a third of the teachers with partners or children often have their relationships with them adversely affected.

He also commented on the effects of stress reactions on teachers' willingness to remain in teaching. He found that 60 per cent of the staff in his investigation wanted to leave teaching.

The cost of this amount of labour turnover is high yet it is only a part of the cost of the occupational stress. Absenteeism, retirement due to stress-related illnesses and reduced effectiveness when teaching should also be included in estimating the cost of stress in the Education Service.

The cost of stress has important human implications which should be considered with the financial. One significant aspect of the human costs is burnout. This condition has been defined in different ways by research workers and writers but one of the clearest definitions is:

> Burnout is a syndrome of physical and emotional exhaustion involving the development of a negative self-concept, such as poor feelings of personal achievement, negative job attitudes, such as being discouraged and depressed about work, and a loss of concern and feeling for people (Pines and Maslach, 1978).

It is a severe form of stress reaction which once it has started is usually difficult to reverse. The signs of burnout include the physical symptoms of chronic exhaustion, low resistance to illness and alcoholism. Mental symptoms are shown by a deep and pervasive cynicism about work, colleagues, children and the education system. Behavioural signs are chronic absenteeism and leaving teaching after a period of sickness.

A significant number of these symptoms can be identified in two reports of interviews with two comprehensive school teachers. In the first interview a teacher told Dunham (1986):

> I have feelings of not achieving anything, it is pointless. I have feelings of depression. I have tension in my head and have lost half a stone in three months. I switch from one decision to another — I will leave, no I won't — I thought I was going crazy. I cannot switch my mind off, my sleep and eating are disturbed. I stopped going to meetings and I cannot face going to school.

Shaw (1986) also interviewed a comprehensive school teacher whose teaching career had been terminated by stress. He left his school at the end of a Thursday afternoon, in October 1984, when he was in a dreadful state, utterly exhausted. He went to bed after tea and awoke about nine o'clock sweating like a pig and trembling. His wife, also a teacher, said 'You simply can't go on like this, it's bloody silly' and he made the decision not to return to teaching. He applied for a breakdown pension and eventually three doctors agreed that he was unfit to teach. He had been teaching for 20 years and he was 42.

In his interview he retrospectively identified the signs of severe stress which at the time he had not recognized:

> I went through a period when I couldn't plan even the next day's work and when teachers were away I was incapable of providing work for their pupils or assisting the supply teachers. I'm sure I look calm but inwardly I

was screaming hysterically. I was in general unable to cope with administration. When I had a free period I wasted it by pursuing trivia.

Recommendations for the reduction of stress in teaching

Kyriacou (1981) has argued that recommendations for reducing staff stress involve two perspectives. The first pays attention to ways of improving coping skills by learning to use a greater range of personal stress management strategies of relaxation, time management or physical fitness activities. The second approach aims to improve the teachers' work situations which will reduce the sources of organizational stress by providing management training courses for headteachers, reducing noise levels in schools, providing more effective induction training for all appointments and developing staff support groups in schools.

The role of social support in reducing and preventing occupational stress has received much support in the literature. Cox (1977) emphasized the need to improve support from senior staff and colleagues as a means of helping teachers cope with stress. Dunham (1980) in a comparative study of teachers in four comprehensive schools in England and West Germany reported that a major recommendation of the teachers in both countries was for much more encouragement from senior staff and improved contact and communication with them. Teachers would then feel more able to discuss their difficulties in a positive manner.

Kyriacou had identified the three main benefits of staff support groups as:

Teachers receive advice from colleagues about professional skills.

They are able to discuss the difficulties which are threatening to become major pressures and suggest successful coping actions.

Good relationships in a caring group encourage teachers to release feelings of tension, anxiety, frustration and anger.

He has argued that it is the responsibility of senior management to initiate the support teachers need: 'Much of the responsibility for improving the social support a teacher receives in schools must inevitably rest with the Head ... It is important that the Head should take the initiative by seeking to find out the problems facing his own senior staff ... and showing himself to be receptive to their difficulties, thereby setting an example which they would be expected to follow' (Kyriacou, 1981).

Dunham (1986) has disagreed with this argument for three main reasons: the severe pressures on senior management teams, it implies a one-directional flow of support from the top downwards, and it increases teachers' vulnerability when support from the top is expected but is not available because of heavy pressures on the senior management team. His model is different in that it seeks to open up pathways of support in all directions in an organization — upwards, sideways and downwards.

He has proposed that each school establish its own stress reduction programme aimed at strengthening three types of resources: personal, interpersonal and organizational. Personal resources are improved work strategies, positive attitudes, out of school activities, exercise and relaxation. One proposal he strongly recommends is for all teachers to be given the opportunity to learn time-management skills. He quoted a head of department who wrote: 'the control of time is crucial to a teacher's well being' and he reported the following framework of techniques which the head of department has evolved over fourteen years of teaching:

— be prepared to write down tasks as they are received;
— construct a weekly list based on order of importance;
— allot tasks to appropriate time slots during the week;
— undertake more thought orientated tasks to times when most fresh. If necessary divide up lengthy tasks into small units;
— look for tasks that can be discarded or delegated;
— identify sources which will enable a rapid and successful completion of a task;
— try to avoid taking on more than is reasonably possible to complete;
— check off tasks once completed;
— try to ensure that some time is left available for emergencies or nothing in particular.

All of the above points related to a day-to-day, week to week basis. Longer term planning is also necessary. This can be assisted by either a long wall calendar showing completion dates, appointments, special jobs. It may, if displayed in a prominent place within the department, act as an effective form of communicating to others and so cut out the need for memos.

Dunham has also strongly recommended that all teachers are encouraged to participate in activities which are directed towards the important aim of becoming physically fit and then maintaining a high level of fitness by physical exercise. He proposed jogging, cycling, fast walking and swimming or any activity 'which makes you breathe heavily but does not cause you to get out of breath' (Dunham, 1986). He has also, optimistically, suggested that teachers might enjoy beginning each day with Jack's Six Minute Loosener! This is a physical fitness programme with six exercises starting with *circular arm swinging' and ending with gently running on the same spot until you have counted 200.*

A more realistic recommendation for many teachers is learning relaxation skills. There are several different methods available, some starting with the feet and working upwards and some working from the scalp downwards. One approach which has been effectively used by many people was formulated by Murgatroyd and Woolfe (1982).

Relaxation training exercises

To practise the routine it is best to lie on the floor or to sit in a position which helps you feel comfortable. Regular practice of this brief routine each day will also aid in the reduction of stress and increase the ability to cope with stressful situations:

Lie down on your back or sit in a chair which supports your back;

Close your eyes and try to blot out any sounds. Think only of these instructions.

Think about your head. Feel the muscles in your forehead relaxing. Let any creases just drop away. Relax your eyelids. Relax your jaw. Let your tongue fall to the bottom of your mouth. Begin to breathe deeply;

Relax your shoulders — let your arms go loose;

Relax your neck — let your head roll until you find a comfortable position;

Think about your left arm. Tense it then relax it. Tense it again and relax it slowly. Concentrate on it from the shoulder to the tip of your fingers. Let any tension in the arm flow from your fingers. Let this arm become relaxed;

Do the same for your right arm;

Think about your left leg from the hip to the knee and from the knee to the tip of your toes. Tense your left leg and then relax it. Tense it harder and then relax it. Tense it harder and then relax it as slowly as you can. Let any tension in this leg flow from your toes. Let this leg become relaxed;

Do the same for your right leg;

Listen now to any sound from within your body — your breathing, your heartbeat, your stomach. Pick one of these sources and focus on it. Exclude other thoughts from your mind;

After about 2–3 minutes slowly open your eyes, sit upright and stretch your arms and legs fully.

These recommendations to learn and to use daily these physical exercises and relaxation skills are helpful to all teachers who want to reduce stress. They provide opportunities for teachers to engage in activities, hobbies and interests which enable them to assume alternative life styles to those they follow in their professional rhythms in school; these have been called the *Principle of Alternating Rhythms* (Bolles, 1981). They need to be considered very carefully indeed for those teachers who are workaholics — neglecting all aspects of their life except work — who are ambitious and impatient and involved in a *chronic incessant struggle to achieve more in less and less time* (Friedman and Rosenman, 1974). The modification of their attitudes to work and time are so important because research clearly demonstrates that these so-called Type A men and women are 'coronary prone', that is, they have an increased risk for all forms of cardiovascular disease leading to heart attacks compared with Type B individuals whose life styles are the opposite of the overdriven Type A patterns.

These proposals for strengthening personal resources might be perceived as merely palliative and peripheral contributions for stress reduction. Teachers who make these comments ask for *direct action* recommendations to help them develop school-based policies. These approaches are concerned with strengthening organizational resources. This can be achieved in a number of ways: effective selection procedures; induction programme for all newcomers including experienced staff appointed to management positions and internal appointments to new jobs; review interviews for all teachers thereby providing satisfaction for important staff needs which include:

— knowing what is expected of them;
— receiving feedback about their work;
— being able to discuss their difficulties objectively and constructively;
— feeling valued by receiving recognition for effort as well as achievement;
— being aware of professional and personal growth.

These recommendations for improvements in selection, induction and review procedures, need to be augmented in Dunham's view by greater in-service training provision so that appropriate opportunities are offered for continuing staff development. For staff appointed to management roles training in team management skills which emphasizes the importance of good relationships should be encouraged. This emphasis on the importance of good relationships in management is supported by research into the characteristics of healthy organizations. In these studies the physical and social conditions in which people should work have been analyzed and they offer clear directions for the development of healthy schools. There are five essential requirements for teachers:

1. They are able to influence the decisions which affect them at work;
2. They have a sense of purpose and direction;
3. They have a strong sense of acceptance and support from colleagues;
4. Their work enables them to feel competent;
5. They are aware of their own professional development.

But in some schools teachers do not find these requirements for a healthy organization and they may have to promote organizational change by learning the skills of assertiveness. Being assertive is not the same as being aggressive. Assertiveness has two significant characteristics: first standing up for your own rights in ways which do not violate the rights of others, and secondly, expressing your opinions, feelings, needs and beliefs in direct, honest and appropriate ways (Back and Back, 1986).

Typical situations in school in which assertiveness is valuable in helping to reduce stress are when a teacher is blamed for a mistake for which he/she is not responsible, or when a member of staff is asked to undertake a new area of work despite being already over-burdened or when a teacher is asked to undertake a task within an unrealistic time constraint (Murgatroyd and Wolfe, 1982).

This recommendation for assertiveness training and the other proposals which have been considered in the final part of this chapter have significant policy implications. They are good reasons for believing that with the development of stress reduction programmes teachers can be helped to cope effectively with heavy work pressures without developing high stress levels. The three aims for these programmes should be preparation, support and prevention. Dunham (1986) claims that with the achievement of these aims staff will be able to accept present and impending challenges with confidence, competence and effectiveness.

Summary and prediction

In this chapter we have identified the major themes in the rapid expansion of research interest in stress in teaching in the United Kingdom in the last decade as set out in the introduction.

Predicting future themes for research studies concerned with stress in teaching is hazardous but four seem to be emerging. These are firstly, specialist studies of stress, for example, headteachers, deputies and pastoral care staff, secondly, appraisal of stress reduction projects, for example, videos and stress packs to evaluate their effectiveness, thirdly, comparative studies of stress management training in teaching and other helping occupations e.g., nursing and social work, and fourthly, the assessment of the financial costs of stress in teaching.

References

ARMES, D. (1985) *The Unhappiest Profession*, London, Armes.

BACK, K. and BACK, K. (1986) *Assertiveness at Work*, London, Guild Publishing.

BOLLES, R. (1981) *The Three Boxes of Life*, London, Speed Ten Press.

COX, T. (1977) 'The nature and management of stress in schools', in *The Management of Stress in Schools*, Clwyd County Council.

DUNHAM, J. (1980) 'An exploratory comparative study of staff stress in English and German comprehensive schools', *Education Review*, 32, pp. 11–20.

DUNHAM, J. (1983) 'Coping with stress in school', *Special Education: Forward Trends*, 10, pp. 6–9.

DUNHAM, J. (1986) *Stress in Teaching*, Beckenham, Croom Helm.

DUNHAM, J. (1987) 'Caring for the pastoral carers', *Pastoral Care in Education*, February, pp. 15–21.

DUNHAM, J. (1988) 'Stress management for home economics teachers', in *Newsletter of Association of Teachers of Home Economics*, Dublin.

FRIEDMAN, M. and ROSENMAN, R. (1974) *Type A Behaviour and Your Heart*, London, Fawcett Publications.

HEBB, D. (1972) *Textbook of Psychology*, New York, Saunders and Co.

KNUTTON, S. and MYCROFT, A. (1986) 'Stress and the deputy head', *School Organisation*, 6, pp. 49–59.

KYRIACOU, C. (1980) 'Coping actions and occupational stress among school teachers', *Research in Education*, 24, pp. 57–61.

KYRIACOU, C. (1981) 'Social support and occupational stress among school teachers', *Education Studies*, pp. 55–60.

KYRIACOU, C. and PRATT, J. (1985) 'Teacher stress and psychoneurotic symptoms', *British Journal of Educational Psychology*, 55, pp. 61–64.

KYRIACOU, C. and SUTCLIFFE, J. (1978) 'Teacher stress: prevalence sources and symptoms', *British Journal of Educational Psychology*, 48, pp. 159–167.

LAWRENCE, J., STEED, D. and YOUNG, P. (1983) 'Monitoring teachers' reports of incidents of disruptive behaviour in two secondary schools', *Education Studies*, 9, pp. 451–453.

MURGATROYD, S. and WOOLFE, R. (1982) *Coping with Crisis*, London, Harper and Row.

PINES, A. and MASLACH, C. (1978) 'Characteristics of staff burnout in mental health settings'. *Hospital and Community Psychiatry*, 29, pp. 233–237.

SHAW, H. (1986) 'A Burnout Case'. *Times Educational Supplement*, 31st January.

Part Five
Support for Special Needs

13
The National Library for the Handicapped Child

Beverley Mathias

Introduction

The National Library for the Handicapped Child was established in 1985 through the initial sponsorship of The Enid Blyton Trust for Children. In 1987 the Library became a registered charity and a company limited by guarantee. The funding for the Library is entirely from voluntary sources, and receives no statutory finance. Children's books for the Library are provided by British publishers, but overseas children's books and all reference books, audio visual and computer software are purchased from funding provided for the purpose. Most audio-visual equipment, reading aids and computer hardware are donated by companies, trusts and other grant making bodies.

From the inception of the Library staffing has been geared to the needs of the user. Both the Director and the Librarian are qualified librarians, while other staff have skills in working with children with disabilities. At present the staffing consists of the Director, the Librarian, one full-time administrative assistant, one full-time general assistant and one part-time assistant.

Use of the Library's facilities are available to anyone who is interested in, or works with, children whose disability affects their ability to read. This means that the staff work with a wide range of children with varying abilities and interests. Some of the children have difficulty with school work, some have a disability such as hearing or sight impairment which affects the way they learn, others have a physical problem which precludes them using print. Some are intellectually handicapped and need slower-paced teaching to attain the same skills as other children. For all children the Library offers a place where they may look at books, play with book-based or language-based toys, use computers, and learn to use mechanical and electronic aids which will assist their ability to read unaided. No pressure is placed on the children, and although the main thrust of material is geared to children aged between 0 and 14 years, the 14–16 year olds can also find books and other items of interest to them.

The Library is a reference collection only and nothing can be borrowed. However, all visitors and enquirers are directed to their own local library service, to local branches of various self-help and charitable organizations, and to the local education authority. Any material which the Library holds is readily available and details regarding suppliers can be given.

The aim of the Library is that all children who visit should feel at ease and not threatened in any way by fear of assessment. The best way to describe how the Library works is to explain the physical layout and shape of the Library, its location within the London University Institute of Education and the ease with which facilities can be used by the children.

Physically the Library is on Level Four of the Institute of Education building in Bedford Way, London WC1, which means it is on concourse level, or half a floor up from Bedford Way. Access for those not independently mobile is via the outer courtyard from Russell Square, which is also the way in for wheelchair bound visitors. This will change as a wheelchair lift is being installed to cope with the half floor difference. The Library occupies a long narrow section of the building. The visitor enters a reception area where books for sale are on display together with a wealth of free material about the Library and other organizations which help the child needing special education. To the right is an open entrance into a room which is 164 feet long and nine feet wide. One wall of this is entirely glass. Off to the left of this room is a large balcony accessible through two sets of french doors. The balcony is safely fenced and is used as a play and lunch area by visiting children.

Inside the Library, at the point where the visitor moves from reception into the long narrow area, there are a number of toys, each offering the child some form of moral support. There are bears to cuddle, dolls to dress, a doll's house, building blocks and construction toys, posting boxes, soft toys of well-known children's book characters, and a large rocket big enough to hold a number of children. There are also a telephone box and a set of dolls, each of whom has a disability which might or might not be mirrored in the child who picks it up. There is an apple which responds to speech, and there will soon be a music centre designed for use by children who are immobilized. Some of the toys are tactile and are of particular value to the child with poor sight, the emotionally disturbed child, and the child with poor motor coordination. A rocking horse and a rocker with a safety seat offer children the opportunity for movement and rhythm. The children are encouraged to play, talk to and with the toys, explore, and most of all to feel at ease. In this way it is hoped that by the time the child has relaxed through play and is ready to explore further, books will no longer be the threatening objects they have become to many of the children.

Librarians and teachers visiting the Library for the first time often remark that the books are no different from those they have in their own collections. The intention of this library is not to have books which are different from those used by children without reading problems, but to specialize in those books which can be read by or with children who have a difficulty with reading. For this reason the arrangement of the shelves is similar to that found in any library used by children. There are one or two minor differences however. The picture books are divided into two sections, one is ordinary picture books of interest to children up to around 7 years of age, in other words, an ordinary picture book collection. The second section is picture books for older readers. These are books never intended for use by young children, but designed and written for children aged between 8 and 13 years. To a child who has difficulty with print, picture books become something it is fun to read, sophisticated in concept and something to share with friends. Thus the child who is having difficulty with text learns that pictures tell part of the story, and that pictures and text can tell a sophisticated and complicated story without being difficult to read. The main section of the picture book collection is subdivided roughly into sizes and specific categories. For instance all board books and rag books are kept with other books suitable for and of interest to very young children, and all the moveable books which flap, squeak, pop and unfold are kept in one place.

Another difference between this library's collection and other libraries for children is that the fiction contains what in some libraries would be regarded as picture books. These are books for early independent readers. Series such as the *Beginner Books* from Collins, the *I Can Read* books from World's Work, the *Red Nose Readers* from Walker Books, the *Happy Families* series from Viking Kestrel and the *Bodley Head Beginners* are amongst the series which in other libraries would not be in the fiction collection at all. Because it is important for the children using this library to feel they can read, any fiction/picture book which falls into this category is shelved with the fiction. The remainder of the fiction is of books which will interest a reader up to around 11 years of age.

There is a further fiction collection, which in other children's libraries might not exist. Because of the wide range of abilities of the children there are those at all age levels who, once they have mastered print and perhaps mechanical aids to reading, streak ahead as independent readers. So this library has a collection of fiction for more experienced readers. This might include young children with poor sight who use large print or mechanical aids, young people with intellectual disabilities who read abridged fiction, children with hearing problems who have mastered reading English. These children need time to become accustomed to reading, but once they learn to read independently they will be interested in the same range of books as any other child. Thus the collection includes abridged fiction, books for younger and older readers, large print, story collections, books about children with disabilities and general fiction for a wide age and interest range. Some of this material will be more complex in sentence structure and perhaps more sophisticated in language than the fiction found on the other shelves. The children who use this collection have become independent as readers and have also become more able to understand text which is not simplistic in approach.

Children who have poor sight can sometimes read without the aid of mechanical and electronic devices if the book is in large print, others need the additional assistance offered by a closed circuit television, a Viewscan or a magnifier. For these children the mastery of print comes first, followed by the desire to read. These children become experienced readers quickly, once they have become accustomed to using the form of print and the application best suited to their needs. Children with hearing difficulty will advance quite quickly if they have internalized language through sign language and then learnt to transfer that to English, which to them is a second language. Once this is accomplished their reading needs are the same as for any child, although they will need assistance as their grasp of language will not be as extensive as hearing children of the same age. Not all children learn to read quickly, and some children never become fluent readers. Some children learn at age 3, others are still struggling at age 13. In this library we want each child to find something he or she will want to read, and to avoid any feeling of intimidation at the quantity or supposed difficulty of books on the shelves. This division of picture books and fiction, while unnecessary in other children's libraries, is essential here if the children are going to feel confident taking books from the shelves to read. The collection of large print books which the library has is not shelved in one place but integrated into the fiction collection. These books although originally published for children with poor sight are of equal value to children with hearing problems, children who have specific learning difficulties and children who simply find it easier to manage reading if the print is large. There is no stigma attached to reading large print, and as the books are attractively presented and look the same as books with smaller print, the children will read them.

Non-fiction books are catalogued in exactly the same way as any other collection of children's books, using the Dewey Decimal System. However, the collection is smaller than those found in school and public libraries because so much of what is published is not suitable for children with reading problems. Some picture books are included in this section. Books by Byron Barton, Peter Snell and the Rockwells are included as they have a simple text which is accurate and suitable as a learning aid. Where possible books with simple texts are used. Some publishers do produce books in two parallel series, one with full text and one in simple text. There are a few titles in dual language, including braille and sign language. A wide selection of folk tales and poetry is also included, although stories and poems which the children will not be able to read for themselves, but which we feel they would enjoy hearing, are included in the reference collection. The non fiction includes some books in braille with thermographic illustrations enabling the blind child to read and to feel, via a tactile surface, the illustrations to the text. A number of these books, and children's books in sign language, are bought in America where the production rate of such titles is higher than in this country.

Physically then, the section of the Library devoted to children's books is in four sections; toys, picture books, fiction and non fiction. At this point along the Library the collection breaks and the remainder of the stock is for use by adults working with and caring for the children.

The Library subscribes to, or receives by donation, over 150 periodicals, journals, and newsletters which come from a number of English-speaking countries. The range is wide, covering newsletters from small groups connected with one particular handicap, to academic journals for professionals involved in education and care work. The collection includes review journals, magazines for use by the children or for parents and teachers, journals for those involved in academic research and many general periodicals containing information about education and reading. All titles are held for one year, many are held for much longer.

Because of the nature of the work done in the Library much of the ephemeral information about rare syndromes, handicaps, illnesses and disabilities which can affect a child's reading is not available in book form. The Library therefore maintains a file of articles and information on these topics. There is also a file of publishers' and suppliers' catalogues plus general files covering topics of interest to those involved in the education of children with special needs.

For those caring for and working with the children there is a reference collection of books and audio visual aids. This is also catalogued using the Dewey Decimal system and covers a wide range of books, multi-media and non-book materials. Books covering such topics as the educational needs of the child with learning difficulties, the problems which might be encountered in children with specific difficulties or handicaps, teaching methods for children with special educational needs, and books about disability. The books are purchased from all over the English-speaking world and at the moment the collection is in excess of 2,000 volumes. Because some of the children are print handicapped and will never be able to read a printed book independently the Library holds a representative collection of taped books, books on video, and also picture books on film strip and slides. These can be used with domestic equipment so that the child can 'read' at his or her own pace, but without needing to use print.

In addition to books the Library holds a range of computer and audio-visual hardware. An IBM PC is used for cataloguing the Library stock, while a BBC B and a BBC Master, a Sinclair Spectrum and an NEC computer are available for both adult and child visitors to use at their own pace. The various ancillary pieces of equipment attached to the computers includes two touch screens, a Concept keyboard and a Touchmaster, variable type size printers and a tracker ball. The software is often non-commercial having been produced with a specific learning disability in mind, although it may also be suitable for use with a wider group of children. Most of the software is geared towards helping the child with language and literacy, reading and understanding of print.

As well as computer equipment the Library has a number of independent electronic devices designed to help children use print and to communicate. The Viewscan uses a laser camera to scan print and then produce it on screen. The operator controls the size of print on the screen and the speed at which the print appears. The Closed Circuit Television (CCTV) magnifies print, picture or object so that the child with poor sight can examine pictures, read text and look at objects with ease. The CCTV has a colour monitor enabling the child to see colour in addition to line. There are also projectors for slides and film strips, each working with a pulsed tape so that the child can watch a picture book without needing to operate the machine. For children needing assistance with spoken language there is a Language Master, and for children without speech the library has a Lightwriter. This is a typewriter with a dual screen which not only presents a message to the operator but also to the other participant in the conversation. In addition the machine will both speak and print anything typed on the screen.

Each item of equipment held by the Library has been purchased because it offers the user additional assistance in reading and understanding print. Most of the equipment is too expensive for the individual to purchase, but much of it can be supplied through schools, or with the help of grant making trusts.

In the two years of the Library's existence the collection has grown to a stock of over 2,000 reference books, 6,000 children's books, five computers and various other items of equipment. Over 4,000 visitors have seen the Library, used the equipment and selected books for their own use by browsing through the collection. While nothing in the Library is available for loan, everything can be handled, assessed, notes made of the supplier and then ordered for the child, school, college or day centre.

In 1986 the Library produced its first printed catalogue. This contained entries for all books processed to June 1986. In 1988 the supplement to this will be prepared. This will include all books, periodicals, software, and audio visual items added to the collection between June 1986 and June 1988. The Library also sells a small selection of books about special needs education and the family care of children with disabilities, handicaps and debilitating illnesses.

As the Library is within the Institute of Education our hours are subject to those which the Institute works. Generally the Library is open Monday to Friday from 10.00 am to 5.00 pm, but it is advisable to check before arranging a visit. Group visits are welcome, but need to be booked well in advance. The address and the telephone number of the Library is as follows:

National Library for the Handicapped Child, University of London, Institute of Education, 20 Bedford Way, London WC1H 0AL. Tel. 01 636 1500 (ext. 599) after hours 01 255 1363.

14
The Voluntary Council for Handicapped Children

Philippa Russell

Introduction

The National Children's Bureau is a leading independent voluntary agency, committed to promoting and developing better education, health and social services for children. The Bureau's well established research programme, its growing body of development work and firm knowledge base, and its unique role in offering authoritative information and research, professional guidance and consultancy, have provided leadership in promoting change and development in children's services. The Bureau has over 500 corporate members comprising the United Kingdom's foremost professional, statutory and voluntary bodies. It therefore provides a unique forum for the discussion and development of policy and practice issues across children's services.

The Bureau was established in 1963 after extensive consultations with all sectors of children's services. Narrow professional territorial interests and sectional conflicts in voluntary as well as statutory services made it essential to provide a collective response to the need to plan effectively and collaboratively for children and families. The Voluntary Council for Handicapped Children was created in 1976 after similar consultations and a range of concerns about failures to work collaboratively to meet the needs of handicapped children as identified in the 1970 Eileen Younghusband Report, *Living with Handicap*.

Under the aegis of the National Children's Bureau, the Voluntary Council is an independently elected Council representing the major national voluntary, professional, statutory and consumer organizations concerned with disability and special needs. The Voluntary Council and the National Children's Bureau have worked closely together on a number of issues and concerns in the field of special educational needs. At a time of major changes and developments in services, with advent of the Education Reform Bill whilst the impact and implementation of the 1981 Education Act are still under review, the Bureau and Voluntary Council are closely involved in the development of new strategies for meeting special educational needs and the multi-professional implications in policy and practice for families and service providers.

Special educational needs — the 1981 Education Act

The 1981 Education Act, perhaps for the first time in special education, introduced the possibility of major developments in facilitating a working partnership between health education and social services, professionals and parents in developing a more pro-active dynamic and creative approach to meeting special educational needs. But a firm recognition of the multi-professional context of special educational needs and the central role of parents in education decision making have posed major challenges in implementation. The National Children's Bureau and the Voluntary Council for Handicapped Children have played a major role in developing policy and practice with regard to the new processes. As the Fish Committee (ILEA, 1985) noted, 'it is necessary for a variety of professionals to accept common aims ... if all inspectors, teachers and professionals in allied fields are to understand and work together to meet the special joint needs of children and young people, joint planning and inter-professional training are vital'.

The 1981 Education Act Research Dissemination and Management Development Project of the University of London Institute of Education (see chapter three in this volume) in collaboration with the National Children's Bureau, has identified key issues for promoting the successful management of change in policy making, structures of provision and professional and consumer representatives in terms of developing services to meet children's special educational needs. The Project has clearly demonstrated the importance of working with those involved with strategic level planning with and between authorities; the professional heads of the services concerned in decision-making about assessment, statements and the allocation of resources and those with direct responsibility for decision-making about supporting resourcing and determining the pattern of special needs in schools. The purpose of the project has been to consolidate the findings from the three DES funded special education research projects and other relevant sources; to identify the 'change agents' in training different professional groups and in developing and evaluating procedures for promoting the management of change. The Project has recognized not only that the 1981 Act and its associated guidance has represented a significant point in the development of services for children with special educational needs, but that it reflects over a decade of emerging policy and practice arising from the Warnock Committee's new philosophy of a broader and more flexible definition of special educational needs. The Warnock Report, like the 1981 Act, gave recognition to the important *interactive* elements of service providers, home and school environment and administrative arrangements which were essential for more holistic approaches to special educational provision. The 1981 Act had a broad commitment to integration, but subsequent implementation has revealed the complexity of supporting children with special needs in ordinary schools. The Education Reform Bill poses even larger questions about prioritizing for special needs and about the major challenges for schools in meeting special needs in the most effective way.

The project has identified a range of key issues, including:

1. The impact on assessment processes, the making of the statement and the allocation of provision of the relativity of definition of special education needs;
2. The respective roles of professional advisers and administrators;
3. Communication, coordination and the monitoring of services both within and between services;
4. The levels and patterns of resource allocation;
5. Support for the development and appraisal of professional and of administrative staff.

The 1981 Act is implemented in the context of separate powers and responsibilities of local government and the quasi-autonomous nature of professional authority and accountability. It has a civil rights perspective in giving parents access to information and to decision-making about their children. But the focus upon the identification of individual *needs* has sometimes caused tensions in terms of joint resource planning between LEAs, District Health Authorities and Social Services Departments. Consumer involvement has not always been as effective as was anticipated. Training has often failed to be multi-professional, whilst resource allocation has taken place in the context of different planning cycles, budget priorities and service goals within the three main statutory agencies. The Project has, therefore, defined as main goals:

1. The promotion of processes to enhance multi-professional working;
2. The development of joint planning and management systems across the education, health and social services;
3. The adoption of joint procedures by existing training agencies and by those responsible for training with authorities and services;
4. The generation of further service development, based on evaluation and the conscious management of change, within authorities, services and other relevant bodies.

If special educational needs are to be perceived as an integral part of a comprehensive education system which provides for a wide range of individual abilities and special needs within a coherent education policy for all children, then education authorities will need to take a more pro-active role in defining educational policies and in drawing up guidelines and timetables for translating such policies into action. We must give careful consideration to the management of change within a *whole* education service, which in turn necessitates creating opportunities for dialogue, discussion and consultation about changes in all children's services and in particular to rationalize and clarify what the Warnock Report recommended.

Promoting informed choice; parental involvement and the 1981 Act

The 1981 Education Act has succeeded in at least commencing a policy of parental partnership and shared decision-making with regard to special educational needs. Recent years have seen the blurring of many of the inter-professional boundaries with an emphasis upon a whole-child, whole-family approach. However, we are aware that 'partnership' has to be put into the changing legal picture, with parents both collectively and individually becoming more empowered in all education decision-making, an empowerment which is explored further below, since there may sometimes be conflicting tensions between apparent *children's* and *parent's* rights. Teachers and schools have traditionally focused upon the *child* as the primary client, whilst recognizing the key role played by parents in maximizing educational progress. For other agencies, in particular social services, 'whole family' approaches may appear in contradiction without explanation and exploration of perceived needs and the resources to meet them. Additionally, whilst the 1981 Act has unquestionably strengthened the role and rights of articulate parents, many 'hard to reach' parents do not utilize their rights to participate in education decision-making and remain marginalized.

Because many families still perceive the assessment system as being deficit-dominated and have negative expectations of the new procedures, it is essential to resolve certain specific issues in order to ensure:

1. The interpretation of LEA policies and procedures on issues such as assessment or integration to parents as well as to relevant professional and voluntary agencies who will be working with families.
2. Some form of 'administrative arrangements for the role of the named person' as envisaged in Warnock, in order to provide a key worker approach to the complex coordination of information which accompanies formal assessment under the 1981 Act.

As part of a process of genuine consumer involvement, LEAs should be encouraged to follow the examples of the ILEA, Haringey and Derbyshire and *ask the consumers* (parents, children and the teaching staff) how they perceive services to be working; what they mean by partnership and what changes and developments should be incorporated into existing arrangements and procedures. 'Asking the consumers' has been a valuable function of the Community Health Councils, as well as voluntary bodies. Although there is no equivalent to the Community Health Council in educational terms, local and national voluntary organizations can work with LEAs in order to undertake such exploratory exercises. The Bureau has recently undertaken a survey of customer satisfaction with special educational provision in the London Borough of Haringey (Berridge and Russell, 1987). We see this style of consumer involvement as of vital importance in LEAs where there are significant ethnic minorities or where major changes in provision are proposed. Parents need to understand the proposed changes. If they do not feel involved, they may resort to confrontation and rejection of change because they sense a general attrition of services, rather than productive change and evolution in terms of local provision for special educational needs.

Evidence from consumer evaluations and the Voluntary Council's work suggests that one of the problems in achieving partnership is that information and advice are offered too late. Parents frequently feel extremely anxious from the first moment that their child is identified as experiencing difficulties. Information, counselling and the 'named person' role may be most effective in these early stages, but in the majority of authorities they are not likely to be available.

Many parents perceive recommendations for provision as being resource rather than needs led. To some extent this appears to reflect anxiety by professionals about being honest over shortfalls in provision. However, as the Derbyshire and Haringey survey showed (Kramer, 1985; Berridge and Russell, 1987) parents would much prefer *honesty* accompanied by an honest appraisal of the child's needs even if there have to be subsequent negotiations to meet those needs in the most effective way.

The first parent advocacy projects in the United Kingdom have raised a number of wider issues about parent representation and the 1981 Act. Traditionally the majority of UK voluntary organizations in the special needs field are 'disability' labelled. For parents of children with emotional and behavioural difficulties or moderate learning difficulties, such 'labels' are unacceptable. Similarly many parents need sensitive support and counselling at the start of assessment and before any clear diagnosis of the cause of a learning difficulty is established. The US parent coalitions are beginning to emerge, through a number of partnership projects such as Parents in Partnership and the Welsh SNAP Project. SNAP (Special Needs Advisory Project) not only involves the three major Welsh disability organizations with the three South Wales County Education Departments, but provides the training and support for parent volunteers in order to facilitate parent participation as, when, and how the parent chooses. The early parent support projects demonstrate the importance of resources; of explicit policies, but they also demonstrate a major shift towards *voluntary* participation in education. Traditionally health and social services provision has attracted a significant input from the voluntary sector. Parent members on joint consultative committees, joint planning teams and on community health councils and district health councils are common. Parent involvement in *education* has followed more slowly. But the clusters of the first advocacy and representation schemes around the 1981 Act indicate an important new trend and further demonstrate that parents can be effective and enthusiastic partners in the assessment of children with special needs *if* they are given information, support and accorded parity of esteem with professionals.

These advocacy projects have clearly demonstrated that good will is insufficient to implement the Warnock model of partnership. A supportive framework for parents will not only offer counselling and personal support but a framework for formulating views and sharing information. The first *Parent Guidelines* on Section 5 assessment and statementing successfully developed and piloted by Sheila Wolfendale (1985) were launched at a seminar at the Bureau in

1985. The concept of a 'parent profile' is exciting and challenging and has been widely utilized in order to help parents use their own expert knowledge of their own child.

Since 1985, a number of organizations offering parent advice and advocacy schemes have met under the auspices of the Voluntary Council to explore common concerns such as the production of accessible and relevant information for parents, with special reference to families from minority ethnic groups; the selection, training and support of the advisers or 'named persons'; policy issues such as confidentiality; quality assurance and monitoring of the services provided and constant appraisal of the various options open for parent support.

Young women with learning difficulties

The 1980s have seen a growth of self-advocacy projects for people with learning difficulties. Williams and Shoultz (1982) emphasized that self-advocacy was not only about feelings, but about translating feelings into positive action. These stages of 'articulation and learning' would enable disadvantaged children and young people to acquire the confidence and competence to make realistic choices and to translate them into action. Self-advocacy, however, also requires a radical reappraisal of professional and family attitudes. It also presupposes a willingness to listen and to encourage honest and often painful personal exploration of attitudes, fears and choices. In 1986 the Bureau's project *Something to Say* established its first group for young women with learning difficulties. Previous self-advocacy projects had concentrated primarily on adults, but the Bureau's pilot work clearly identified the need to help young people with learning difficulties during the transition to adult services and to support young *women* who could be 'lost' and marginalized in disadvantaged inner city environments. The project was designed to explore the use of group work in sharing experiences, developing inter-personal skills and enabling the young women to become actively engaged in the world outside through the completion of group tasks.

The group's chosen task was to produce a book about themselves and their experiences and feelings. *Play Back the Thinking Memories* (National Children's Bureau, 1987) demonstrates the group process and the often limited life styles and expectations of the young women. Through the group they had the opportunity to explore their own pain and grief — at loss of self esteem and stigma at school where they were often teased, bullied and called names like 'handicapped' and 'spastic' and at problems and restrictions in their own lives. The young women devised two mythical women, 'Miss Can' and 'Miss Can't' to visualize their self image and their feelings about the successful. The project showed the importance of supporting young people with learning difficulties in acknowledging problems in their personal relationships and homes and at accepting the pain. Reaching the end of their special needs college courses or youth training schemes, they had a sense of lacking control and choice over what should be the next step. One girl said she was 'scared of life'. The group showed that a collective model of self-advocacy can promote self-awareness in young people with learning difficulties during transition to adult services; that the friendships created within a group are particularly important and that 'speaking out' can be a positive experience within a safe setting.

Promoting self-advocacy requires skills, training and support. It also necessitates exploring a range of models for involving young people in decision making. The Young Women's Group has clearly shown the possibility of collective action to discuss difficulties, look to the future and cope with the pain which is associated with disability and restrictions on the usual expectations of young adults in an urban society. As the Group said in its book:

To all those who have mocked us we say:
We would like it if you wouldn't call us nasty names. We're just humans, you know.

To all those who have mocked us we say:
We're not stupid. We can read. Even though we're slow at other things.

To all those who have mocked us we say:
Try and make friends with us.
Try and help us with things we find hard.
Don't bully us, we've done nothing to you.

We want to forget the past. And live a new life. And think about the future instead. The good time — the bad times are over.

The experiences of grief, loss and a bereavement process are well documented with parental acceptance of and adaptation to disability in children. Similar experiences and feelings are clearly identified by the young women in the Bureau project, which clearly demonstrates the importance of enabling young people to explore their difficulties and disabilities and to accept services and support as informed consumers.

Promoting informed choice: involving children and young people in decision-making

The House of Lords decision on the Gillick case in 1985 clarified an important principle with regard to the position of children and young people, their families and the wider community. The judgments of the majority of the Law Lords hearing the case represented a definitive break with the widely held view that children are always under the control of their parents until they reach the age of majority. Three important points emerging from the case were identified by the Children's Legal Centre, namely:

1. That parental powers are for the *protection of the child*. In the words of Lord Scarman, 'parental rights exist only so long as they are needed for the protection of the person and property of the child'.

2. That the *parents' powers change as the child develops*. In principle the child's gradual development towards maturation had been recognized in law (Lord Denning in the Appeals Court of 1969 commenting that '*parents' rights are dwindling rights: parental power starts with a right of control and ends with little more than advice*'). But the Gillick case formally encapsulates that principle as a right and accepts that children acquire the ability over a period of time in order to make responsible decisions about their life.

3. That the Law Lords recognized that *parental powers will depend upon the understanding of the individual child and NOT on any fixed date for the notional achievement of maturity*.

These three principles do not denigrate the central role of parents. Rather they recognize the natural evolution of parent-child relationships within families. A child-centred approach accepts that individual children will differ in their readiness to take control of their own lives. It will not force premature responsibilities or duties. It does however imply that in future decisions must be shared not imposed. It also argues for a very different professional approach to helping families where there are unresolved difficulties and where there are varying perceptions of the needs and rights of children and/or their parents.

An important outcome of accepting the principle of 'informed consent' must be preparation and training for all consumers. The 1981 Education Act has shown the difficulties encountered by unprepared and ill-informed *parents* to take important decisions about their children and to share with professionals real and valuable knowledge of individual children. A project on client participation in decision making at the National Children's Bureau (Gardner, 1987) has replicated the findings of the Dartington Research Unit that 'parents of children in care often feel frozen out by the care process'. A NAYPIC survey of young *children* in care found that without preparation, attendance at meetings related to care reviews was unproductive. The majority did not feel part of a process and only a small number saw their reviews 'as an occasion they contributed towards'. A University of Sheffield study, which examined the view of parents, and young people and social work staff at three stages in the process of decision making on care arrangements, found a total lack of client involvement in many decisions (e.g. placement) and a misunderstanding by social workers of their clients' perceptions of care and the related proceedings. There was general client approval for those social workers who drew up and used clear plans and agreements. As the DHSS *Code of Practice on Access to Children in Care* noted, 'success (in terms of participation) is much more likely if parents are involved from the beginning of assessment, discussion and decision making'.

Achieving a high degree of participation for children, young people and parents will require skill, training and support. The Disabled Persons Act, with its provision for representation of disabled person *and* carer formally recognizes such a need, and regulations, yet to be produced, will be crucial in ensuring that representation is a reality. Advocacy and self-representation are widely promulgated, but often with unclear views of strategies and consequences. Family members who have never felt empowered to make decisions or express opinions about their own lives will be particularly vulnerable unless there are clear guidelines and policies. Certainly the growth of advocacy will entail closer cooperation with the voluntary and consumer groups which have expertise and long-term experience of representing individual interests. Advocacy will necessitate a radical re-examination of the way in which schools and children's services identify the wishes and feelings of children and young people with special needs or children in care when making decisions about their welfare. The House of Lords judgment in the Gillick case confirmed the right of the under-16s to give or withhold consent to medical treatment, and by implication to other forms of professional services, if 'they have sufficient understanding to do so'.

The concept 'sufficient understanding' is in itself troublesome and open to many interpretations. The concepts of control and choice have been explored in the Bureau's project on decision making by young people in care. Gardner (1987) identified a *process* of decision making which ensures sufficient understanding. The criteria for such informed decision making were:

1. Collecting, surveying and comparing different pieces of information — *exploring*:
2. Seeking out trusted or knowledgeable people — *consulting*;
3. Making projected plans and considering consequences — *predicting*;
4. Carrying through a chosen plan — *persuading, supporting, negotiating*.

The project identified a number of key issues in supporting genuine consumer involvement. Carers, as well as consumers, needed support since choice presupposes a dialogue and consultation. Special meetings, group work and other events can be organized so that young people feel that their views are valued. Training groups for teenagers were particularly appreciated. The young people, like parents struggling with participation in the procedures of the 1981 Education Act, needed solidarity and reassurance in feeling parity of esteem with powerful professionals.

Lack of information also often inhibited participation. Many young people were uninformed about the purposes of medical examinations. Placement decisions without adequate information seemed arbitrary and often felt like failures. The project has posed major questions about *who* controls choices; about the legal and moral responsibilities for parenting a child when the overall care is divided up and — most important of all — about the feasibility of young people making choices and exercising control in all the important decisions in their lives.

The child as witness

The Criminal Justice Bill introduced for the first time the concept of closed circuit television in the courts as a means of helping children to give evidence with as little stress as possible. It has been widely recognized that the impact of a traditional court appearance can have long-term traumatic effects upon children and families and two other proposals recommended that video-recordings of children's accounts of alleged incidents might be admissible in court. Such evidence would have the great advantage of permitting evidence to be taken soon after the event and whilst the child's memory was fresh and uninfluenced by any subsequent suggestions. The National Children's Bureau, in its response to the Home Office on *The Use of Video Technology at Trials of Alleged Child Abusers* (NCB, 1987) pointed out that research evidence confirms the reliability of children's testimonies and the quality and weight of evidence which children can give to courts either as witnesses or as victims. The Bureau has held a number of seminars in order to explore the most effective use of video-recorded interviews, recognizing the need to conduct such interviews properly in order to ensure that inappropriately leading questions are avoided and that the child's perspective is adequately represented. Because research evidence suggests that the reliability of a child's testimony is comparable with that of adults in the presentation of accurate information in evidence, the Bureau continues to promote the necessity of the law adjusting its procedures, where necessary, to accommodate the particular needs of child witnesses so that the best quality and most complete evidence may be put before a jury. A second issue for reform includes the need to remove the present restrictions relating to the age of witnesses, the corroboration requirements and the necessity for them to understand the nature of the truth. Since judges will retain the power not to admit evidence which they feel is prejudicial to the defendant, it is clearly time for the 'present largely artificial, unhelpful and counterproductive restrictions to be lifted, thus allowing children's evidence to be given the weight it merits in each individual case, thus enhancing the probity of British Justice' (Davie, 1987).

Another area of concern lies in the need for the introduction of Family Courts. Any serious discussion of the contribution of the child as witness necessitates exploration of the *context* within which a child might be witness and the need to provide a family court system which would bring family matters under one roof; provide properly trained and specialist judges; provide a non-adversarial atmosphere, of particular importance during matrimonial disputes, and where decisions could be made more quickly. There can be little doubt that the Cleveland situation would have been less stressful if parents and children had been able to use a Family Court. Equally, the notion of a child as witness in a *criminal court* must be balanced by the child as an informed participant during *family* issues which require resolution or conciliation by a court. The growing concern about child sexual abuse represents the tip of an iceberg in terms of listening to children; of valuing their perspective, of recognizing the validity of their views within a legal framework. However, improving the legal framework within which children's issues require resolution will be unsuccessful without wider recognition of the need to encourage consumer participation by parents and children in a range of decision-making processes and much more effective arrangements for access to information to facilitate informed decision-making and to clarify procedures.

Investing in the future — child health services

A major concern in meeting children's special needs has been the development of effective child health services. In 1987, the Policy and Practice Review Group of the National Children's Bureau published *Investing in the Future*, a review of child health in the United Kingdom ten years on from the publication of the Court Report (DHSS, 1976). The Court Report set a blueprint for the development of more family-orientated, preventive and integrated child health services, emphasizing the important contribution of such services to all aspects of a child's social, physical and educational development. *Investing in the Future* was greeted by the British Paediatric Association as providing 'a singular service to paediatrics'. The report, based on wide consultation and discussion with a multidisciplinary professional and voluntary audience, made major recommendations to ensure that child health services were, indeed, 'fit for the future' on the Court model. Amongst these recommendations, the Policy and Practice Review Group proposed:

1. *Increased parental involvement.* Parents should be seen as having a major contribution to make to maintaining their children's health. They should possess a standard health record, available whenever professional help was needed, to ensure that they were informed consumers and partners in any decision making;

2. *Immunization.* At school-entry parents should be required to provide evidence of their child's immunization against the major diseases;

3. *Preventive Services.* Effective prevention requires a primary health care team basis, with a consultant community paediatrician within each team;

4. *School Health Services.* School health services need more systematic organization, including designated doctors and nurses for each school. Much clearer medical examinations procedures and transfer of records between schools are required;

5. *Adolescence.* Young people need a personal advisory service with confidential counselling within secondary schools. Each health district should have an adolescent ward, with readily available services from psychologists, social workers, psychiatrists and other relevant staff;

6. *Ethnic Minorities and Socially Disadvantaged Groups.* The Districts need to plan services to specifically address the needs and problems of specific ethnic groups and other minorities. Professionals and policy makers need to work with such groups in identifying their needs and work together to promote better child health;

7. *Child Development Teams.* These essential teams covering chronic disabilities should be created in all districts and provide access to psychologists, social workers and therapists. The transition to adult

services poses major problems for young people with disabilities. The marked reduction and shortfall in services for young disabled adults should be balanced by the introduction of teams to work with young people with disabilities during the transition to adult services and to ensure continuity with the arrangements and products of the child development and district handicap teams working with children;

8. *Psycho-social aspects of child health*. All professionals working in child health and nursing services need more input into initial and in-service training about the psychological and social problems they meet and the impact of these on child health.

Children and AIDS — a cause for concern

In February 1987, the Voluntary Council for Handicapped Children convened the first national conference on Children and AIDS at the National Children's Bureau. The need to examine AIDS and HIV infection in the context of children and young people had quickly become apparent to the Council and Bureau members. The Conference offered the first forum within which to discuss a range of issues relating to AIDS which were specific to children and their families. A number of concerns were identified, in particular the need for a central resource on information about AIDS and HIV and an emerging policy and practice to work.

The first group of children to be directly affected by AIDS in the United Kingdom were the haemophiliac children who received infected blood products. These children were in general in mainstream schools and their management has not posed major problems. However the work of Jacqueline Mok, a Community Paediatrician in Edinburgh, has clearly identified a number of progressive neurological and developmental difficulties in children who were affected *in utero* or in the perinatal period because of maternal infection. This new group of special needs children show a wide spectrum of symptoms which have been generally classified as 'paediatric AIDS'. Their needs will have major implications for all caring professions and for the local education authorities whose services they may use. Some children will in effect constitute a new disability group and in the USA some states have already designated AIDS as a disability which entitles the child or adult to disability services.

AIDS has major implications for the education services as infection control has become slack in most children's services in recent years. AIDS, together with the re-emergence of the much more infectious hepatitis B and meningitis, have refocused attention on the need to reconsider health and safety arrangements in children's settings. In as much as the AIDS virus is not susceptible to any treatment, nor to prevention by immunization, health education has also assumed a new significance. Appropriate health education will in turn challenge schools, requiring explicit information on sex education and on intravenous drug abuse which may offend parents and, with the Education Reform Bill's shift of responsibility to governing bodies, governors of schools. The moral and social implications of changing behaviour mean, in practice, a constant reappraisal of health education in schools and the presentation of educational materials in a language and format which is acceptable to the young people concerned and to their families and local communities.

AIDS has implications for children and young people with special needs. Sections 134 ff. of the DES guidelines note that whilst the transmission of the HIV virus between younger children and neurologically or mentally handicapped children who lack control of their body secretions is very limited, 'in the light of experience with other infectious diseases the theoretical potential for transmission would be greatest amongst these children'. In the USA difficulty has already been experienced with infected mentally handicapped children who were incontinent or who occasionally scratched and bit or chewed toys and equipment. Young disabled people may also not have the same access to information as their able bodied counterparts. There is growing concern about the need to provide accessible health education programmes for people with communication difficulties and to identify teaching materials which can be used with children and young people with learning difficulties. The concept of community care and a much greater community presence for people with a range of difficulties necessitates a realistic reappraisal for the children and young people who will develop AIDS and for whom very special care and support will be needed.

Effective health education and the successful management of AIDS in affected children and young people will require not only information, with appropriate educational materials, but improved collaboration between community, school health and hospital child health services; social services, particularly when a child is in care, and the education authority. The American experience shows the impact of a concerted community response in high risk areas like San Francisco. But it also indicates the crucial importance of access to information and the effective networking of policy makers, practitioners and the statutory and voluntary sector in constantly developing and reviewing practice. Because of the anxieties expressed about the absence of a focus for concerns about *children* and AIDS, the Bureau is hoping to establish a special unit to provide specific information and guidance on children and AIDS. The Bureau's and Voluntary Council's national network and corporate membership provide a unique base from which to disseminate information and guidance and to develop new training materials. The Bureau has already established an Under-Fives Unit and a national database on training and resource materials on child sexual abuse. The case for a special unit on AIDS similarly is strong. Promoting authoritative information, guidance and leadership in children's services has never been easy. The complexity and social implications of the AIDS virus will pose major challenges over the next decade.

Conclusion

The National Children's Bureau and the Voluntary Council are unique amongst the voluntary, and professional, organizations in the special educational needs field because of their broad span of interests and multidisciplinary composition. The Select Committee on Special Educational Needs concluded that 'it seems clear to us that a successful implementation of the 1981 Act is very much dependent on the development by the LEA of a clear and coherent policy arrived at in a way which enables it to command the support of those — parents, teachers and voluntary organizations — who are most affected by it'. To this view, we would add 'the support of the administrators, the network of professional staff, drawn from health, education and social services, as well as the local communities who will have new powers through the 1986 Education Act and the new Education Bill with regard to the direction that arrangements for special educational needs within mainstream schools will take'.

The National Children's Bureau and the Voluntary Council, through their membership and contacts, can take a holistic and independent view of current policy and practice issues in the field of special educational needs. We are, therefore, constantly under heavy demand to respond to a wide range of issues and concerns in the context of the 1981 Act and in particular to advise parents, voluntary organizations and local authorities on procedures relating to the assessment of special educational needs. Our membership provides a forum for effective and dynamic exploration of uncertainties and concerns and enables the positive identification of good practice and new developments.

As the 1981 Education Act, and the Education Reform Bill, continue to pose major challenges in the field of special educational needs, we see our role developing as a catalyst for the complex networking of resources and broad strategic overview necessitated by these changes and challenges in the special education field.

Notes on Contributors

Robert Cameron is Tutor for Advanced Professional Training in Educational Psychology at Southampton University. His special interests are in organizing in-service professional development courses for educational psychologists, evaluating home teaching schemes for families with special needs, helping staff to promote organizational change in schools. He has published over forty articles related to these themes. He has co-authored *Behaviour Can Change*, 1981 (with E. V. S. Westmacott), and *The Portage Approach to Special Needs: Theory and Practice*, 1987 (with M. White). He has also edited *Working Together: Portage in the U.K.*, 1982, and *Portage: Pre-schoolers, Parents and Professionals*, 1986.

Jim Docking is Principal Lecturer in Education at Roehampton Institute of Higher Education, London. The theme of his doctoral thesis was a developmental study of the attribution of responsibility. Prior to taking up a career in teacher education he taught history in comprehensive schools in Yorkshire and Coventry. He now has special interests in pupil behaviour and discipline, in social and moral education, and in parent involvement in schools. He has written an important book called *Control and Discipline in Schools*, 1980 with a completely revised edition appearing in 1987.

Jack Dunham is Tutor in Further Professional Studies at the School of Education, Bristol University. He was formerly Lecturer in Psychology at the University of Bath and has worked as an educational psychologist in the Bristol Child Guidance Service. His main interest and expertise has been in stress management in schools. He has authored *Stress in Teaching*, 1984, and co-authored *Stress in Schools*, 1976, (with J. Simpson and D. Gilling-Smith). He has in press *Improving Stress Care in Residential and Day Care Settings* (with L. McDerment). He is a member of the Parole Committee at Leyhill Prison and member of the Working Party on Stress in the Public Sector at the Health Education Authority in London.

Jennifer Evans is the Senior Development Officer to the Decision Making for Special Needs Project, London University, Institute of Education. She has a particular interest in policy implementation in education, inter-professional and inter-service relationships, and parental issues. She has contributed to the volume *Special Educational Needs in Ordinary Schools* by Cohen, A. and Cohen, L. (1987), and is a co-author of the book *Policy and Provision for Special Educational Needs: Implementing the 1981 Act*, Cassell, 1988.

Brian Goacher is Research Officer to the Tunbridge Wells Health Authority. He was previously engaged with research into the implementation of the 1981 Education Act, a DES sponsored enquiry carried out at the London University Institute of Education. He has special interests in research methodology, teacher induction, educational policy-making, and multi-professional working. His publications include *Mixed Ability Teaching in Mathematics*, 1977; *Mixed Ability Teaching: Problems and Possibilities*, 1981; *Profiling: The Sharing Experience*, 1983; *Recording Achievement at 16 +*, 1983; *Selection Post-16*, 1984; *School Reports to Parents*, 1984; and co-authored *Policy and Provision for Special Educational Needs: Implementing the 1981 Education Act*, 1988.

Ron Gulliford recently retired as Professor of Education and Head of the Department of Special Education, Birmingham University. Throughout a distinguished career he has had a special interest in learning difficulties, the curriculum, and in teaching. His publications have included *The Education of Slow Learning Children* (with A. E. Tansley), 1960; *Backwardness and Educational Failure*, 1969; *Special Educational Needs*, 1971; *Teaching Materials for Disadvantaged Children* (with P. Widlake), 1975; *The Education of the Handicapped Adolescent: Integration and the Training of Teachers in Three Countries*, OECD Paris, 1984; and *Teaching Children with Learning Difficulties*, 1985. He was President of the Association for Special Education from 1962–4 and Honorary Editor of the Journal of Special Education from 1965–80. From 1966–72 he was a member of the Secretary of State's Advisory Committee on Handicapped Children. He was a member of the Lewis, Vernon, and Younghusband Committees, and also member of the Training Sub-committee of the Warnock Committee.

Seamus Hegarty is Deputy Director at the National Foundation for Educational Research. His main areas of professional interest are the integration of pupils with special educational needs, research methods, and international studies and cooperation. He has written and reviewed extensively in the professional journals and written *Recent Curriculum Developments in Special Education*, 1982; *The Making of a Profession: Hearing Therapists in the NHS*, 1983; and *Meeting Special Needs in Ordinary Schools*, 1987. He has also co-authored *Educating Pupils with Special Needs in the Ordinary School*, 1981 and *Integration in Action*, 1982 (both with Pocklington, K. and Lucas, D.); *Students with Special Needs in FE*, 1981 and *Stretching the System*, 1982 (both with Bradley, J.); *Learning Together*, 1984 (with Hodgson, A. and Clunies-Ross, L.); *Learning for Independence*, 1984 (with Dean, A.); *The Best of Both Worlds: A Review of Research into the Education of Pupils of South Asian Origin*, 1985 (with Taylor,

M.); *Supporting Ordinary Schools*, 1988 (with Moss, D.); *Joining Forces: Links between Special and Ordinary Schools*, 1988 (with Jowett, S.). Additionally, Dr Hegarty has edited *Training for Management in Schools*, 1983; *Research and Evaluation Methods in Special Education*, 1985 (with Evans, P.); and *Developing Expertise*, 1988. He is a member of the following committees: FEU Special Needs Advisory Committee, CNAA Teacher Education Research Degrees Committee, and SCDC Arts in Schools Monitoring Group. He is editor both of the *European Journal of Special Needs Education* and *Educational Research*.

Beverley Mathias is Director of the National Library for the Handicapped Child based at the London University Institute of Education. She specializes in children's books and reading difficulties of children with special educational needs. She was trained in librarianship in Australia and also worked in this field in New Zealand before coming to Britain. She has compiled *Pudmuddle Jump In*, and the *Hippo Book of Funny Verse*, both in 1987. She is Special Needs Adviser to the publishing company, Franklin Watts, and a member of the Mother Goose Judging Panel.

Roger Morgan is Deputy Director of Social Services in Oxfordshire. For his doctorate he researched into childhood enuresis at Leicester University and later worked at the Leicester University Child Treatment Research Unit. As Senior Research Officer with Kent Social Services Department he initiated and evaluated projects on the community care of the elderly, the placement of difficult teenagers, and child abuse. He has a special interest in children's reading difficulties, introducing and pioneering in Britain the technique and procedure known as Paired Reading. He has written widely in the psychological, medical and educational journals on behavioural techniques with children. He has published *Childhood Incontinence*, 1981; *Behavioural Treatments with Children*, 1984; and *Helping Children Read*, 1986, and *Help for the Bedwetting Child*, 1988.

Margaret Peter has been editor of the *British Journal of Special Education* since 1974. This is published by the National Council for Special Education. She trained as a journalist, working for regional newspapers as well as freelancing, and has pursued a career in the Civil Service and with a Voluntary Organization. She became Editor of *Special Education* in 1965, a journal published jointly by The Spastics Society and the Association for Special Education. She specializes in methods of communicating research and specialist knowledge to a wide audience in the field of special education. In 1970 she wrote the opening chapter in *Living with Handicaps*, the Report of the Working Party on Children with Special Needs, National Children's Bureau, and was co-editor of the NCSE (1982) publication called *Signs, Symbols and Schools*. She is a member of the Executive Committee of the National Council for Special Education and a member of the Advisory Board for the *British Journal of Disorders of Communication*. She is a regular contributor to *The Times Educational Supplement*, professional journals, and has contributed chapters to a number of books.

Colin Robson is a Professor in the Behavioural Sciences Department at Huddersfield Polytechnic. Trained in science teaching, he worked in London schools, then as a university lecturer in experimental psychology before taking up a post as Head of the Polytechnic Education Department. He has expertise in the field of evaluation methodology and a special interest in special educational needs. He has co-authored *In-service Training and Special Educational Needs: Running Short School-focused Courses* (with Sebba, J., Mittler, P. and Davies, G.), 1988; and chapters in *Staff Training in Mental Handicap* (Eds. Hogg, J. and Mittler, P.), 1987, and *Research and Evaluation in Special Education* (Eds. Evans, P. and Hegarty, S.), 1985. He was until recently chairman of the CNAA Special Educational Needs Panel and is currently chairman of the CNAA Teacher Education Research Degree Sub-Committee.

Philippa Russell is Principal Officer to the Voluntary Council for Handicapped Children at the National Children's Bureau, London.

Judy Sebba is Honorary Research Fellow at the Hestor Adrian Research Centre, Manchester University. She has a special interest in in-service work in the field of special educational needs, and in profound and multiple learning difficulties. She has published *Profound Retardation and Multiple Impairment*, Volumes 1 and 2, 1986 (both with J. Hogg) and *In-service Training and Special Educational Needs* (with C. Robson, P. Mittler and G. Davies). She is Specialist Adviser (Education) to the British Institute of Mental Handicap; Consultant Evaluator to the MENCAP Profound and Multiple Handicap Project, and a member of the Committee of Profound Handicap, International League of Societies for Persons with Mental Handicap.

Delwyn P. Tattum is Reader in Education at South Glamorgan Institute of Higher Education. He has a wide range of interests and expertise relating to pupil welfare in schools. These include problems of deviance, disruption, truancy and bullying. He is also interested in whole school approaches to school discipline, pastoral care and personal and social education curriculum. His publications include *Disruptive Pupils in Schools and Units*, 1982; *Management of Disruptive Pupil Behaviour in Schools*, 1986; and *Bullying in Schools* (with David Lane), 1988.

Keith Topping is Educational Psychologist and Director of the Kirklees LEA Paired Reading Project, Huddersfield. He has a very wide range of expertise including in-service training, the role of parents and other non-professionals as educators, peer tutoring, management systems for disruptive adolescents, and organizational psychology. He has written *Educational Systems for Disruptive Adolescents* 1983; *Parental Involvement in Children's Reading* (edited with S. Wolfendale), 1985; *Parents as Educators*, 1986; and *The Peer Tutoring Handbook*, 1987. He is currently engaged in completing an extensive research programme on parental involvement in reading in Britain.

Mark Vaughan has been responsible for the running of the Centre for Studies on Integration in Education since it was established by the Spastics Society in 1982. The aim of the Centre has been to raise public, professional and political awareness to the issue of integration in education and to promote good practice in schools, through LEAs, and with increased parental participation. In 1988 the Centre was relocated in North London where Mark Vaughan continues to direct its activities.

Klaus Wedell is Professor of Educational Psychology and Special Educational Needs at the London University Institute of Education. In recent years he has been extensively engaged into research related to the implementation of the 1981 Education Act and is currently Consultant to the 1981 Education Act: Research Dissemination and Management Development Project at London University. He has researched and written widely on matters relating to educational psychology, special educational needs, and more recently, on government policy in relation to special education. He has jointly authored *Meeting Special Educational Needs: the 1981 Act and its Implications*, Bedford Way Papers No. 12 in 1982, (with J. Welton and G. Vorhaus), and *Policy and Provision for Special Educational Needs: Implementing the 1981 Education Act*, 1988, (with B. Goacher, J. Evans and J. Welton).

John Welton is Professor of Education and Head of the School of Education at Oxford Polytechnic. His special interest and expertise is in the field of education management. He has co-authored *Rational Curriculum Planning* (with J. Walton), 1975; *Cultural Minorities and the Multi-Cultural State*, (with Alcock, A. and Taylor, B.) 1979; and *Policy and Provision for Special Educational Needs: Implementing the 1981 Education Act*, (with Goacher, B., Evans, J. and Wedell, K.), 1988. He is a Council Member of the British Educational Management and Administration Society.

Alison Wertheimer is a freelance researcher and writer specializing in mental handicap and learning difficulties. She has worked as an editor for Cassell and Company and as translator for Humpreys and Glasgow, publishers. She was Policy Officer for MIND from 1973–79 and Director for seven years with the Campaign for People with Mental Handicaps. In 1980 she was a member of a national working party on bereavement and mental handicap for the King's Fund Centre. She is a member of the Disability Alliance Management Committee, 1981–86; Executive Committee member of the Centre on Environment for the Handicapped, 1981–84; member of the Clients Rights working party of the National Council for Voluntary Organisations, 1983–84; and member of the Independent Development Council for People with Mental Handicap, 1983–87. She has worked and lectured in America and Canada and acted in a consultancy role to the Western Massachusetts Department of Mental Health.

Index